D1594279

Robert Nozick

Philosophy Now

Series Editor: John Shand

This is a fresh and vital series of new introductions to today's most read, discussed and important philosophers. Combining rigorous analysis with authoritative exposition, each book gives clear and comprehensive access to the ideas of those philosophers who have made a truly fundamental and original contribution to the subject. Together the volumes comprise a remarkable gallery of the thinkers who have been at the forefront of philosophical ideas.

Published

Thomas Kuhn
Alexander Bird

John Searle
Nick Fotion

Charles Taylor
Ruth Abbey

Robert Nozick
A. R. Lacey

Robert Nozick

A. R. Lacey

PRINCETON UNIVERSITY PRESS
PRINCETON AND OXFORD

Published in North and South America by
Princeton University Press, 41 William Street,
Princeton, New Jersey 08540. All rights reserved.

First published in 2001 by Acumen
Acumen Publishing Limited
15a Lewins Yard
East Street
Chesham
Bucks HP5 1HQ, UK

Library of Congress Control Number 2001088391

ISBN 0-691-09044-0 (hardcover)
ISBN 0-691-09045-9 (paperback)

Designed and typeset in Century Schoolbook
by Kate Williams, Abergavenny.
Printed and bound by Biddles Ltd., Guildford and King's Lynn.

www.pup.princeton.edu

10   9   8   7   6   5   4   3   2   1

Contents

Preface

Like the other books in the series this book intends to give the student or interested layman a critical introduction to a major modern philosopher, covering his main works so far and discussing at least some of the main criticisms they have received. My own limitations, however, prevent me from treating Nozick's more technical work on decision theory, especially in his early Dissertation. I have tried not to presuppose too much by way of philosophical background, although the argument does get fairly intricate at times and may then require some sympathetic hard work. The bibliography gives full details of the works mentioned in the text or in the guides to further reading.

Two readers, Dr Simon Hailwood of the University of Liverpool and Professor Scott Arnold of the University of Alabama, have provided some very helpful suggestions for improvements, mainly on the earlier chapters, and the summaries are in partial response to Professor Arnold. Dr Hailwood in particular made many detailed comments on the text, which have improved it considerably and saved me from a number of misinterpretations and errors. I am grateful to my colleagues for help on individual points, to the libraries of King's College and the University of London, in particular, for their resources and helpful staff, and especially to Mrs Elizabeth Betts for heroic typings and retypings of my manuscripts. Dr John Shand, the series editor, invited me initially, and he and later Steven Gerrard have shepherded me through the project.

A. R. Lacey
February 2001

Chapter 1
Introduction

Introduction: analytic philosophy

Nozick is a fox, not a hedgehog, to borrow Isaiah Berlin's colourful way of classifying thinkers. (The reference is to the seventh-century BC Greek poet Archilochus, who wrote: "The fox knows many tricks, the hedgehog only one – but it's a good one".) By far his most widely known book is *Anarchy, State, and Utopia*, his first major publication, published in 1974. This has been immensely influential, not only in philosophical circles but in practical politics as well, especially in Great Britain and the United States, where it has offered stimulus and support to the resurgence of free market capitalism that has occupied the closing decades of the twentieth century. But Nozick himself has a different view of it: "Others have identified me as a 'political philosopher'", he writes on page 1 of his latest book, *Socratic Puzzles* (*SP*), "but I have never thought of myself in those terms. The vast majority of my writing and attention has focused on other subjects". He goes on (p. 2) to describe his method of work. He doesn't pay close attention to the criticism his work receives, and then reply to it with a succession of revisions and modifications, but gets on with something else instead. This is partly, as he makes clear, because he doesn't want to acquire a defensive attitude to his own ideas, but partly because his natural inclination is towards exploring rather than consolidating. This might suggest a certain flightiness or dilettantism in approach; but such a suggestion would be quite misleading. When he engages with a topic his work is intense and penetrating and shows an enviable ability to think through the hidden implications of the view he is considering and of alternatives to it.

So far he has published six books, including two volumes of essays, one original and one of reprinted articles etc. As well as political philosophy these have covered ethics, epistemology, methodology, the theory of choice, metaphysics, philosophy of mind, philosophy of religion, and what might be called the philosophy of life. In at least two of these areas, apart from political philosophy, namely epistemology and philosophy of mind, he has contributed notable ideas that are at the forefront of current thought.

Nozick was born in New York in 1938, as a Jew of Russian extraction, and came to philosophy in the late 1950s against a background of analytic philosophy. He discusses his attitude to this in an interview with Borradori in her book *The American Philosopher*, which consists of interviews with nine American philosophers (together with valuable and illuminating editorial material by Borradori herself). The term "analytic (or analytical) philosophy" is used in somewhat varying, although related, senses. In the 1920s and 1930s the logical positivists pared philosophy right down by insisting that any utterance which is to be meaningful in the primary sense of being used to assert something (as against asking, commanding, expressing attitudes, etc.) must be either a tautology of logic or mathematics or else verifiable by appeal to sense experience (helped by the laws of logic and mathematics where necessary). This approach, which seemed to leave no room at all for philosophical statements properly so called, did not last long. (Its main British representative, A. J. Ayer, declared on television in 1960, "Logical positivism is dead".) But its influence was, and still is, immense. Analytic philosophy, as understood by Borradori and Nozick, grew out of it, widening its horizons so far as meaningfulness went, but keeping a piecemeal approach to its problems, rather than trying to construct large-scale systems, and maintaining a certain isolation from other disciplines, both humanistic and scientific; philosophical questions were philosophical and must be pursued for their own sakes and by philosophy's own methods, not those of the sciences or arts. It is this isolationism that proved to be one of its weakest points. Its insistence on rigour had always allied the analytic movement to the sciences, despite their differences, and philosophy of science was always a popular and highly respected part of the subject. Problems about space and time, matter and substance, life and the lifeless, body and mind, and many others, cannot be solved without taking account of the data of the sciences. In the case of the physical sciences at least, this had generally been acknowledged from the start. But there is a difference between accepting scientific conclusions among the premises of an argument and finding that the process of arguing itself involves an ongoing appeal to the sciences at almost every step. Philosophical and scientific questions remain different, but the supposed sharp borderline between their methods tends to become eroded. Philosophers may not themselves conduct experiments, but their method may involve frequent second-hand investigations into empirical questions by asking their colleagues in the laboratory next door.

In the case of ethics and politics, analytic philosophy thought it should confine itself to examining the nature and status of the subjects themselves, the meanings of their central terms, the role of truth and falsity in them, the structure of arguments in them, and so on, leaving substantive views in them to moralists and politicians since it was assumed that any position on these substantive questions could be combined with any view on the properly philosophical questions (often described as those of metaethics). For instance, it was assumed you could discuss whether "Abortion is wrong" was an assertion of something as being true or an expression of an attitude etc., independently of whether you agreed with it. If you did, the question would concern what you were doing in so agreeing. But this independence too proved illusory, and philosophers came to realize they had to enter the arena and discuss the substantive issues.

A further feature of philosophy in its analytic guise was its attitude to its own history. There are two attitudes in particular that one can take to the history of philosophy. One can study it for its own sake, trying to understand the positions of earlier thinkers in the terms in which they themselves would have understood them, emphasizing the questions they emphasized and bracketing one's own views and interests. The danger of this, from the point of view of philosophy itself, is that it tends to separate itself from the rest of the subject and become something merely antiquarian, apart from probably being impossible to carry out without just slavishly repeating what the earlier thinkers said. The second approach is to subordinate the enquiry to one's own philosophical interests, choosing philosophers for study according to how their interests coincide with one's own, treating them as though they were contemporary colleagues who were simply talking in a rather antiquated language, but who were "really" trying to say the sort of things we think they should have said. The dangers of this are obvious enough, and it leads one to wonder what the point is of studying them at all. Of course these approaches need not be, and seldom are, held in such extreme

3

forms. They are rather tendencies one can steer between, veering in varying degrees to one side or the other.

Naturally enough, in view of what we saw earlier, analytic philosophy veered towards the second approach. The history of philosophy has always been an important part of the syllabus in analytically inclined universities, but with a tendency to treat it as a foreshadowing of the truth, or as a source of building materials rather than from a conservationist point of view. Of course analytic philosophy was not alone in its guilt here, and was far from the worst offender. One can think of how the history of philosophy was treated in Soviet universities, or even by a philosopher as eminent as Aristotle, at least as often interpreted, who explicitly described the utterances of one of his predecessors (Empedocles) as "lisping" attempts at the truth (*Metaphysics* 985a5; cf.993a15, *On Coming to Be and Passing Away* 314a13).

Before going on, a further word about the term "analytic philosophy". It can also be used more widely to denote the general method and spirit that has dominated most anglophone philosophy throughout the twentieth century, in contrast to "Continental" philosophy, so called because of its prevalence in France and Germany in particular, and also to various Oriental etc. systems. In this sense analytic philosophy's main features are an insistence on rigorous step-by-step arguments with full attention (ideally!) to criticism at every stage, combined with a certain aversion, although less marked than in the narrower version, to large scale system-building, and in particular to the development and presentation of systems without much attention to criticisms until the whole thing is finished. In fact, a certain comparison in respect of narrowness of scope could be made between analytic philosophy, especially in the narrow sense, and Continental philosophy: while analytic philosophy tends to ignore, or at least soft-pedal, the philosophies of the past, Continental philosophy (and many Oriental philosophies too) soft-pedal the need for rigorous critical examination of the individual steps of the argument as they are taken, using the tools supplied by logic where necessary. Analytic philosophy in the wider sense, however, including much of what is sometimes called post-analytic philosophy, is wider in scope and more tolerant than its narrower cousin, just as that in turn was wider and more tolerant than logical positivism.

In Nozick's discussion with Borradori, "analytic philosophy" is used in the narrow sense, which I will therefore normally adopt in what follows, simply noting that much, although not all, of what Nozick wrote after abandoning analytic philosophy in this sense would still count as analytic philosophy in the wider sense, both in terms of many of its features and in terms of the subjects chosen for discussion.

Changes of interest

Nozick tells us (Borradori 1994: 76) that in his youth he was "quite interested in issues of social and political philosophy"; but he really began his philosophical career, as he goes on to say, in the sphere of philosophy of science, largely because of the influence of his teachers as an undergraduate at Columbia, notably Morgenbesser, and later, as a graduate at Princeton, Hempel. We will see shortly the importance that the influence of Hempel, undoubtedly an analytic philosopher, had on turning him away from analytic philosophy. This interest in philosophy of science did not lead to any book on the subject, but he turned instead to the related subject of decision theory, concerning "rational choice when it comes to accepting or rejecting a scientific hypothesis" (Borradori 1994: 77), leading to his Ph.D. thesis on "The Normative Theory of Individual Choice" (later published as a book in 1990). Even after that he toyed fruitlessly with an attempt to solve the free will problem (*SP*: l) before finally returning to political philosophy and getting down to *Anarchy, State, and Utopia* (*ASU*).

Throughout this period Nozick regarded himself as an analytic philosopher, if perhaps a rather loosely anchored one (Borradori 1994: 78). One feature he has always shared with analytic philosophy is a certain distancing from history, despite his growing and lasting interest in certain Oriental philosophies which he traces to his empiricist background that insisted you should "take your experiences seriously" (Borradori 1994:79). Among the great historical figures he acknowledges only Socrates as his master (Borradori 1994: 80; cf. *SP*: 2–3) and says he has "always started again from zero" (ibid.). In reflecting on his own reading of Quine, he remarks how he was struck "by the difference between thinking independently about a subject and thinking that is focused upon someone else's ideas. When you approach a topic through the route of someone's theories, that person's mode of structuring the issues limits how far you can stray and how much you can discover. You think within their 'problematic'" (*SP*: 8). Of course, as we can see from the case of someone like Descartes, this does not mean that one is not in fact influenced by one's predecessors – otherwise the growth of philosophy would follow a very uneconomical course. Indeed Nozick himself says, when discussing what problems he is proposing to tackle in *Philosophical Explanations* (*PE*), "other philosophical views are scanned and searched for help" (*PE*: 21). This is different from using the views of some one philosopher as one's basis.

Nozick's change of approach: proof and explanation

Nozick's development after *Anarchy, State, and Utopia* brings us to a fundamental change in his whole approach to philosophy. Up to this time, as we have seen, he was firmly if not very enthusiastically in the analytic camp. But the Introduction to his second book, *Philosophical Explanations*, offers a different style of philosophizing, aiming at explanation rather than proof. It was this emphasis on explanation that linked this development to his teacher Hempel, whose most important contribution to philosophy of science consisted in a thorough examination of the notion of explanation, although with Nozick the notion led in a quite different direction from the analytic interests of Hempel. What Nozick objects to is the alleged coercive nature of philosophy in the analytical and similar traditions; *Philosophical Explanations* begins with a subsection called "Coercive Philosophy". One thing Nozick objects to is attempts to "deduce [one's] total view from a few . . . intuitively based axioms" (*PE*: 3), whereby "One brick is piled upon another to produce a tall philosophical tower, one brick wide"; if the bottom brick is removed the whole thing falls to pieces. He wants to replace this "tottering tower" model by one based on the Parthenon: "First we explore our separate philosophical insights, column by column; afterwards, we unite and unify them under an overarching roof of general principles or themes" (ibid.). Apart from the exaggeration of "one brick wide" – he speaks himself of "intuitively based axioms" (plural) – this is a fair enough point. Long arguments of a purely deductive nature do indeed incur this risk of collapse, because it happens so often that an argument is valid (having its conclusion follow from its premises) without being sound (having all its premises true as well). But it is not clear how far analytic philosophy faces this danger, although its parent, logical positivism, may do so in so far as it depends on the verification principle.

But Nozick wants to go further than this. The main idea is a remarkable one. He is against the whole enterprise of proof as an aim of philosophy because he thinks of it as trying to force people to believe things, and "[i]s that a nice way to behave toward someone?" he asks (*PE*: 5). He emphasizes the way in which we describe arguments as "powerful" or "knockdown" and as carrying "punch" or "forcing" people to conclusions (*PE*: 4). He supports this by appealing to the way children think of arguments as involving raised voices and anger. There is certainly a sense of the word "argue" in which it does mean this, although it is hardly its main sense, and certainly not its original one, which is something like "make clear" or "prove", as in expressions such as "His treatment of his enemies argues his natural generosity". But the more important point is the one about what Nozick sees as the coercive nature of argument. That there is some plausibility in this is shown by proverbial remarks such as "The man convinced against his will is of the same opinion still". Nozick points out that as a means of getting people to believe things, coercive argument has its drawbacks because of the weakness of the sanctions at the philosopher's disposal. If the hearer "is willing to bear the label of 'irrational' . . . he can skip away happily maintaining his former belief". If the philosopher wishes to pursue the matter he can only do so by "produc[ing] reasons for accepting reasons" – which begs the question. In the last resort the hearer could simply "sit there silently, smiling, Buddhalike" (*PE*: 4).

This is all very well but perhaps the irrationalist is getting away with too easy a victory. The difficulty of giving an ultimate justification for appealing to reason was clear already to Aristotle, who tackled the problem in Book 4, Chapter 4 of his *Metaphysics* by offering the earliest version of a kind of argument later associated especially with Kant and known as a transcendental argument. Taking the law of contradiction (which forbids the acceptance of any pair of contradictory statements) as the basis of rational argument, Aristotle says that of course we cannot force anybody to accept it by offering a proof of it because any such proof – indeed any proof at all – must rely on it, so that we should simply be begging the question. But if we are brought to a stand here so is our opponent, and far more radically. If he refuses to say anything then we cannot do anything with him – but why should this worry us? We cannot convince the table in front of us, but that is no problem. But as soon as our opponent tries to assert anything we have got him, for he is already committing himself to the law of contradiction. He cannot speak or even think coherently without so committing himself. At this point he will probably accuse us of smuggling in the word "coherently"; perhaps he just prefers to think incoherently. "I accept that the law of contradiction is valid", he may say; "it's just that I also think it's invalid." But if he asserts something and at the same time asserts its opposite, he has not achieved anything; whatever his purpose was in asserting it he will have frustrated that purpose. Of course he may have some ulterior purpose, as when a criminal might utter a contradiction to convince a court that he was of unsound mind, but then he has merely uttered the contradiction and not seriously asserted it, or even seriously thought it. I could utter a mere string of words such as "Over not yellow the when", but I haven't asserted or thought anything. Indeed, without the law of contradiction one could not use words at all, for what would they mean? Whatever I want my words to mean, if I allow at the same time that they do not mean that, then I have not even uttered a string of words, but merely a string of noises, like an animal.

Having shown, as I hope, that the law of contradiction is essential to thought, I had better add that there is a school of philosophers who partially reject it. These are the dialetheists with their associated notion of paraconsistency. But even they do not reject the law entirely. They merely think that some contradictions are true, not that any old contradiction is so, and so they can consistently allow that their own assertions are subject to the law, at least as far as anything said so far goes. Their main motivation is to deal with the logical paradoxes of Russell and others. Dialetheism, which came to prominence during the 1980s, is highly controversial, but it is not relevant to discuss it further here.

So Nozick's smiling Buddha would, to all intents and purposes, not be a human being at all. This part of Nozick's argument has consisted in saying that we cannot force a human being to be rational, and our answer has been that indeed we cannot, but that if he is to be a human being at all he must be at least partly – and we might say mainly – rational already; he will have lapses as we all do, but they must be the exception. Even the stupidest of our philosophical friends thinks and behaves rationally in most of his daily living. It is not true then that we are helpless in the face of the irrationalist.

Coercion

But is it anyway fair to regard the philosopher who aims at proof as using force against his opponents? Perhaps there is a sense in which someone who compels you by rational argument to come to a certain conclusion is using force or coercion, but it is not the normal sense in which we talk of coercing people. Indeed, it is hard to see how what we do could be coercive if, as Nozick has been saying, it is impossible to compel people to come to certain conclusions. Perhaps the charge is that we try to do such things? But there is surely a fallacy here (which is why I called the idea "remarkable" when introducing it at the start). We normally talk of coercing people when we make them act against their better judgement, or in some sense take the decision out of their hands. The qualification "in some sense" is necessary because the person who is coerced is still the agent of his actions; I do not coerce you into killing someone if I push you off a cliff so that you fall on top of them; you would not be pardoned because of extenuating circumstances, but acquitted. Nevertheless if you are coerced you are interfered with from outside. But your reason is not outside you. If you do a mathematical calculation you may feel "compelled" to come to a certain conclusion, perhaps an unwelcome one. But this is no infringement of your freedom. If we could choose what conclusion to come to in rational arguments the whole notion of rationality would collapse. Why should it be any different if the considerations that lead you to the conclusion are presented by someone else? It is true that they may compel you to consider something you would not otherwise have considered – once they have brought it to your attention you may find it impossible to ignore it. But this is not the same as compelling you, once you have thought of it, to conclude things from it that you would not otherwise have concluded.

Coercion is a topic Nozick discusses in one of his early articles (in 1969, reprinted in *Socratic Puzzles*). It raises two questions in particular: What is it and when, if ever, is it morally justifiable? It is the first of these that is relevant here.

We have seen that to be coerced is not the same as having one's behaviour literally forced, so that the action is taken completely out of one's hands. A coerced action is still an action and must depend on a choice, even though the choice may be "not fully one's own", a notion Nozick discusses at the end of his article (*SP*: 42–4). A question he does not discuss here is what constitutes a choice. Could there be a choice that was not at all one's own? Could my action depend entirely on my choice or volition, but that choice itself be entirely determined, e.g. through drugs or hypnotism? Or would there be no choice at all here, and so no real action? This leads to the problem of free will, which we will return to later. But Nozick does allow (*SP*: 44) that coercion may admit of degrees. Typically it might be said that you are coerced into action if you are presented with considerations that make it unreasonable to expect, although not strictly impossible, that you should act in any other way. I coerce you if I point a gun at your head. Nozick discusses various other conditions and complications, such as whether I must have certain intentions, or even know of your existence; whether you must have certain reasons for acting as you do; whether you are coerced into doing certain other things, either as means to or as consequences of your coerced action; and whether there is more than one type of coercion. In particular he distinguishes between threats and offers: why is it more natural to say that threats coerce than that offers do? Because, he thinks, normally we (or strictly "the Rational Man") welcome being presented with an offer, but not being presented with a threat. (Cf. here his later distinction between forcing and inducing in *The Examined Life* (*EL*) 175n.) The "normally" is important. We may welcome a threat if it gives us an excuse for doing something we wanted to do anyway. As for unwelcome offers, consider Bernard Williams's "Pedro" example (Smart and Williams 1973: 98–9): Pedro is about to shoot 20 hostages when a foreign visitor arrives. To honour the visitor, Pedro offers to set the other hostages free if the visitor will himself shoot one of them. Hardly a very welcome offer! Nozick does not mention this particular case, but it is a feature of his work that he is constantly sensitive to the possibility of exceptions to his claims and the need to modify or fill them out, and he often draws attention to specially awkward cases without attempting to resolve them (e.g. *SP*: 336 n.14, with text at *SP*: 20).

Nozick distinguishes coercion from two related notions, being unfree not to take the course in question, and having no choice about whether to take it. He starts his article with examples of not being coerced into an action but still being unfree to avoid it, and of being coerced into an action but still free to avoid it. But his examples involve some ambiguity in the notion of being free. Suppose I know I will be caught if I rob a bank; I am not thereby coerced into not robbing it (no threats are involved), but I am not free to rob it. Or suppose I am coerced by threats into doing something, but the threatener was bluffing; then really I was free not to do it. I am free, it seems from this last case, if I can act without suffering certain untoward consequences. But in the former case whether I am free depends on whether I know I can so act. In another example I am imprisoned and so not free to go to Chicago, though I am not coerced into not going there. Here my lack of freedom depends on physical impossibility. In a fourth example I am not free to murder someone in an audience I am addressing, though not coerced into not doing so. Here it is not clear whether this is because I would be apprehended or because I am not morally free to murder. Later (*SP*: 34–5) the question concerns what I should be free to do, where the context suggests "should be allowed to do". Nozick implies that he is aware of these distinctions (*SP*: 333 n.1), but does not discuss them.

On the notion of having no choice, Nozick merely presents a couple of examples en passant of cases where it might be said that someone "had no choice" while refusing to say they were coerced (*SP*: 24, 30). A more obvious example, where no threats or offers are even in the offing, might be that of the proverbial philosopher deciding whether to rescue an accidentally encountered drowning child from a river on a chilly day. In this case, moreover, though one might "have no choice" the action would clearly be "fully one's own".

The core of coercion then is the existence of a threat. How does this affect what we were saying about proof and persuasion? To be threatened is, at least, to be faced with the prospect of some unwelcome consequence if one does or fails to do something. But what sort of consequence? Presumably in the case of philosophical argument believing something one does not wish to believe. If the proof really is a proof one will end up believing something true, and therefore, assuming one is genuinely engaged in philosophical argument, something which at least under that description (i.e. as true) one would wish to believe. Is the threat then that if one refuses to accept the proof, or perhaps if one refuses to enter into the argument at all, one will end up believing something false? The former is presumably the relevant case, since we are concerned with methods of philosophical discussion, not methods of getting people to enter into such discussion. But Nozick, as we saw, raised the question of the threatener's intentions. If these do not include bringing about the unwelcome consequence if the threat is not complied with (and the hearer knows this) then we have not a threat but a warning, and that does not constitute coercion, or not in the primary sense (cf. the "mother's heart attack" example at *SP*: 21).

But perhaps the real objection to the appeal to proof in philosophy is that it involves not coercion in the proper sense, but an attempt to foist unwelcome truths on the listener. Although I normally want to hold true beliefs (if we did not the whole notion of belief would collapse), some truths I might prefer not to know, e.g. that I have a fatal disease, or that some long cherished philosophical view of mine is false. Take the latter case (what we say will apply a fortiori to the former). Suppose you present a sound argument (a valid argument with true premises) that my view is false. I need not listen, but as we saw just above, your attempts to make me do so are not what is under discussion. Once we exclude this, and concentrate simply on what you say, then surely we would only talk of coercion, force, or anything in that area, if you try to brainwash me; or browbeat me by appealing to my emotions or using emotive language; or by using fallacious but plausible arguments; or by any other such rhetorical devices. But in those cases you would not be appealing to my reason but trying to bypass it, or in the case of deliberate fallacy distort it. You would not be appealing to proof but to something else, a misuse of reason. As we saw earlier, I may be compelled by reason to come to a certain conclusion, but this is no violation of my integrity as a rational person. It is interesting that in *Philosophical Explanations*, Nozick brings as an ally Hannah Arendt's description of Lessing: "He . . . wanted to coerce no one either by force or by proofs. He regarded the tyranny of those who attempt to dominate thinking by reasoning *and sophistries*, by compelling argumentation, as more dangerous to freedom than orthodoxy" (*PE*: 651 n.2, italics mine; cf. text at *PE*: 5). Either Arendt or Lessing (or both) was surely pretty muddled.

A kinder view of what Nozick is doing (suggested to me by Hailwood) would say that he is really concerned with the sort of aggressive arrogance that some philosophers may adopt in trying to control others and force them to believe what they themselves believe, as against inspiring people to think for themselves by showing how things can "fit together". There may be something in this, although if this *is* Nozick's point he is rather asking to be misunderstood by his extended and exclusive development of the point, and his emphasis on attacking what appears to be a particular type of deductive argument (the "tottering tower" model) rather than a manner of conducting the argument.

Explanation and understanding

What then does Nozick want us to substitute for appeal to proof as a way of doing philosophy? We have seen that *Philosophical Explanations* contrasts proof with explanation. Here we must avoid a possible misunderstanding. In rejecting proof as the aim of philosophy Nozick is not rejecting all appeal to deductive argument. Not only would that be completely at odds with his acknowledgement of Socrates, but for his mentor Hempel the primary kind of explanation has a deductive structure whereby to explain a phenomenon is to deduce it from certain initial conditions by using general laws, and Nozick's own work is of course packed with rational arguments of one sort or another. His point is presumably (he doesn't attack this question head-on) that this use of rational argument is subordinate to an over-all aim that is persuasive rather than coercive. One might wonder whether this subordinate use of rational argument can avoid his own objections to proof as the final aim. If rational argument is essentially coercive it will presumably still be so when used in a subordinate role, even if its coerciveness is then confined to a limited sphere. But be that as it may, this tendency reaches its culmination in one of his later books, *The Examined Life*, of which he says, "I was presenting one person's thoughts in the hope that it would stimulate alternative thoughts in other people. I wasn't asking the readers to accept what I was writing as the truth about these topics, but as a vehicle that could help them to think more deeply about those questions" (Borradori 1994: 74).

A page later Nozick talks of his desire to "structure the enterprise of philosophy around the activity of understanding" (Borradori 1994: 75). In *Philosophical Explanations* he compares explanation with understanding. They differ because explanation shows how the explanandum is connected to other actual things, while understanding "locates it in a network of possibility" (*PE*: 12). Even a hypothesis known to be false can produce some illumination, he thinks (*PE*: 11), but it "will not explain how something *is* possible" (*PE*: 12). Philosophers are often condemned for appealing to eccentric or bizarre possibilities that no-one would take seriously. Nozick himself certainly does so quite frequently, and he defends the practice because to ban it might mean that philosophy "could not lead us to radically new and surprising truths or insights" (*PE*: 12). It might be added that the implausibility of philosophical examples often depends on their gross oversimplification or artificiality, which may well be justified in order to bring out some underlying principle that could get lost in a welter of detail. Compare the way problem-setters in elementary mechanics tell us to ignore friction or air resistance.

When he introduces explanation as a philosophical aim, Nozick emphasizes problems which ask "how something is or can be possible" (*PE*: 8). He adds a long list of such problems about free will, knowledge, motion and other topics, including philosophy itself. In each case some everyday conviction is apparently excluded by a philosophical argument (as, for example, Zeno's paradoxes seem to exclude motion, see "Guide to further reading" for Chapter 1). Since we face an apparent inconsistency between the apparent excluder and the everyday conviction, we have three choices: we could deny the conviction, deny the excluder, or deny the inconsistency. What determines which choice we take, particularly between the first and the other two, Nozick calls an "interesting issue" (*PE*: 9); but to discuss it further here would take us into a general discussion of scepticism. He does, however, point out that simply to offer a proof of the everyday conviction, assuming one is available, would still leave us not understanding how it was possible in view of the apparent excluder. Clearly he has a point here. Most people would regard ordinary experience as sufficient proof of the reality of motion, but that does nothing to dispel our puzzlement about Zeno's paradoxes.

Explanation produces understanding, since the actual is a fortiori possible (*PE*: 12). In view of this interest in understanding, we might expect Nozick to give considerable attention to Verstehen, the process by which we allegedly acquire understanding of another's actions or of a historical event by imaginatively projecting ourselves into the minds of the agents concerned. He does indeed devote two short discussions to it (*SP*: 123–5; *PE*: 636–8) in which he points out that its reliability is subject to empirical checking since we can make predictions about others' behaviour on the basis of it and then see whether these are borne out; and also that its use depends on our having similar insight into ourselves (since it involves putting ourselves into others' shoes), and that this insight can similarly be checked by seeing if our predictions of our own behaviour are borne out. But Verstehen is, of course, of limited use in general philosophy, since it is concerned only with the behaviour of other animate beings; it is therefore of interest mainly to philosophy of psychology and philosophy of history.

Truth and the aim of philosophy

But despite this emphasis on understanding, Nozick insists that the primary aim of *Philosophical Explanations* is more modest and limited to explanation, although that will produce some understanding. To aim directly for understanding, he thinks (*PE*: 21), may simply leave us with a morass of mere possibilities that will not explain what actually does enable us to have free will or knowledge, etc. However, at this point he admits to what might seem a disconcerting pluralism. He envisages a "basketful" of admissible philosophical views that are mutually incompatible but none of which should be rejected completely. Does this turn him into a relativist? No, he claims, because not all views are admissible, and those that are admissible are ranked – at least partially. But even those of higher rank need to be supplemented in certain respects by those of lower rank. He disclaims any attempt to provide a neutral way of ranking the views; he will simply describe "how things look from within the view I rank first" (*PE*: 22).

Does this simply replace relativism with subjectivism? Any view one puts forward is simply one's own view. Others may contrast my views with the truth, but I cannot contrast them myself, except in the sense of admitting that I may later need to alter my present view. But if a higher ranked view needs supplementing by a lower one, why not construct a yet higher one containing the acceptable elements of both? Is the point that such a view could be inconsistent? That might remind us of complementarity in physics, according to which photons etc. are both particles and waves, and thereby have inconsistent properties since, for example, particles are located at definite discrete points while waves are not. I cannot discuss the physics case in detail, but two points suggest themselves. First, things can consistently have apparently inconsistent properties in different respects or from different points of view. And secondly we may well find it necessary to say inconsistent things, but if so, we must regard this a mere stepping stone to a consistent theory perhaps requiring quite new concepts. Scientists often use theories they know are strictly false, either because they have no alternative until some Einstein comes along, or because they are simpler and near enough to the truth for the purposes at hand; they measure their tennis courts by Euclidean geometry because its errors when applied to the physical world are undetectably small at that scale. The situation in philosophy is no doubt vaguer and more confused, but it is hard to see why it should differ in principle.

All this, however, must not be confused with a different point about the aim of philosophy. In a typical expression of his views about method Nozick says: "Rather than force somebody to believe by constructing an incontrovertible argument, it is more morally legitimate and more epistemologically creative to stimulate the interlocutor to alternative ways of thinking" (Borradori 1994: 18–19). This and similar exhortations (e.g. *PE*: 7) suggest a procedure of presenting different views, perhaps favouring some rather than others but pointing out the merits and defects of them all. Seen as a pedagogic method this need not end in either relativism or subjectivism, but it leads us on to the question of Nozick's attitude to truth.

Despite saying that he has "always started again from zero" (Borradori 1994: 80) Nozick cannot see how to "start philosophy in a neutral way, making no philosophical assumptions, remaining neutral among all possible philosophical views" (*PE*: 19). But his attitude to the search for truth is in fact somewhat ambivalent. He insists that "The goal is finding out the truth, after all" (*PE*: 20), and says that *Philosophical Explanations* aims by and large not at understanding but "at explanation, at truth" (*PE*: 21). Yet he says of the explanations he tentatively puts forward, "not only do I not ask you to believe they are correct, I do not think it important for me to believe them correct, either" (*PE*: 24), and later he says, admittedly of his least coercive book, *The Examined Life*, that he "wasn't asking the readers to accept what I was writing as the truth about these topics, but as a vehicle that could help them to think more deeply about those questions" (Borradori 1994: 74). What are we to make of all this? How can someone say both that their aim is to pursue truth and that it does not matter whether their readers or even they themselves believe what they are saying?

Three remarks suggest themselves. First, readers who "think more deeply" are presumably intended to aim at, and hopefully arrive at, the truth in doing so. Secondly Nozick presumably thinks it true that the things he says will help them in this aim. And thirdly he certainly gives the impression of aiming at truth in his own philosophical discussions, even though what he says is often avowedly inconclusive. To assert something is to present it as true, and to assert it tentatively is still to tentatively present it as being true. *Philosophical Explanations* decries "the aesthetic view of philosophy" (*PE*: 20 – despite the final subsection of *PE*: "Philosophy as an Art Form"); and although in *The Examined Life* he "just wanted to probe more deeply into what made life meaningful and valuable" (Borradori 1994: 73) he was evidently concerned with the truth about what did so.

The unity of Nozick's philosophy

I started by calling Nozick a fox, not a hedgehog. How much unity then can we expect to find in his philosophy? Despite not being keen on engaging with his critics he does modify his views from time to time. But he is not one of those, like Russell or Wittgenstein, who hold radically different views at different times. His philosophy therefore does not fall apart at different periods of his life in the same area. But the focus of his interest changes, and it may not always be obvious what his approaches in the different spheres that engage his attention have in common. Let us return for a moment to coercion. We shall see later that in another sphere, that of personal identity, he takes and indeed initiates a "closest continuer" or "closest relative" view. We have seen that for Nozick a coerced action is still an action, and so involves choice, even if this is "not fully one's own". But whether an action influenced by other people is voluntary may depend on something outside the agent, namely whether they had a right to act as they did (*ASU*: 262), and, as we shall also see later, when our actions are influenced by outside forces whether we deserve punishment may depend on whether those forces are personal or impersonal (*PE*: 395–6). These views are examples of an "externalism" akin to that explained at the start of Chapter 5 (in this book) that pervades Nozick's philosophy. But for more on Nozick's "externalist" view of coercion and how he uses morality to define it, see Wertheimer (1987, especially 251–5, 264–6).

A more important and pervasive respect in which Nozick has a unified philosophy is brought out explicitly by himself. His first published book, *Anarchy, State, and Utopia*, was notoriously libertarian and anti-coercive in outlook. As we saw earlier, he had not at that stage developed his rejection of analytic philosophy, but it was perhaps by a "natural outgrowth in continuity", he thinks (Borradori 1994: 75), that he came to be anti-coercive in philosophy too. In *Philosophical Explanations* itself he compares the philosophical pluralism we have just been discussing with the pluralistic framework for utopia that he had developed, as we shall see later, in *Anarchy, State, and Utopia*, although he did not have that earlier discussion in mind in forming his later views (*PE*: 654 n.15). We will return briefly to the unity of Nozick's philosophy in Chapter 7 ("Interlude: the unity of Nozick's philosophy").

In what follows we will partly consider Nozick's philosophy in the order in which he developed it, but subject to the need to divide the field into coherent and manageable chunks that each have some unity of their own. We will start with *Anarchy, State, and Utopia*, which will occupy us for two chapters, corresponding to its ethics and its politics respectively. This more or less reverses the treatment these subjects receive in the book itself, but it seems best to start by saying something of the moral basis of the system before going into the structure erected on it as a basis. Nozick does modify and develop his views later, especially in the moral sphere, so the third chapter says something about that. The order of the next few chapters, dealing with topics mainly covered in *Philosophical Explanations*, is rather arbitrary, but we start with the area where Nozick is best known after his political views, namely epistemology; there he introduces the notion of "tracking the truth", and also says some things about scepticism and evidence. As mentioned previously, Nozick's 1963 Ph.D. dissertation on decision theory was finally published as a book in 1990. Much of this is a fairly technical treatment of certain positions in decision theory and game theory. Some readers may be pleased to learn that I am not competent to discuss these and, in general, shall not attempt to do so – with one exception. This is the famous paradox of choice known as Newcomb's Problem (see below, Chapter 6), which Nozick introduced into print and discusses in three different places, starting with the dissertation. This chapter also discusses various issues arising in his latest main book, *The Nature of Rationality (NR)*, where among other things he offers an evolutionary account of the nature of rationality. A substantial part of *Philosophical Explanations* is devoted to metaphysics and philosophy of mind. Here Nozick's most original contribution is his "closest continuer" theory of personal identity, which also has implications for other metaphysical problems such as that of the "ship of Theseus" and which we mentioned briefly above. There are a few other problems too about the self which are treated in the same chapter. Among the questions traditionally most associated with metaphysics are those about what exists and about God. In particular, the question why there is something rather than nothing occupies Nozick for quite a time, and he discusses God in the context of a treatment of infinity in general. The last of our three chapters on metaphysics (Chapters 7, 8 and 9) concerns free will, a topic which, as we saw earlier, he spent quite a lot of time on before turning to political philosophy, and to which he returned in *Philosophical Explanations*. Our final chapter then winds things up by looking briefly at some more general topics on philosophy and life.

Summary

Although often known primarily, to his dismay, as a political philosopher, Nozick has contributed substantially to epistemology and the metaphysics of identity and has also examined at some depth, albeit to a far more mixed response, other metaphysical topics. His initial interest in methodology was followed, after a fruitless foray into free will, by his political philosophy, but then led him, paradoxically through the influence of the analytic philosopher Hempel, to abandon analytic philosophy – at least in the narrower of its two senses – and develop a more irenic outlook aiming at explanation and ultimately understanding rather than proof. This leads us to discuss how he treats coercion and how he relates it to proof, and whether he can avoid an over-irenic devaluing of rationality and the essential role of the law of contradiction, falling into a certain relativism or else subjectivism. Perhaps he can avoid all these when his approach is properly understood, but then he will risk veering away from his insistence that the aim of philosophy is to seek the truth, a risk from which, it seems, he can be at best tentatively defended. Finally, we ask to what degree there is any unity to Nozick's philosophy, a topic we will return to briefly later.

Chapter 2

Anarchy, State, and Utopia: *the moral basis*

Introduction

When *Anarchy, State, and Utopia* was published, it received a mixed reception to say the least. Most reviewers praised it as an elegant and elaborate presentation of a very distinctive position, but the position itself was vigorously attacked from all sides, although some assailants admitted to illumination while some were shocked. In the Introduction to his *Reading Nozick*, Paul (1981: 3) quotes a review by Barry who castigates Nozick for a "sort of cuteness that would be wearing in a graduate student and seems to me quite indecent in someone who, from the lofty heights of a professorial chair, is proposing to starve or humiliate ten percent or so of his fellow citizens . . . by eliminating all transfer payments through the state, leaving the sick, the old, the disabled, the mothers with young children and no bread-winner, and so on, to the tender mercies of private charity, given at the whim and pleasure of the donors and on any terms that they choose to impose" (Barry 1975: 331–6). Nozick would no doubt reply that this is to blame the messenger for the message. If the conclusions he comes to are the right ones they had better be uttered, whether from lofty heights or from the abyss.

So what are these conclusions? To start with a nutshell account, Nozick holds that each person is a separate individual with inviolable rights to live as he chooses, provided only that he respects the similar rights of other individuals. These rights include the rights to be free from interference, to own and use at one's own absolute discretion legitimately acquired property, to enjoy the fruits of contracts freely entered by both sides, and to enforce these rights unless one has contracted such enforcement out. But they do not include the right to any uncontracted assistance from others, and one's obligations to others are correspondingly limited. Only to avoid "catastrophic moral horror" (*ASU*: 30n.) may these rights be violated. This of course is only what I have called it, a nutshell account, but it forms the basis of what Nozick must set out to defend.

As the Barry quotation illustrates, Nozick's position is often regarded as hard and inhumane. Nothing that he says in any way discourages private charity, which he would certainly wish to encourage, but as Barry again makes clear this is humiliating to the recipients, and although certainly necessary to some degree in most practicable societies can hardly be thought of as anything but a most unfortunate necessity. Nozick himself describes in his Preface (*ASU*: ix–x) his initial aversion to believing "anything so apparently callous toward the needs and suffering of others". The force of argument reluctantly compelled him to accept the philosophy of *Anarchy, State, and Utopia*, though as we shall see his arguments at this point are in rather short supply. His initial reluctance disappeared as he became accustomed to his conclusions and their consequences, although he acknowledges that this puts him in some bad company. In later works he does modify some of his conclusions, but for the moment he must follow the argument where it leads: "it may be that correctness in ethics is not found in what we naturally think". A later passage (*EL*: 280) makes clear that he is quite capable of seeing the evil in capitalism and the good in communism.

The sheer force of reason then is what Nozick takes, or perhaps would like to think of himself as taking, as impelling him on his journey. But how exclusively can he follow this course? Reason needs premises, and even Kant, the most rationalistic of moral philosophers, would not have got far had he not bowed in reverence to the authority of the moral law.

What then are Nozick's premises? It has often been pointed out, including by Nozick himself, that he says very little by way of an ultimate moral justification for the whole system. The Preface to *Anarchy, State, and Utopia* warns us not to expect "a precise theory of the moral basis of individual rights" or "a precise statement of the principles of [his] tripartite theory of distributive justice" (*ASU*: xiv), and he ends his first chapter by saying that such a task might take a life-time, adding, however, that "[t]hat task is so crucial, the gap left without its accomplishment so yawning, that it is only a minor comfort to note that" he is no worse than Locke in that respect (*ASU*:

9, cf. 153). This apparent casualness has indeed been pounced on by critics, and Paul (1981: Introduction) says that only in *Anarchy, State, and Utopia*, among the various books that espouse a similar philosophy, is that philosophy left "without ethical support" (Paul 1981: 17) – although Paul defends Nozick's limited aim of merely obtaining credibility for a currently unpopular view by deflating various alternatives to it (1981: 5, 13–4). Similarly, Davis in an otherwise critical article regards the "hints we are given" as "enough to ask of the first version of any high-level philosophical theory" (Paul 1981: 345); Nozick himself claims that he is no worse than Rawls in this respect (*ASU*: 230). Still, it might be thought that a controversial theory, as Nozick's undoubtedly is, calls for something a bit more positive by way of support than merely an attack on its rivals, or even hints, and fortunately for a chapter with the title of this one we are not left entirely in the dark about the basis of Nozick's moral system.

There are basically two approaches to ethics relevant to us here – teleological and deontological – associated with the terms "good" and "right" respectively, although the distinction between them is not always as sharp or as obvious as it might seem. For the teleologist the main aim in life should be to pursue the good, whatever that might consist in, and the justification for our claims and duties will be forward-looking. For the deontologist there are rights and duties that arise from and are justified by certain situations. Their justification is backward-looking. The rights can, and no doubt usually do, involve the production of good. I have a right to be paid a salary by my employer, because salaries are a good thing. Of course other things must be true too if I am to deserve my salary, but the justification for my employer's duty to pay me is not that by doing so he will promote the greatest good – he might well produce more by giving the money to charity. If I have promised to do something for you I shall presumably benefit you if I do it; otherwise the promise would in a sense lose its point, but I still have a duty to fulfil it unless I am released from it, either by you or by some relevant circumstance such as your death. (We are of course ignoring many complications irrelevant here, such as whether a superior duty can override the promise.)

In these terms Nozick is decidedly a deontologist, although he makes rights rather than duties the foundation of his system. People have rights, and other people have duties to respect those rights, which cannot, without some further ado, be overridden. The "further ado" is the source of some complication, if no more, to his system, which we will look at later. Deontologists are not bound to ignore teleology altogether. They can allow that we can have a duty to produce good, but they deny that this is the overriding consideration. Our duty often tells us to produce less good than we might, as in the employer case above. Nozick can well allow that I have a positive duty to give to charity. What he would insist on is that I also have a right not to give to it, or at least a right not to be compelled to give to it. Here we need to distinguish between what we might call morally enforceable duties and purely moral duties. (Whether a duty is legally enforceable depends on the legal system and raises other issues.) I might have a moral duty to give to charity, but also a right not to be forced to do so. I might even have a specific duty on this occasion now to give to an urgent relief project which only my great wealth can make possible, while still having a right not to be forced to do so; I might still say I am "within my rights" in refusing, even if I risk being condemned as piggish. It might be worth adding that in his discussion of Ayn Rand, written shortly before *Anarchy, State, and Utopia*, Nozick quotes the following sentence from Mortimer Adler: "I would like to add in passing that those who regard their duties to others or to the community as independent of their obligation to make a good life for themselves are either sentimentalists or thoughtless do-gooders". Nozick's reaction, one surely eloquent enough, is to add two exclamation marks of his own (see Paul 1981: 228 (= *SP*: 384)). Paul's version does not make clear that the exclamation marks belong to Nozick, not to Adler (see the original, Nozick 1971a: 302). To be fair to Adler, he adds the words "who often do more harm than good – not only harm to themselves but also to others and to the community itself" (Adler 1970: 172).

The role of the individual

"Individuals have rights, and there are things no person or group may do to them (without violating their rights)." Such is the opening sentence of *Anarchy, State, and Utopia* and it sets the tone for the whole. But what are these rights? Who has them, and where do they come from? We have already been warned not to expect too much here (*ASU*: xiv), and Nozick has been criticized for relying simply on moral intuitions, which others might not agree with, and offering no more than "a reconstruction or systemisation" of them (Wolff in Paul 1981: 80), although it is hard to see what else he could rely on in the last resort; demonstrations of ultimate moral premises are, to say the least, hard to come by. But he does say something. As for who has rights, Nozick insists that only individuals can have them. Individuals can transfer their rights by various processes, and a group of individuals may have a right to do something that no member of the group separately has a right to do, but only because different individuals who separately had a right to do part of the thing in question each transfer these rights to the group. Suppose I own a riverside acre of land and you own an adjacent acre and we each wish to construct a marina that will require two acres. I can use my acre but not yours and you can use yours but not mine, so if we combine, the pair of us will have a right to build the marina although neither of us had that right separately; but the pair of us will not have any rights except those that derive in this way from those we have separately. (The example is mine, but see *ASU*: 89.) The same applies, in Nozick's view, to larger combinations and organizations, such as the state. But the situation will be more complex because the members of an organization such as a state, assuming it is a legitimate one, have transferred to it not merely simple rights like that of owning land, but also the right to carry out certain functions, particularly defensive ones, which will involve the right to take decisions on matters that were not accessible to the original holders of the rights, and which they could hardly be in a position to decide upon individually even if they had the relevant knowledge. The setting up of the state will occupy us at length later, but the point is that there are, for Nozick, no emergent rights of collective entities.

The significance of individuals is that they alone are the subjects of experiences, and so the bearers of interests. Individuals may undergo certain evils to attain greater goods, but "there is no *social entity* with a good that undergoes some sacrifice for its own good". There are only individuals, each of whom has only his own experiences, and for each of whom "his is the only life he has". "Talk of an overall social good covers this up" (*ASU*: 32–3; *ASU*: 228 refers to Rawls (1971: 27) for the same point). "This root idea, namely, that there are different individuals with separate lives and so no one may be sacrificed for others, underlies the existence of moral side constraints" (*ASU*: 33).

In view of the charge of inhumanity so often brought against Nozick it is hard not to see in these remarks, which form one of the foundations of his whole system, an emphasis on what must be at the root of any humane philosophy or charitable enterprise, and this must surely have contributed to the acceptance that Nozick's ideas have often received, especially in recent years. It is ironic that, although as we saw above he is fully in favour of charitable enterprise, the working out of the implications of these ideas has seemed to lead so far in the opposite direction.

The basis of rights

The separateness of individuals forms part of the basis for Nozick's doctrine of rights, and he uses it in a significant way to argue from moral form to moral content – significant because one way of making progress in ethics is to argue that if morality has a certain structure (in this case a deontological structure involving side constraints) it must also have a certain particular content: "the form of morality includes F (moral side constraints); the best explanation of morality's being F is p (a strong statement of the distinction of individuals); and from p follows a particular moral content, namely, the libertarian constraint [prohibiting aggression against another]" (*ASU*: 34, omitting footnote).

This, however, is only a start, as Nozick is well aware. What is the point of having rights? This may seem an odd question. A legal system might give one a right, e.g. to make a "citizen's arrest" in certain circumstances, in order to promote a secure society. But moral rights are not "given" in this way. They either exist or they don't. But we can still ask what their point is, in the sense of what principles govern their existence or non-existence, and indeed why we should bother about them at all. Rights are presumably things we welcome having, which suggests they have some connection with promoting our interests. Some people have talked of a criminal's right to be punished, a right criminals are seldom seen to assert. Plato in his dialogue *Gorgias* does not talk in terms of rights, but does claim that it is in the criminal's own interest to be punished because that will purify him and make him a better person. Whatever we may think of this argument there is another that has been offered in modern times for a right to be punished, and one that brings us nearer to Nozick. A few decades ago, when retributive punishment was rather out of fashion, it was sometimes said that criminals were really the product of their inheritance and environment so that it was more humane to regard them as needing treatment rather than punishment. Where this might be said to violate the criminal's rights is that it treats him as less than a fully rational and responsible human being. Perhaps some criminals really are like this (psychopaths), but most presumably are mentally normal, and normal people surely think they have a right to respect for their full human status, even if there might be occasions when they would find it prudent not to trumpet that right too loudly.

It is this sort of consideration that makes Nozick forbid "paternalistic aggression", embarked on for its victim's benefit, for "there are distinct individuals, each with his own life *to lead*" (*ASU*: 34, his emphasis). He explicitly asks what constraints are based on, and refers to the meaning of life as offering the best hope for an answer (*ASU*: 48–51). Only a being with the capacity to shape his life in accordance with some overall plan can have or strive for meaningful life (*ASU*: 50). Nozick then raises various questions, such as "Why are there constraints on how we may treat beings shaping their lives?" (ibid.), which he hopes "to grapple with . . . on another occasion" (*ASU*: 51). It is not obvious just where he does this, although *Philosophical Explanations* (748 n.19) refers back to this passage and insists that the link he was bringing out between ethics and the meaning of life was intended to go via the moral push rather than the moral pull. These notions of push and pull we shall meet in Chapter 4, and in Chapter 10 the meaning of life and the relations between meaning and value, but the associated text to the present note (*PE*: 612) makes the point clear that it is the meaning of the agent's own life that his behaving ethically will increase, not the meaning of the person's life whom he is behaving ethically towards. This of course leaves wide open why "being responsive to the value of others, as value", which "would be reflected back into [the agent's] own value" (*PE*: 612), should involve treating the others in question as the bearers of, and only of, the libertarian rights expounded in *Anarchy, State, and Utopia*.

In line with this Nozick thinks we would reject the offer of an "experience machine" as a substitute for living our ordinary lives, where this is a machine that simulates any experience we might desire, rather as pilots are trained in flight-simulators, although the machine could make us believe the simulated situation was real. In fact he pushes this idea further, envisaging a machine that enables us not just to feel but to be a certain way – to be an eminent mathematician perhaps, not just to enjoy the reputation of being one. Here the machine does not merely produce feelings, nor even simulate actions (give us the experience of climbing Everest), but enables us really to do things. How does it differ, he asks (*ASU*: 44n.), from our relying, as we must do, on our genetic inheritance and early environment, neither of which do we "deserve"? He does not answer this except by pointing out that if machines were available to make us, at the touch of a button, able to conquer each obstacle as we came to it there would be nothing left for us to *do* at all (except pressing buttons perhaps).

P. Singer (Paul 1981: 52) makes a criticism which is this: Nozick has not refuted the possibility that the only ultimately valuable things are experiences, and we only want to do or be other things in order to improve experiences, whether our own or other people's, which the machine would make superfluous, so that he has not refuted that version of utilitarianism which relies on this approach (let alone others which don't); the utilitarian could say that *if* everyone had a machine there would indeed be nothing left beyond experiences for us to treat as valuable. Nozick, I think, would reject this, saying that my experiences while (or after) climbing Everest or solving crosswords only have value for me if I presuppose that I really am doing those things; it is not enough that I merely believe that I am. Nozick discusses this more explicitly elsewhere: see his rejection of a life based on deception when discussing Rand's egoism (Paul 1981: 221 (= *SP*: 263). Also we might ask whether we could "experience" climbing Everest without climbing it (or doing something similar in a simulation chamber, with extreme cold, low oxygen, etc.). Can we "experience" stamina, endurance and will-power without actually displaying them? (Does dreaming affect this? I suggest not, but must leave this to the reader.)

Two more points arise. First (based on a private remark by Hailwood) is there any likelihood of an experience machine mentality arising as the computer-based virtual reality scenarios beginning to appear are developed more and more? And secondly is deception always so bad? We often do not welcome being burdened with, say, the knowledge that we have a fatal disease. Furthermore some people take comfort from believing in a life after death. If they are wrong they will never discover this fact. Given that the arguments on either side are necessarily inconclusive, are they irrational to go on believing it? Could we say they are intellectually irrational but pragmatically rational?

The issues Nozick raises are fascinating and important, but the underlying point is that what we value is authentically *leading* our own lives. What Nozick brings out is the obscurity of this notion. Perhaps something depends on our not departing too far from "normal" procedures, e.g. by using performance-enhancing drugs, but what is normal will inevitably alter as technology advances, and perhaps we must just hope that each new procedure will always leave obstacles to be overcome, and perhaps generate new challenges of its own. At any rate, Nozick ends up by basing moral constraints on "that elusive and difficult notion: the meaning of life" (*ASU*: 50–51), as we have seen, a topic on which he says more in Chapter 6 of *Philosophical Explanations*, as we shall see in our own last chapter, but Nozick's discussion there is mainly at a rather abstract and general level, although he does discuss the significance of death and annihilation.

We shall see later that Nozick bases value primarily on the notion of organic unity, and his own philosophy will display a greater unity if we can connect what he says about topics like the experience machine and the meaning of life with that notion. One way of doing that here might be to argue that his rejection, in general, of the experience machine depends on the unity achieved by connecting our experiences so far as possible with the real world.

Animals and angels

An interesting side-issue which Nozick discusses here, and which any moral theory should define its position on, concerns the treatment of animals. He does not discuss whether animals have rights, but we might distinguish saying that some creature has a right to a certain treatment and saying that it is right so to treat it and wrong not to (cf. *PE*: 719 n.84). The latter need not entail the former. Perhaps something only has a right if it is capable of recognizing rights in general, both its own and those of others; infants have rights in virtue of what they will become later, just as people still keep their rights while asleep. But even if animals don't have rights it may still be right to treat them only in certain ways. For Nozick we can kill them for important purposes, such as if they are dangerous, or needed for our proper nourishment (which he thinks they are not), but not for mere amusement or trivial purposes (hunting is wrong: *ASU*: 37). We can perhaps kill even people, if they are a threat to us, however innocent; this is one of several issues he "tiptoe[s] around" (*ASU*: 34–5). But more importantly for our purpose, he insists that we should only be willing to take account of things other than felt experiences in the case of people but not of animals if we can find some principle to justify this in the case of people and show that it does not apply in the case of animals (*ASU*: 45). He then asks whether, if animals can sometimes be sacrificed for the sake of people, there might be higher beings for whom people themselves could be sacrificed. But here things get complicated. Nozick in fact treats these higher beings as going well beyond the intellectual and moral development we have reached, which they reach as children (*ASU*: 46). The trouble with this is that it is not radical enough. A mere increase in intelligence, moral insights, or sensitivity, however vast, would surely not justify sacrificing us for their purposes. We do not sacrifice children or imbeciles for our own.

Normally when talking of animals' behaviour we do not regard them as morally low grade, like delinquent children; we think that morality does not apply to their actions at all (there may be marginal exceptions in the case of the higher primates). If there are any beings "higher" than us, how do we know that the concepts relevant for describing them are not as alien and inaccessible to us as morality is to the mental life of animals? (For a discussion somewhat, although only somewhat, along these lines see *PE*: 443–4.) How do we know indeed that terms like "mentality" itself or "concepts" or "interests" are not superseded in their case? Or keeping the terms, since *we* cannot otherwise describe them, how do we know that they would not regard morality as inapplicable, not because they were wicked but because they thought in totally different terms? Of course all this is in a sense unintelligible to us, but that is not surprising. We are similarly unintelligible to animals, and "whereof one cannot speak, thereof one must keep silent", as it was famously put (the final words of Wittgenstein's *Tractatus*).

Keeping, however, to the possibility that there are beings significantly "higher" than us without being unintelligibly so in the way just described, Nozick makes an interesting methodological point when he says (*ASU*: 47) that there could be two moral theories, one saying our rights were absolute and the other saying they could be superseded in the interests of higher beings but not in the interests of other humans, which gave the same judgements in all actual situations but diverged when it came to certain possible situations. This is like, but also unlike, the notorious "grue" problem that Goodman (1954) raised with his "new riddle of induction". It is like it because we have two theories which coincide for all actual cases but diverge for certain possible ones (which might become actual in the future). It is unlike it because in the inductive case the actual cases provide our only reasons for holding either of the theories, so that it is hard to justify choosing one rather than the other, but it matters because our aim is to predict, whereas in the moral case we already have access, through our thought-experiments, to the reasons for holding either of the theories, but as long as there are no higher beings around it does not seem to matter which theory we hold. But Nozick points out that it would start to matter if we did meet such beings, because on one view but not the other it might be *our* duty to sacrifice one of our number in their interests.

Welfarist criticisms of Nozick

Nozick's reliance on the separateness of individuals to ground his theory of rights has met substantial criticism, mainly on the grounds that he tries to extract too much from it. Scheffler and Nagel both argue that he focuses too exclusively on one kind of rights, which Scheffler distinguishes as liberty rights rather than welfare rights. Scheffler produces an alternative conception of natural rights – natural in the sense that they depend upon the bearer's possessing certain natural attributes such as "the capacity for forming a plan of life" (Paul 1981: 152). According to this, "every person has a natural right to a sufficient share of every distributable good whose enjoyment is a necessary condition of the person's having a reasonable chance of living a decent and fulfilling life", provided only that his having it is not at the expense of someone else's being prevented from having such a share (Paul 1981: 153). Such rights include "adequate food, clothing, shelter, and medical care" (ibid.), as well as, in modern societies, education, for rights, although "natural" may differ in different societies (Paul 1981: 167 n.7). Scheffler does allow some right to liberty, and insists that natural rights are not the whole of morality, but the vagueness of terms such as "adequate", and variability of rights according to social conditions, make the implementation of these rights a matter of considerable dispute and uncertainty. They are indeed overridable, but "only in extreme circumstances" (Paul 1981: 152). They will require positive action on other people's part, not mere refraining from violations, but "[t]he refusal of an able-bodied person to do any kind of work *might* suffice to override that person's natural welfare rights" (Paul 1981: 161). Would that count as an "extreme circumstance"? At any rate he thinks that Nozick's argument from form to content will not do, and that his own conception of natural rights is better able than Nozick's own to provide the conditions that Nozick wants for a meaningful life.

Rather similarly, Nagel accuses Nozick's appeal to the meaning of life of being out of focus for defending the rights he is interested in, for it concentrates on rights to avoid suffering certain things and to have certain opportunities, while the rights he wants to establish "are rights not to be deliberately treated or used in certain ways. . . . The relation between the possessor of the right and the actor, rather than just the intrinsic nature of the possessor and of his life, must enter into the analysis of the right and of its basis" (Paul 1981: 198). Nagel also insists that rights differ in their stringency. To kill me to avoid some great evil is more impermissible than to violate my property rights for the same purpose (Paul 1981: 196, 199).

A further development of the distinction between liberty rights and welfare rights is made by P. Russell, who argues that Nozick doesn't distinguish need from equality of material resources as a justification for distribution, and does not distinguish among needs themselves between non-essential needs, e.g. for a haircut (an example Nozick uses in arguing against the justifiability of distribution by needs) and essential needs, e.g. for medical treatment. If the ability to lead a meaningful life is the basis of rights, and essential needs are those needed for that purpose, then essential needs should form a basis for rights. Russell concludes that this makes charity an obligation, albeit an "imperfect" obligation in that we may not have enough resources to fulfil all charitable obligations and no-one has a right to what cannot be provided. Here it differs from generosity, which it is up to us to exercise as we will. But charity, he thinks, is a matter of justice and can be enforced. The obvious way to do this is through taxes, and so some redistributive taxation is justified, despite Nozick's notorious rejection of such an idea (*ASU*: 169): "Taxation of earnings on labor is on a par with forced labor", because it means in effect that some of a person's working hours are spent in earning enough to pay the tax. He admits that there is more flexibility than in ordinary forced labour, and that there is no need to work at all beyond the point where an individual's earnings reach the tax thresholds, but he does not think this affects the fact that people are subject to aggression in being taxed. Some people have expensive tastes, while others prefer the values of leisure and so do not need to work beyond the tax threshold. If it would be wrong to seize the leisure of the latter, why, he asks, is it not also wrong to seize the money of the former (*ASU*: 170)? We will return later to this question of redistribution, but for the moment we might think that if Russell is right and charity is an enforceable obligation, it need not be as humiliating to the recipients as my initial quotation from Barry would suggest. But I am not sure that "charity" is really the word that Russell wants. It is only the enemies of the welfare state, of whom Russell is plainly not one, who talk of "charitable handouts" in connection with its payments – but this too we will return to later.

Libertarian criticisms of Nozick

Before going on, we can note that Nozick's attempt to derive rights from the separateness of persons has been criticized not only by welfarists but also from his own libertarian side of the fence. Welfarism is associated with the political left because of its emphasis on collective action in aid of the individual, but is also sometimes called welfare liberalism because of its emphasis on the liberties of the individual, in opposition not, or not only, to the constraints of socialist collectivism but to the reining in of the individual in the interests of authority based on tradition, as associated with conservatism and part of the political right. Liberalism tout court, without the qualifier "welfare", is associated economically with an emphasis on free trade and an absence of embargoes and tariffs between nation states, and is seen as somewhere between right and left – right because of its emphasis on free trade and left because of its opposition to authoritarian controls, in both the social and economic spheres. Socially, it claims to be neutral between different value-systems and ways of life – without much chance of success, it is often said, because it clearly represents a value-system itself. (Welfare liberals too can be neutral if, like Rawls, they have a neutrality of aim in that they want basic institutions and public policy that do not favour any particular conception of the good.) Libertarians also oppose authoritarianism, but are seen as forming the other part of the political right because of their opposition to restraints on individual behaviour in the interests of welfarism. One kind of anarchism is an extreme form of libertarianism. Another kind, communistic anarchism, puts a lot of emphasis on "mutual aid" (the title of a book by the anarchist Kropotkin), but only at the voluntary level, and libertarian anarchists can consistently engage in cooperation or mutual aid, although it will be less central for them and they will not depend on it. (For a good but brief discussion of the topics of this paragraph, to which it is much indebted, see Wolff 1991: 136–9, and also Kymlicka 1990: 155 n.l, and on the different kinds of anarchism see Miller 1984.)

Libertarians tend towards some sort of egoism but not necessarily of a crude hedonistic form; they concentrate rather on forms of self-realization. Nozick describes the libertarian Rand's position as a "constrained egoism", the constraints being provided by other people's rights (Paul 1981: 218 (= *SP*: 261)), and goes on to criticize her for being unable to maintain this view consistently. In fact, as he makes clear at the start of his article (Paul 1981: 206 (= *SP*: 249)), he regards Rand as giving inadequate arguments for a basically sound position. (In the article following Nozick's in Paul (1981), Den Uyl and Rasmussen criticize Nozick for misinterpreting Rand and not doing justice to the kind of egoism she holds, but that need not concern us here.)

Another libertarian is Mack, who holds a view similar to some extent to Rand's, which he calls "eudaemonistic egoism". This, he thinks, lets him provide a foundation for libertarianism, which Nozick fails to do. Mack thinks the mere separateness of persons and the fact that each has his own life are not sufficient to generate rights (although the reason he gives is the rather odd one that these are "alterable" facts that might be circumvented by "unifying all persons into a great social organism" (Paul 1981: 288)). What we need is rather the "value, desirability, or rightness of persons being separate beings" (ibid.). Justification must stop somewhere, and he admits that "[p]erhaps . . . rights exist without being grounded in anything. There simply are these deontic claims which are accessible to the morally insightful" (ibid.). But this sort of intuitionism he finds unsatisfactory, and he goes on to elaborate the notion of an "objective" proper end for each person, based on a Thomistic view of the nature of man, whereby if there are certain requirements for the existence of something, that thing functions well only if it promotes those requirements. The argument avowedly involves "the derivation of a fundamental normative claim from non-normative premises" (Paul 1981: 291–2). This of course introduces an old ethical chestnut that has plagued us ever since Hume (1739–40: 3.1.1, last paragraph). Not only is promoting the requirements of his own existence an objective end for each individual, which therefore generates obligations for him, but promoting or at least not violating them becomes an objective end for all other individuals too, and so generates the first individual's rights, violation of which by other individuals would constitute what Paul calls a "pragmatic contradiction" (Paul 1981: 17; see Mack himself in Paul 1981: 290–91). Whether this can really serve to generate interpersonal rights and obligations, and also whether the resulting system can really be called a version of egoism, whatever we take "eudaemonistic" to mean, are large questions that we need not go into any further here. But if Mack's position is not sustained then, to that extent anyway, Nozick is absolved from not having come to such a position as the basis for his own theory.

The nature of rights

Another feature of Nozick's approach that has called forth substantial criticism, a feature underlying much of the discussion of the last few pages, is his view of the nature of rights themselves. This is that rights are absolute. If you have a right at all, then you have it, full-bloodedly and subject only to the restriction that you do not violate the rights of others. (Actually we shall see an important and far-reaching qualification of this later, but that does not affect the initial conception of what a right is.) If you have a right not to be treated in a certain way, e.g. killed or robbed or enslaved, this might seem fairly plausible, but an important set of rights for Nozick are ownership rights, and this raises the question of what ownership consists in. Nozick thinks of ownership rights, or property rights, as absolute, in the sense that if you own something you can do what you like with it – subject again to not violating others' rights: I can use my knife as I like, but not plunge it into your chest (*ASU*: 171). But why should ownership not be a matter of degree? Ryan produces the example of holding an academic post. This gives the holder many rights, for instance to his salary, but he cannot sell the post or bequeath it to his children (Paul 1981: 328–32). Similarly if I own a room in college I have a right to occupy it and keep books in it, and keep my colleagues out, but I cannot alter it structurally or chop its furniture up for firewood, or sell it.

Similarly why should there not be limits on the amount of property I can own, or the length of time for which I can own it? We shall see later that Nozick does allow some limitations of the former kind – although only in special circumstances – and limitations of the second kind may follow from the contract by which I acquired the property in the first place; the flat I live in is mine for 99 years only, because I bought it in a fair and free contract of a kind common in England. Contracts are an important path to ownership for Nozick, and nothing he says debars them from resulting in limited ownership, including implicit limitations: my flat may be taxable. Of course I have an absolute right to the fulfilment of a legitimate contract, subject to any restrictions in the contract itself, but this says no more than that I have an absolute right to whatever the contract allows me an absolute right to.

We have already seen something of Nozick's attitude to taxation, and of Russell's argument that it would be justifiable on Nozick's own terms if it is needed to satisfy those welfare rights that are essential for a meaningful life. It might be thought that an obvious argument in favour of taxation can be made from the interdependence of civilized living. Owners of fat-cat salaries sometimes defend themselves by insisting that they have earned them by the work they have done. But this work has been done against the background of a complex modern society. If they tried using the same talents to do the same work in a "state of nature" they might find the salaries not forthcoming, and also that their talents did not let them produce work which *would* be valued by their fellows in such a state. Company chairmen need not flourish in the jungle.

Nozick deals with this sort of argument in a section on the "principle of fairness", which he derives from Hart (1955) and Rawls (1971) (*ASU*: 90–95; see especially *ASU*: 95, and also *ASU*: 265–8). The section starts with a discussion of Hart's claim, which Nozick rejects, that all special obligations (or special rights – we could express the point either way), must be enforceable or we could not distinguish special rights from their absence. (This discussion spawned a rather intricate debate in the journal *Analysis*; see Steiner 1981b, 1982; Wilson 1981; Miller 1981.) Nozick then turns to the principle of fairness itself, which he describes as holding that "when a number of persons engage in a just, mutually advantageous, cooperative venture according to rules and thus restrain their liberty in ways necessary to yield advantages for all, those who have submitted to these restrictions have a right to similar acquiescence on the part of those who have benefited from their submission. Acceptance of benefits (even when this is not a giving of express or tacit undertaking to cooperate) is enough, according to this principle, to bind one" (*ASU*: 90, omitting footnote).

Nozick rejects this principle, even when it is modified to ensure that the benefit one gains outweighs the costs of one's cooperation.

But there are certain ambiguities in his discussion. Of the two sentences quoted above the first mentions simply being benefited, while the second mentions acceptance of benefits. Does it matter whether one takes positive action to accept the benefits, or merely refrains from cutting oneself off from them? What if you cannot avoid the benefits? Nozick raises these questions but does not answer them, and although he has officially finished the discussion of enforceability (*ASU*: 93) he slips back into it (*ASU*: 95).

Some of what Nozick says is plausible enough. Why should I contribute for benefits I have not asked for, especially if the contribution outweighs the benefit? But is this really enough to cover such issues as taxation and the upkeep of society in general? Is there not a difference of degree that is massive enough to affect this issue? In Nozick's example if I refuse to contribute, and others do likewise, we would lose the benefits of entertainment over a public address system. Well, we could do without those I imagine. But Nozick himself mentions the far-reaching nature of our dependence on other people in general. Without them we would not even have a language, for instance. We shall see in the next chapter how he envisages the development of a legitimate state, with its limitations. For the moment I am asking whether there is not a difference between having benefits, even genuine ones, foisted on one without being consulted or allowed the choice and receiving the sort of benefits that are virtually a condition of living at all in any kind of human way, and which it hardly makes sense to talk of having a choice about. Even rugged individualists of the John Wayne type, as they have come to be called, following J. Wolff, had to be brought up to learn a language and the arts of looking after themselves. I spoke above of a difference of degree, and where there is that there will normally be many intermediate cases. If you really enter wholeheartedly into the benefits of public entertainment, and arrange much of your life around them, then it is more plausible to say you have an obligation to contribute, but we need not look for a sharp boundary to your obligations if, as Nozick's critics often point out, rights and therefore obligations corresponding to them vary in stringency. (For an argument that Nozick cannot reject a revised principle of fairness without jeopardizing his theory of property rights, see Arneson 1982.)

One might think from all this that rights are the supreme value for Nozick, but this would be misleading. Rights are not values at all for him but side constraints, and we must beware of adopting a "utilitarianism of rights" (*ASU*: 28) whereby our goal is to minimize the violation of rights. It is commonly argued against ordinary utilitarianism that it cannot cater for such moral intuitions as that it would be unjust to punish an innocent man as a scapegoat to prevent a lynch mob running riot and inflicting great evils on many people. Nozick adapts the same example by talking of the mob as violating the rights of many people: would we be justified in violating the rights of one innocent person to prevent this? A utilitarianism of rights would presumably say yes, but for Nozick this would be equally counterintuitive. This is surely right. Having accepted the injustice of the first case we would hardly change our minds if some-one pointed out that sacrificing the scapegoat would not only save many people from great evils, but also save them from violations of their rights. A side constraints view is just that and not a maximiz-ation of anything, whether of goods or the preservation of rights. To this extent the separateness of individuals does have a role to play.

The theory of justice I: justice in transfer

Nozick's theory of distributive justice is an entitlement theory, which has three parts: justice in acquisition, justice in transfers, and the rectification of injustice. His general slogan is, "Whatever arises from a just situation by just steps is itself just" (*ASU*: 151). We are here concerned with justice in transfers, the central core of the theory, on which he spends most of his time; we will come to the other two parts later. He contrasts his entitlement theory with end-state theories and patterned theories, where justice consists in the promotion of some end-state or pattern respectively. End-state theories we have already looked at, in effect, in discussing welfarism, and the nature of rights. Patterned theories are those which take the phrase "to each according to his –" and fill in the blank with some term such as "needs", "merits", "deserts", "virtue", "IQ", or whatever (*ASU*: 159–60). (We might think his own theory took the form "to each according to his previous transactions", but perhaps this is what Nozick means to exclude (*ASU*: 156) by insisting the blank be given only "natural" fillings.) Nozick then argues that patterned theories are inconsistent with liberty because liberty will always upset patterns. He relies largely on his notorious "Wilt Chamberlain" example which has been hotly attacked ever since, notably by Cohen (1977). Suppose we take egalitarianism as our preferred pattern, and suppose we achieve it, and everyone has equal resources. Wilt Chamberlain is a famous sportsman who exercises his liberty by demanding 25 cents from everyone who sees him play. A million people exercise their liberty by paying this, and he ends up with a quarter of a million dollars – far more than anyone else. The pattern has been broken. Plainly the argument can be generalized to almost any use of our resources. Are we to preserve the pattern by restricting liberty? It is here that Nozick makes his famous remark: "The socialist society would have to forbid capitalist acts between consenting adults" (*ASU*: 163).

Against an extreme egalitarianism, barring any departure from exact equality, this argument is certainly just. But what egalitarian in his senses would hold such an extreme view? Among the many criticisms of the argument that have been made by Cohen and others (e.g. Kymlicka 1990: 98–102), are that Chamberlain could be taxed (which we have already discussed); that wealth is power, so that accumulations of it could themselves restrict liberty; that people might wish to live in a certain sort of society, and might not make the choices they do (on how to spend their money) if they realized the implications of making them; that even if small inequalities are acceptable it does not follow that large ones resulting from series of them are (Quest 1977; cf. Lederkramer's (1979) reply that the difference between large and small inequalities is irrelevant to Nozick's notion of entitlement – although Quest's argument may well make one wonder if entitlement *is* an adequate basis for justice). Also Sorensen (1986) offers an argument similar in kind to Quest's but not open to Lederkramer's objections. Cohen also uses the "wealth is power" argument to turn the tables on Nozick by claiming that it is capitalism that restricts liberty. This last argument returns us to Nozick's notion of coercion which we met in Chapter 1, and to a feature of it which was not very relevant there – that a person is only coerced or forced as a result of someone else's illegitimate action. Nozick agrees, says Cohen, that anyone forced to work or starve is forced to work, but he only *is* forced if his employer has acted illegitimately. This definition, however, does not satisfy Cohen, nor J. Wolff, who points that on it "a criminal rightfully imprisoned is not forced to remain in jail. And miners, trapped underground by a rockfall, are not forced to remain where they are until they are rescued" (Wolff 1991: 85). Nozick could deal with these cases, especially the last, if he appealed to different notions of force, as indeed he must if he allows, as he does, that at least some obligations can be enforced. For if I force you to fulfil your obligation then surely you are forced, even though I act quite legitimately? But this does not solve the real issue about whether capitalism involves exploitation and that involves injustice. Nozick sometimes points out that workers often have other alternatives – difficult perhaps but not impossible such as setting up their own factories – but don't adopt them. But this has not always been so (not in nineteenth-century capitalism). At one point he seems to argue that if workers are not exploited when there are other alternatives available which they don't take, then neither are they if those alternatives disappear without the workers knowing it (*ASU*: 254–5), which is like arguing that if you don't leave a room you are free to leave you are still free to leave if someone quietly locks the door on you (for more on this see "Guide to further reading" for Chapter 9).

An important point about the relations between rights and liberty has been made by J. Wolff using Ryan's argument about university posts that we saw earlier. Let us call the sort of rights I have over my room in college weak property rights, and the sort of rights that let me transfer my property at will to anyone I please and have inviolable possession of it strong property rights. (Even strong property rights do not let me do absolutely anything with it; I still cannot stick my knife in your chest.) Nozick claims that liberty upsets patterns (*ASU*: 160–64), but Wolff distinguishes two concepts of liberty (Wolff 1991: 93ff.) On one, which he calls Lockean, I am free to do whatever I ought to do, a view often summed up in the slogan, "Freedom is freedom to do as you ought". On this view therefore a moral demand is no restriction on my liberty. On the other view, which he calls Hobbesian, freedom is freedom to do as I like, a notion holders of the first view often call licence as opposed to liberty. On this view a moral demand does restrict my liberty. Nozick is a Lockean on liberty, and so can regard the obligations imposed by his entitlement theory as no restriction on liberty. But his entitlement theory involves strong property rights, and so he claims that taxation etc. do restrict liberty. Wolff then asks why a Lockean on liberty should not adopt weak property rights, thus allowing the legitimacy of taxation etc., and equally claim that these new obligations do not restrict liberty. A Lockean on liberty can never use liberty to challenge a moral claim, for either the claim is sound, and so does not restrict liberty, or it is unsound, but this must be shown on independent grounds (Wolff 1991: foot of 96). If Nozick were to switch to a Hobbesian view of liberty he could say that taxation does indeed restrict liberty, but so now would the obligations of his own entitlement view. In fact Wolff goes further and says a Hobbesian on liberty might well think that liberty positively requires patterns, for more liberties might be gained by restricting a few. He gives an example, becoming topical in Britain, of privatizing roads. This gives me the liberty to own a road, but at the expense of having to pass numerous toll gates when driving. "Socialist joint ownership of roads would seem to enhance liberty rather than impede it" (Wolff 1991: 99). (Nozick would probably reply that, at least where those who gain liberties are different from those who lose them, this involves a "utilitarianism of liberties".)

Wolff concludes that liberty cannot be used to ground rights as Nozick wants without circularity, since on his Lockean view of it liberty itself cannot be defined without reference to the rights and obligations it is supposed to ground. On one point, however, Wolff is criticized by Hailwood, who agrees with him in general but thinks he ignores one feature of Nozick's view: liberty is not just "the right to do what you have a right to do" (Wolff 1991: 100), but "a natural right to do what you have a natural right to do" (Hailwood 1996: 36). Hailwood criticizes Wolff for using this circularity to criticize Nozick's claim that liberty upsets patterns. The criticism would only work, Hailwood thinks, if Nozick based his rights on some pattern (socialism, utilitarianism, etc.). But Nozick in fact treats rights as "natural", so the real criticism of him is whether these rights can be made plausible, especially when the Lockean theological basis is removed.

Blurring the distinction

So far we have made a sharp distinction between teleological and deontological approaches and placed Nozick firmly in the latter. But this picture may need some modification for two reasons. First, he himself sees the situation as rather more complex, and secondly it is not obvious just how consistently he holds the views that he does hold.

Earlier we saw Nozick raising the possibility that there are higher beings than ourselves and that it might be that we could legitimately be sacrificed for their interests but not for the sake of other people. He asks (footnote at *ASU*: 46) whether this is a teleological view giving people infinite worth relative to other people. He thinks it is not, because a teleological theory, that maximizes total value, would allow some people to be sacrificed for others. (His sentence does not have commas after "theory" and "value" but the sense and context seem to demand them.) But the view is not purely deontological, since it lets us be sacrificed for higher beings, and so he concludes that "[t]his illustrates our earlier remark [at *ASU*: 29 note] that 'teleological' and 'side-constraint' do not exhaust the possible structures for a moral view". In fact he has considered a number of different moral structures in his earlier article "Moral Complications and Moral Structures" (in *SP*).

A further reason supporting Nozick's blurring of the teleological/deontological distinction has been given by Pettit (1988), followed by Hailwood (1996: 52–3). Consequentialists (or teleologists) have often argued that they can recognize rights, but mainly on various practical grounds, such as those underlying rule-utilitarianism (for some references see Pettit 1988 n.1). Pettit offers an argument that recognizing some rights as such may be essential, not merely advisable as a means, to achieving the best consequences. He takes the example of children who may only feel secure if they know that their parents' love for them, which involves recognizing them as the bearers of certain rights, is unconditional, and not existing merely as long as their parents think it will have the best consequences, or even the best consequences for the children themselves. It might be thought that the parents could get the best of both worlds by employing deception and pretending that their recognition of the children's rights was absolute when really it was subordinate to their views on the children's welfare, but this, Pettit thinks, would be a flimsy device and likely to be seen through. The argument, as Pettit recognizes, is parallel to the "paradox of hedonism", that in many cases aiming directly at maximizing one's pleasure is a way of ensuring that one fails to do so.

The second reason for modifying our classification of Nozick is partly that he wavers about it himself and partly that his theory commits him to modifying it. In a notorious passage (*ASU*: 30n.) he writes: "The question of whether these side constraints are absolute, or whether they may be violated in order to avoid catastrophic moral horror, and if the latter, what the resulting structure might look like, is one I hope largely to avoid". Actually he does say a bit more, although not much, in the long footnote to his earlier article on Rand. Here, while deprecating (as he does in *ASU*) the idea of writing constraints into the goal to be achieved, which would tend towards a "utilitarianism of rights", he raises the possibility, without much enthusiasm, of other structures, such as a "side-constraint structure with principles governing the setting aside of the whole structure" (Paul 1981: 224(= *SP*: 380)). Also Pettit, in the article just mentioned

(1988: 46–7), allows the possibility of a limit K of good (including presumably the avoidance of evils); rights may be violated for goods greater than K but must remain inviolate where no such goods are in the offing. But this returns us to our discussion of alternatives to teleology and deontology, so let us pass on.

The theory of justice II: justice in acquisition and Locke's proviso

We have been discussing justice in transfers, which Nozick says most about, but defending this won't get us far if the goods we transfer were not justly acquired in the first place. Justice in acquisition is where Nozick is most obviously in danger of compromising his libertarian and deontologtical stance, and he has to bring in what he cheerfully describes as "an additional bit of complexity" (*ASU*: 174), because he realizes the need to avoid certain grossly unacceptable monopoly situations, such as Rashdall's example of appropriating the only waterhole in the desert (*ASU*: 179n.) (could one justifiably do so, if it only had enough water for one?). To deal with this he brings in Locke's famous proviso that one can appropriate resources only if there be "enough and as good left in common for others" (*ASU*: 175; see § 27 of the second of Locke's *Two Treatises of Government*; although *ASU*: 55n. treats it as a "proviso on transfers and exchanges"). But this leads Nozick to introduce a certain paradox, which Wolff (1991: 108) calls the zipping back argument. Suppose that all (useful) land is already owned but Z (perhaps born too late) owns none. Then Y (the last appropriator) could not legitimately take any without leaving none for Z. So X could not take any without leaving Y unable legitimately to take any, and for similar reasons neither could W, and so on back to A (the first appropriator). This has some analogy to the paradox of the unexpected examination, or perhaps better that of taking the last cake at a tea-party, since all but Z *can* appropriate, but not legitimately. To deal with this Nozick weakens the proviso to insist merely that the appropriator leave enough for others to *use* (*ASU*: 176). This obviously leads to a weakening of property rights, since now an owner must allow others at least some use of his property where relevant (as Nozick realizes: *ASU*: 179).

The general idea is that others must not be left worse off than they would be otherwise. But this raises various problems: otherwise than what? This is the problem of the base line (*ASU*: 177), which has led to much critical discussion (see especially J. Wolff). Nozick seems to assume the base line is a state of nature with no appropriation at all. This would indeed allow a lot. Even the poorest today are probably better off than they would be in such a state of nature, and it is hardly surprising that Nozick ends up by saying a free market system won't violate the proviso (*ASU*: 180). But there are other alternatives, such as socialist joint ownership, and other complications (see J. Wolff 1991: 112–14).

Hailwood, while criticizing Nozick on other grounds, defends his choice of base line because the problem is to defend private property *given libertarian rights*, "one of which is the right to use natural resources" (Hailwood 1996: 42), which appropriation by others might hinder. Use is a natural concept while appropriation is a conventional one. Animals can use things but they cannot own them. So rights to use should come before rights to own, because ownership already presupposes rights and so cannot ground them, which use might. So it is reasonable to regard rights to own, and to appropriate, as growing out of rights to use, which in this sphere are rock-bottom rights. This gives a further justification for the weakening of the proviso, and also perhaps for Nozick's choice of base line, although Hailwood makes another criticism (1996: 43) in saying that when Nozick considers what makes someone worse off he confines himself unduly to material values; a John Wayne type might well prefer liberty to wealth. (This is incidentally a criticism which Ehman (1980) makes at much greater length of Rawls in the first section of his article; however, it would be unfair to say that Nozick ignores this in other contexts.)

Kirzner (Paul 1981: 394–407) points out further complications for the proviso when we consider discovery, whether after diligent searching, perhaps with advanced techniques, or accidentally (but only someone with Fleming's knowledge could have "accidentally" discovered penicillin), or by adding value to already known objects; similar problems arise when we exploit knowledge that only we possess, whether we got it through being in a privileged position ("insider trading" etc.) or otherwise. Nozick considers such questions but only briefly (*ASU*: 181–2). Would, for instance, a brilliant scientist who discovered a cure for cancer by synthesizing certain common materials have a right to charge what he liked for it, with people dying all round him? Nozick says yes, because he does not violate the proviso (of course Nozick could still condemn him morally; see p. 22–3). We might ask who paid for his laboratory and his education – but that would return us to the principle of fairness. Nozick, as we saw, downplays the proviso as largely otiose, but it is not obvious that he sees the effect Kirzner claims discovery etc. have on needing the proviso at all, and on the acquisition/transfer distinction (Paul 1981: 401).

Nozick insists that the proviso "is not an 'end-state' principle; it focuses on a particular way that appropriative actions affect others, and not on the structure of the situation that results" (*ASU*: 181; cf. *ASU*: 27, 114). Maybe, but the appeal to the proviso at all has a distinctly teleological flavour (J. Wolff 1991: 111–12), and even if he followed Kirzner in abandoning the proviso the position would be much the same concerning compensation (see *ASU*: 345 n.14). Finally Brock (1995) argues that Nozick's acceptance of the proviso commits him to redistribution to help the needy.

The theory of justice III: rectification and compensation

Justice in acquisition then raises problems for Nozick which make him tend in a teleological direction, and this tendency continues in the third part of his theory of justice: rectification of past injustices. This presupposes the first two parts, and so is less important (but see Davis in Paul 1981: 348), but it raises the same issues as the closely related notion of compensation, which plays an important part in the escape from anarchism in Part One of *Anarchy, State, and Utopia*. The extent to which Nozick's use of compensation leads him into "teleologism" is brought out in detail by Mack's first article in Paul (1981), a difficult article on a difficult chapter (Chapter 4) in *Anarchy, State, and Utopia* (Paul's summary (1981: 11–12) is helpful).

Generally it is wrong to violate rights, and if you do you must compensate your victim, as well as meriting punishment; compensating does not make your action right. Sometimes, however, even a virtuous person may violate rights; for Nozick, though, he must still pay compensation (cf. R. P. Wolff in Paul 1981: 87). Why not simply allow any violation provided compensation is paid? Partly because this would lead to fear, and to people being treated as means rather than ends, and liable to have their rights violated at any time. But also for another reason, which requires the notion of compensation to be examined.

Compensation for Nozick comes in three grades. In the lowest grade people are compensated only for disadvantages actually incurred, even though they may be left worse off than they would have been otherwise. (Nozick is vague about this distinction. Sometimes a person counts as disadvantaged only if that person is disadvantaged *as compared to others* in the situation (*ASU*: 87; cf. *ASU*: 144n.), while later he talks of people being "somewhat disadvantaged, but no more than everyone else" (*ASU*: 146n.)). The second grade is awkwardly called "full" compensation and so sometimes "merely full" to distinguish it from the third. Here people are given enough to make them indifferent between being violated and compensated or left unviolated. The third grade is "market" compensation. Suppose my house is compulsorily purchased for a motorway. Full compensation will give me just enough to buy an equally satisfactory house elsewhere. But on the open market (with no motorway) I might have made a profit beyond this, so market compensation would be what I could have got on the open market. (My new house, although equally good for living in, might have a lower market value.)

Normally in a voluntary exchange both parties gain something; the benefits of exchange are divided between them; the reason for not allowing all violations if compensated is that merely full compensation (the only practicable kind there) unfairly deprives the person compensated of his share of these benefits.

Exchanges where both parties benefit Nozick calls productive. Unproductive exchanges are those that leave one party no better off, or more exactly, where one party would have been no worse off had the other party not existed, and also no worse off had the exchange been impossible for some reason. Unproductive exchanges can then be prohibited, with suitable compensation paid.

In the above motorway example the exchange would presumably be unproductive. I would be no worse off, as far as this situation goes, if the roads authority did not exist, and also no worse off if for some reason the exchange were impossible. So if I cannot be given market compensation (because of the indefiniteness of its amount perhaps) the appeal tribunal could prohibit the exchange, with merely full compensation (or even less: *ASU*: 87, 145) for the roads authority. (The fact that in a Nozickian state perhaps no motorways would ever get built might or might not be a good thing. The case would be different, however, if I had nothing to gain by keeping my tottering old house except to extract compensation from the roads authority; then it could go ahead, paying me merely full compensation.)

It is here that Mack sees a significant shift in Nozick's view of what justifies prohibition, from a purely deontic view to an outcome-based or teleological view (see especially Paul 1981: 186–7). Nozick may confuse the issue somewhat by concentrating as he does on cases where we can legitimately prohibit, with due compensation paid, actions which risk violating rights, even though perhaps no rights are actually violated. Originally actions could only be prohibited if, and because, they violated rights. Now we have cases where actions which in fact violate no rights can be prohibited, but violation is still in the offing. However, Mack (Paul 1981: 180–83) constructs several cases where on Nozick's principles actions can be prohibited, because unproductivity is involved, even though no rights violations are in the offing. Here Nozick seems to have no grounds for justifying prohibition except the social effects of unproductivity.

(Terminologies differ. One can talk of border (or boundary) crossings, and call illegitimate ones violations and legitimate ones infringements (Thomson in Paul 1981: 132)).

Mack's criticism is of a kind sometimes called "internal" because it accuses its target of internal inconsistencies and so of self-refutation, rather than of merely not satisfying certain demands from outside, such as that it should pay more attention to equality or welfare. Another, avowedly internal, critique of Nozick is made by Kavka (1982), from a standpoint quite different from Mack's libertarianism. Like Mack, Kavka fixes on the difference between full and market compensation, but constructs a dilemma for Nozick whereby if he relies on full compensation, as he does in justifying acquisition, this leaves the door open for justifying redistribution too, whereas if he opts for market compensation he can no longer justify acquisition.

Yet another internal criticism is Steiner's (1981a) argument that libertarianism itself demands a certain element of socialism, because it involves minimizing non-contractual restrictions on individuals, and this implies that for later generations appropriative rights cannot rest on historical principles but on certain end-state principles which can be indefinitely extended into the future (1981a: 568). Even Nozick himself, as Steiner reminds us (1981a: n.19), allows that the socialist is right in saying the worker can claim the entitlements of his labour, but wrong in saying what those entitlements are (*ASU*: 154–5). Nozick also ends his discussion of distributive justice by saying: "Although to introduce socialism as a punishment for our sins would be to go too far, past injustices might be so great as to make necessary in the short run a more extensive state in order to rectify them" (*ASU*: 231). How short a run, and how much more extensive?

However, this distinction between internal and external attacks, although emphasized by Kavka, should perhaps be seen rather as a matter of degree, if attacks based on demands for welfare etc. appeal, as they often do, to Nozick's own appeal to the meaning of life.

Steiner's emphasis on future generations, which comes even more heavily in his brief note in Paul (1981), is constantly repeated in discussions of acquisition and rectification and the proviso but space prohibits further discussion here. See especially Lyons in Paul (1981), and Davis (ibid.), who also points out (Paul 1981: 353) that entitlement is to particular objects, but over time these may be stolen and destroyed, and compensation can only take the teleological form of restoring the loser to a level equivalent to what he enjoyed previously.

Elsewhere Steiner (1978) criticizes Nozick's use of compensation for appropriation. First, A surely need not compensate everyone who *might* have used what he had appropriated, if only one person could – but which? Secondly, if we assume only B could, then A must compensate B for not getting the thing in question, but he may deduct what B would have had to compensate A with, had B appropriated the thing. But B could similarly deduct, when compensating A, what B would have lost had A appropriated the thing, and so we have a vicious circle, and the compensation is "entirely indeterminable" (final words). It seems that if A and B could equally benefit from the thing, the compensation either (if he takes it) must pay the other is equal and so therefore are the deductions they can make, which equal the compensations, so that the compensation A (if he takes it) must pay oscillates between the thing's value for B and that minus its (equal) value for A, i.e. between the thing's value and zero. A possible solution would be that A should appropriate it and pay B half the thing's value, so that they end up with half each, although it might then be hardly worthwhile for either of them to do the appropriating – provided one of them did (they could toss a coin perhaps). Of course this solution would only work for this simple case where there are just two contenders and they could equally benefit from the thing; other cases would be complicated, if not worse. How far does ownership depend on ability to use? *How much* of America and Australia did the Indians and Aborigines own? I may own my eight discs, but do I own the whole of my desert island when the exploiters arrive (to refer to a famous British radio programme)? (See, for example, *ASU*: 174). We shall meet compensation again later.

A different criticism that deserves to be briefly noted is made by Ehman (1980) who emphasizes that the market *presupposes* ownership regulations, and creates rather than preserves rights. He also points out that Nozick criticizes Locke's "mixing one's labour" criterion of rightful acquisition, but then assumes a pre-legal "natural" market.

Nozick on Rawls

Probably the most significant contribution to political philosophy since the war, more so even than *Anarchy, State, and Utopia*, is Rawls's *A Theory of Justice*, which appeared in 1971 (three years before *ASU*), and Nozick devotes some 50 pages, along with a number of scattered references, to discussing it. We have already met it briefly in his discussion of justice as fairness.

Like Nozick, Rawls rejects teleology (1971: 330), although not in the extreme fashion that Nozick claims to do (with mixed success, as we have seen). He is a contract theorist, but the contract is hypothetical and made between bloodless idealized figures who will later become embodied and have to live with the result. They are ignorant of almost everything about their future selves, but they know some general laws of psychology and economics, and are intelligent, rational and non-altruistically prudent – but not necessarily selfish: they know they will have friends and families who must accept as reasonable the principles they choose (Rawls 1971: 155); they do not take account of morality because they are supposed to be generating it, or at any rate social justice. The principles they unanimously choose then become the principles of Rawls's theory of justice, and are plainly meant to represent our reflective intuition, while providing a basis for morality in enlightened self-interest. In fact the choosers follow a "safety first" policy of maximizing the position of the worst off in the relevant respects (liberty, welfare or whatever) – a "maximin" policy which aims to maximize the minimum good (or "minimax", if looked at as minimizing the maximum evil). When the choosers apply this policy they choose first a principle of liberty, which (very roughly) requires equal liberty for all, and then (but only when the principle of liberty is satisfied) the "difference principle", which says that an equal distribution of goods is to be preferred unless an unequal one would be better for all the parties concerned. (For a general summary of his position see Rawls 1971: 302–3, and for the difference principle, Rawls 1971: 75–6.)

Rawls's theory is a "patterned" theory, the desired pattern being a distribution curve of welfare etc. with its deepest dip as shallow as possible, and so we can expect Nozick to criticize it. A minor point is that Rawls focuses on worst-off groups rather than individuals (*ASU*: 190); this is presumably because Rawls is concerned only with social justice and the general economic set-up, not with personal relations or individual psychology, although there are indeed difficulties about how to define the groups.

In a more serious criticism (*ASU*: 190–97) Nozick argues that Rawls fails to defend the difference principle. The argument is to this effect: it is all very well to say the poor should be benefited because they have less than the rich, but in another respect they may already have more, namely that they may well gain more than the rich do from living in a single society with the rich rather than if rich and poor lived in *total* apartheid. Why then should the rich consent to changes that would benefit the poor more still? (Cf. especially *ASU*: 194–5, and the discussion of base lines above.)

This raises an issue about what the choosers are supposed to be doing. They are to choose prudentially (not necessarily selfishly), but also to be practical and choose principles their descendants (any of whom they might turn out to be identical with) would accept. But is this not to base justice, which is what in effect the choosers are choosing, unduly on psychology? Why should justice depend on what the rich, or anyone else, would choose (gifted with the knowledge, denied to Rawls's choosers, that they *are* rich)?

Nozick's point, however, is rather different. For Rawls justice is fairness, so if both rich and poor gain from cooperation but the poor gain more, it would seem fair that any new arrangement should favour the rich rather than let the poor gain even more still. But this seems counterintuitive, and for Nozick the trouble lies in letting fairness put constraints upon the holdings that arise from voluntary social cooperation. Appealing to fairness leads to an intuitively unfair result. The issue evidently depends on whether the absolute value of holdings is considered, which would favour helping the poor, or their relative value compared with some previous or hypothetical base line, which in the example would favour helping the rich. At first sight the former might seem the obvious choice, but we do in fact often use relative criteria in assessing people's well-being. (Hence, to take contemporary English examples, the widespread approval of SERPS, and the definition of poverty in terms of half the average income. Also this may depend not on envy but on expectation and imagination.) Nozick seems to prefer abandoning this issue, at least in the context of social justice.

Nozick makes many other criticisms against Rawls: that he begs the question against the entitlement theory (*ASU*: 202–3), and could not defend distributing by entitlements as against distributing inversely to them (*ASU*: 201), and is open to Nozick's notorious compulsory eye-transplant objection to favouring the worst off (*ASU*: 206); that he relies on a certain procedure (appeal to the original choosers' choices) to generate principles of justice, whereas the principles so generated cannot include any procedural ones (*ASU*: 207–9); that he cannot, as Nozick can, cater for what Nozick calls the "addition" and "deletion" conditions (*ASU*: 209–10); with finally a long argument against Rawls's treatment of natural endowments and related notions (*ASU*: 213ff.). But this chapter is already overlong, and the above discussion must serve simply as an example.

Summary

Nozick sets out to elaborate and defend an uncompromising libertarianism, which most, but not all, of his critics have accused him of giving no adequate moral justification for – a charge he is inclined rather disarmingly to accept, even though it is only partly valid. He is a deontologist rather than a teleologist, and bases his system on the rights of the individual, from which any rights that a group or an authority may have must be derived. We all have duties to respect these rights, and may have other duties too, such as those of charitable aid, but these latter are not to be enforced, although open to moral pressure and persuasion. Individuals are separate, and have each their own lives to lead. This gives morality its form, the moral side constraints, whose content is the libertarian constraint prohibiting aggression, including "paternalistic aggression". This constraint is ultimately based on "the meaning of life", which Nozick thinks involves rejecting the view that only experiences have value, a rejection he has been accused of not establishing. Further topics we discussed here include the "experience machine" and our relations to non-human creatures, both inferior and (if we met any) superior.

Criticisms of all this have come from both directions, from welfarists and from more extreme libertarians, or (one kind of) anarchists. Welfarists have argued in particular that Nozick stresses liberty rights at the expense of welfare rights; however, the basis he claims in "the meaning of life" can serve to justify both of these if it justifies either. The main libertarian criticism has been that Nozick's justification for rights is inadequate, and a Thomistic justification has been offered. Underlying some of these criticisms is the charge that Nozick has too absolute a view of rights, which leads to his rejection of taxation and of Hart's views on the free-rider problem. He also rejects what he calls a "utilitarianism of rights".

The theory of justice itself has three parts – justice in acquisition, justice in transfer, and rectification of injustice – of which justice in transfer gets most attention. The foundation is entitlement rather than end-states or patterns. Nozick uses his Wilt Chamberlain example to argue that liberty upsets patterns, but this faced many criticisms, such as the claims that capitalism restricts liberty, which leads to a discussion of exploitation, and that on Nozick's Lockean view liberty cannot ground rights without circularity (although this claim has itself been criticized). However, we saw some reasons both in a criticism (by Pettit) and in Nozick's own writing for blurring somewhat the line between deontology and teleology. The discussion of justice in acquisition revolved mainly around Nozick's use of the Lockean proviso, which leads him to modify his absolute view of ownership (where Hailwood defends him), and also has a certain teleological flavour, and leads to problems in the case of discoveries. The discussion of rectification led us to a complex discussion of compensation and its three grades, where several critics have seen teleology creeping in, especially when Nozick admits the massive need for compensation for historical injustices. These and other criticisms have been called "internal" to Nozick's system, and Steiner constructs a certain paradox for the case of appropriation, as well as emphasizing future generations.

Finally we sampled Nozick's criticisms of his great rival, Rawls.

Chapter 3

Anarchy, State, and Utopia:
the political outcome

Introduction

The moral basis of Nozick's system rests firmly on rights then: rights of acquisition, rights of transfer, and rights to compensation. It is a system of individuals, separate and inviolable, who may be "social products" in that they benefit from the doings of their contemporaries and their ancestors, but who owe no "general floating debt which the current society can collect and use as it will" (*ASU*: 95). Morally speaking we enter society from the outside, already fully formed. What sort of society then do we enter?

The main thought for Nozick is that, other things being equal, the less government we have the better. His task is to steer a course between the Scylla of anarchism, the absence of all government, and the Charybdis of the welfare state, or (horror of horrors!) socialism – although to be fair Nozick may have in mind by "socialism" something nearer to communism with its command economy and class war rather than simply the idea that society has a responsibility to care for its less fortunate members, even though he rejects that too. Individuals may have a moral obligation to do so, but it is not an enforceable one. The big names of anarchism belong rather in the nineteenth century than the twentieth (Bakunin, Kropotkin, Proudhon, Stirner, for instance). But anarchism has its defenders today as well, as we have seen already, and some of the most vigorous attacks have come from them, e.g. R. P. Wolff (author of *In Defense of Anarchism*), in Paul (1981). It may seem ironical that Nozick, who is so much nearer to anarchism than most contemporary political thinkers, should be subjected to so much attack by those that might be thought of as the nearest to being his natural allies, but perhaps it is a case of the well known phenomenon that heretics are in greater danger of attack than infidels – they are seen as "letting the side down".

Anarchy, State, and Utopia is divided into three parts: the first reckoning to establish the minimal state in the face of the pull of anarchism; the second to show how the moral basis of the theory does not allow any further development of the state; while the third, which we will come to later, draws some implications designed to make the system appear more palatable. The second part we have already mainly dealt with, and it is to the application of the moral basis in the first part that we now turn. To some extent this involves reversing the order of Nozick's own discussion; the moral basis comes in both parts, but its discussion focused more naturally on why we could not go beyond the minimal state, while Nozick starts, not unreasonably, by asking how we get to the minimal state in the first place.

Whether there should be a state at all is what Nozick describes at the outset as "[t]he fundamental question of political philosophy" (*ASU*: 4). Since Plato's *Crito* attempts have proliferated throughout the ages to justify the state by appeal to some sort of social contract, and we might expect Nozick to follow suit, in view of the importance of contracts in his theory of justice. Most contract theorists have realized that no actual contract of the relevant kind ever took place – and would hardly bind successive generations even if it did – and so they have resorted to tacit contracts, which, as by Plato, one is deemed to have signed if one has continued to live in the state without emigrating. But this is pretty artificial, if only because emigration is for most people not a real possibility, and it savours of situations where a woman is "deemed" by a town council to have made herself voluntarily homeless because she ran away in despair from a violent husband. Some contract theorists, including more recent ones like Grice (1967) and Rawls, have tried to base political obligation – and indeed our obligations in general – on a hypothetical contract, where there is not even the pretence that an actual contract occurred; for Grice we have a duty to do something if it would be in everyone's interest that everyone should contract to do it in the relevant circumstances, while for Rawls, as we have seen, rules or institutions are just if they are what his original choosers would unanimously agree upon.

Explaining and justifying: the program

Nozick's approach is to start from "a nonstate situation in which people generally satisfy moral constraints and generally act as they ought", and then to argue that: "If one could show that the state would be superior even to this most favoured situation of anarchy, the best that realistically can be hoped for, or would arise by a process involving no morally impermissible steps, or would be an improvement if it arose, this would provide a rationale for the state's existence; it would justify the state" (*ASU*: 5; a footnote adds that "a theory that presents a state's arising from a state of nature by a natural and inevitable process of *deterioration* . . . would not 'justify' the state, though it might resign us to its existence"). This has some relation to a contract view because of the prominent part played by contracts in the "morally permissible steps", although the contracts will be an accumulation of individual contracts taken over a substantial period and not a single general contract. Actually the formulation just quoted has three clauses, of which the first and third emphasize that the state would be "superior" or "an improvement" if it arose, while the footnote adds that a state of which this was not true would not be justified. This suggests a teleological approach unusual for Nozick. The justification of the state, one would think, should not for him depend on how beneficial it would be if it did arise. But the passage quoted is unusually wide in scope, and most of the time it is the second clause, about "no morally impermissible steps" being involved, that he emphasizes.

This does, however, raise a problem about just what Nozick is trying to do, and whether what he provides, even if he provides it successfully, can count as justifying the state. Since neither he nor anyone thinks that the state – any actual state – did arise by the squeaky clean process he goes on to present, what is the point of presenting it? It is not as though we were in a state of nature, wondering how we could properly escape from it. We are already at the far end of whatever process brought us to where we are. This, it might be thought, does not put Nozick in any worse position than Grice or Rawls, neither of whom relies on any actual historical process. But the trouble lies in the purely historical nature of Nozick's entitlement theory of justice, which neither Grice nor Rawls shares. Nozick does of course have as part of his theory of justice a principle of rectification, but we have already seen that this principle would have a lot of work to do if we were to try to rectify the current effects of the actual injustices of history (*ASU*: 231).

However, perhaps Nozick is not trying to justify any actual state but simply to show how a state *could* be justified. In fact some of what he says suggests he is not even trying to do this, but simply to explain something, which has led R. P. Wolff to complain that Nozick's task is indeed to justify a state, not to explain it (Paul 1981: 80). It is not clear just how he sees these tasks as related. He says (*ASU*: 6) "In addition to its importance for political philosophy, the investigation of this [just mentioned] state of nature *also* will serve explanatory purposes" (emphasis mine). But since this appeal to explanation occupies a large part of what follows, and since the main point of *Anarchy, State, and Utopia* is plainly to justify a certain political outlook, he must surely think this attempt to explain a certain situation will have some relevance to justifying it.

So why might Nozick think this? He calls explanations in other terms of a whole realm, e.g. the political realm, "fundamental", and borrows Hempel's notion of a "potential" explanation as, roughly, one which would be correct if everything it said were true and operated. A fundamental explanation using no false facts or mistaken laws can still be "process-defective" if it would explain a certain phenomenon had not the process it says produced it been pre-empted by another process which produced it instead, and such process-defective fundamental potential explanations include the one he is about to develop for the political realm, as he rather vaguely calls it. (For all this see *ASU*: 6–9.) What he goes on to explain is the growth of a Nozickian state, but the defect of the explanation is hardly that something else produced that state instead, although something else (the actual course of history) did produce *a* state, or set of states. But perhaps this does not matter. A Nozickian state is *a* state, and perhaps the point is that the account to be offered would explain the growth of *at least* a Nozickian or minimal state.

But another ambiguity looms. Does Nozick mean that, given certain initial conditions (a "state of nature") a minimal state would develop, or merely that it could? "Could" gives a much weaker claim than "would". Sayward and Wasserman (1991) point out (Corlett 1991: 261–3) that the "could" interpretation can be trivialized because those in a state of nature *could* simply agree to set up a minimal state without further ado, however implausible it might be that they would (cf. J. Wolff 1991: 47–8). They add that Nozick usually says "would", and that he dismisses "could" as inadequate (*ASU*: 119) – although part of what he says is that "[e]xplaining how a state *could* [emphasis mine] arise from a state of nature without violating anyone's rights refutes the principled objections of the anarchist" (*ASU*: 119); he does not explain how it does so. The situation is slightly muddied by a further ambiguity in the use of "could". When B. Williams asks: "What weight is there in the fact that we *could*, relative to certain wildly idealized psychological assumptions, reach the state without violating anyone's rights?" (Paul 1981: 33), this is compatible with his meaning that (for Nozick) we *could* reach the state from scratch by making certain assumptions, and that if we do make them we *would* reach it. The "could" interpretation could be saved from trivialization if we interpret "could" to mean "could by some reasonably plausible process", but it seems pretty clear in fact that Nozick intends "would" (*pace* R. P. Wolff in Paul 1981: 80).

So what is the relevance of talking about what would happen in certain circumstances for one who holds a historical entitlement view of justice? Here we must remember that Nozick's target in the first part of *Anarchy, State, and Utopia* is not welfarism, which he is so famous or infamous for opposing, but anarchism. Suppose he can show that if we start from a state of nature a Nozickian state will inevitably develop; then there is not much point in the anarchist hoping to achieve a state of nature – even if he succeeded the state of nature he achieved would be unstable and disappear again. At this point we could answer a possible objection: either the state of nature once existed or it didn't. If it did, why has it not led to a Nozickian state? If it didn't, why bother to talk about it? We could answer the first point by returning to the idea that the proposed account is to explain the growth of *at least* a minimal state; and to the second we could now say that whether the state of nature did exist is irrelevant if it is something that the anarchist might still hope to achieve.

However, the above account will not do as it stands. The most we have done so far is show how to "justify" the existence of some state or other by demonstrating that it is inevitable since a state of nature would not last. But this would take no account of Nozick's requirement that there be "no morally impermissible steps". Nozick wants to show more than that some state is inevitable. Perhaps he wants to show that if a state did arise by just steps from a state of nature it would be justified, as opposed to all the other states that might have arisen, and indeed do exist, which in his eyes are certainly not justified. But now we face the opposite danger, of ignoring his use of "would" rather than "could". After all, how could he deny on his own terms that if a state did arise from a state of nature by just steps it would be justified, however likely or unlikely its arising was?

Perhaps his position is this: if we start with a state of nature, some political state will inevitably ensue. If we add in (as he does) that people in general act justly, then the state that does arise will be a just one. Perhaps remaining in a state of nature would also be a just outcome, but since that is not an option we can ignore it. If this is so, he has two aims fused together: showing that some state will arise anyway, and showing that if people generally (not always) act justly the state that arises will be justified. The nub lies in the "not always". Trivially, for Nozick, if people always act justly the outcome will be just, but so it will without this if they usually do. Nozick is not, on this view, trying to justify any actual state, but to point us in the direction of a just state by showing that even for a non-anarchist it is not an impossible ideal. The justification of the minimal state, were one to arise, would consist in showing that, however it actually arose, it could be regarded as though it had arisen inevitably from a certain initial situation (the state of nature plus a certain assumption) *without involving any morally impermissible steps*.

E. F. Paul (1981), while accepting Nozick's general moral frame-work, argues that this historical approach is irrelevant, and that whether a state is justified should be asked with reference to some given period of its history, and answered according to its behaviour during that period, however it originated. Roughly, if it limits itself to protecting Nozickian rights then it is justified. On the view I have been sketching Nozick does not make the state's justification depend on its actual origin, but perhaps he would think of Paul's view as not by itself a sufficient answer to the anarchist. Anyway, let us turn to the account he actually offers of how a state of nature generates a political state.

The execution I: the state of nature

What is a state of nature? For Hobbes, notoriously, it was a state where life would be "solitary, poor, nasty, brutish and short" (1651: Part I, middle of Ch. 13). Locke is more optimistic. In the second of his *Two Treatises of Government* (Ch. 2), he describes it as a state that "all men are naturally in, . . . a state of perfect freedom to order their actions, and dispose of their possessions and persons as they think fit, within the bounds of the Law of Nature" (§1), and "though this be a state of liberty, yet it is not a state of license", for "[t]he state of Nature has a law of Nature to govern it" (§6). Locke clearly assumes that not only do men have obligations in a state of nature but that in general, at least, they will obey them, being motivated to do so at least partly by the need for cooperation.

Nozick is closer to Locke than to any other of the classical theorists, and he takes over this conception of a state of nature, including the idea that people in it will act morally (according to Nozickian principles of morality, which they will presumably know by intuition) for most of the time but not all of it. That most of us most of the time act reasonably morally without thinking about it, and without meeting either inner struggles or external sanctions is certainly true. (For an eloquent exposition of the point see Bergson 1935: Ch. 1.) If we did not, family and social life would be impossible, although there are morals and morals: Hitler believed in kindness at least to animals, if not to Jews, and Himmler was meticulously honest in his personal affairs.

But just what is a state of nature? The use Nozick makes of it, to *generate* a political state, suggests it is a condition prior to all political institutions, where individuals are entirely independent although in contact with others in competition for the same resources. But how far is this anything but an ideal limit? We have seen already how he admits that even such things as language depend on socialization (*ASU*: 95): isolated individuals would hardly he human at all, and could hardly have any conception of either property or rights. To survive biologically they must at least be in families, and to avoid disastrous "inbreeding" some contact between families must exist. The idea that society developed from a set of (fairly) noble but unsocialized savages is historically absurd and presumably impossible. Nozick, of course, is not committed to the historical reality of this, but does the possibility of his model depend on its possibility?

But perhaps this is to confuse being prior to all political institutions with being prior to all socialization. Locke ends his discussion of the state of nature by imagining himself asked "as a mighty objection, where are, or ever were, there any men in such a state of Nature?" and pointing to "all princes and rulers of 'independent' governments" (§14), or as we might say, dictators. We can ignore some here irrelevant details of Locke's own views, but the point is that being in a state of nature is a relative matter, and individuals who have had ample opportunity to get socialized on their home ground can still find themselves in a state of nature in regard to certain other individuals. (On Locke's "princes" , one might ask why no minimal world government has arisen, and despite various international agencies none looks likely. Nozick might say that rulers do not behave morally, although on his own view of a state of nature they should do, at least generally. But the case is complicated because morality may apply differently to rulers, since they risk not just themselves but their subjects.)

At any rate a realistic state of nature – if it is to be of any use to Nozick or anyone else – must consist of individuals already socialized. The question then is: how much more is involved? Locke's state of nature involves having "possessions" and Nozick quotes this with evident approval (*ASU*: 10), but does this not involve a set of concepts that imply an organized society, however small and local? Where in fact does a state of nature leave off and something else begin? The point is not just that the transition may be very gradual, but that it is not clear what it is from and to. As Williams writes, after discussing Nozick's appeal to boundaries and their crossing, "There is . . . a persistent doubt about whether the State of Nature can really be got off the ground without taking for granted conventions and institutions of a kind which the State of Nature does not itself provide" (Paul 1981: 32). But let us turn to the process of growth itself.

The execution II: growth of the state

The basic process is fairly simple. People in a state of nature find it convenient to form groups for mutual protection, pooling expenses. Several such groups of various sizes appear, and people naturally gravitate to the biggest and most powerful, which becomes the dominant agency. Eventually this agency acquires a de facto monopoly of power in its area, except for that needed for immediate self-defence (*ASU*: 26). It now has become what Nozick calls an "ultraminimal" state, or, since it only has a de facto monopoly of power and does not claim a *de jure* one, a "statelike entity" (*ASU*: 118). One further step is needed before we reach the full minimal state, traditionally often referred to as the "night-watchman" state, because so far it only provides protection for those who insure themselves with its services. The rest (the "independents", or John Wayne types) are left to fend for themselves. The agency has to defend its clients against them, which involves prohibiting them from various activities (to be mentioned later). But it is now morally obliged to compensate them, which it does by offering them its protective services at its own expense, i.e. at that of its existing clients. It has now become a fully fledged minimal state, satisfying the two conditions Nozick insists on

– of having a monopoly of power in its area, and of offering its protection to all the inhabitants of that area.

Practical objections

Such is the basic idea, although the details are messy, especially in the later stages. Most of the criticisms that have assailed it have focused on the later stages, accusing them of being morally confused or inadequate; however, the earlier stages too have been accused of being impractical and unrealistic.

On the practical front, how will the agencies behave? Williams (Paul 1981: 32–3) suspects they would be "partial towards their clients, hypocritical towards potential clients, and horrible towards confirmed non-clients". He also suspects (hesitantly) that although Nozick's individuals sometimes act wrongly, his agencies always act morally (Paul 1981: 33; cf. Sampson 1978: 96). Actually Nozick does allow that rogue agencies may appear (*ASU*: 17), but he thinks they would become unpopular and wither. He could point out that the agencies, or their agents, would not have the same personal motives for wrongdoing as would private citizens, although this would only mildly reassure anyone knowing the behaviour of many actual police or commercial bodies. R. P. Wolff brings various other practical objections, deploring Nozick's "complete failure to take account of the most obvious and well known facts of human motivation and social experience" (Paul 1981: 90–91); however, both he and Williams think this of minor importance because they take the "could" interpretation of what Nozick is doing.

If the agencies can misbehave, or simply be misinformed or use unreliable procedures, even with the best of intentions, the obvious question is: who will control them? At first they will be subject to economic control, since clients will leave, or not join, those perceived as inadequate, but this will get progressively harder as they get larger and fewer in number, and especially when there is only one (Nozick briefly mentions these issues in his discussion of utopias, but says he has nothing special to add (*ASU*: 329–30 with n.13)). Wolff compares the dominant agency to something like a telephone company: if I disapprove of its activities I can ask the government to control it, whereas for Nozick "the dominant protective agency *is* the government!", which as a device for guaranteeing our liberties etc. he calls "a trifle feckless" (Paul 1981: 93). Would we be worse off than trying to control our own government? Well, the different parts of the agency might be subject to control by each other and we could complain to the agency about the behaviour of the sub-contractors it will no doubt use; but democratic governments are subject to election and fearful for their popularity, which a Nozickian government, however minimal, will not be (but cf. J. Wolff 1991: 58). Nozick must rely heavily on the premise that the individuals running the agencies will be at least as generally moral as he takes them to be in their private lives – and even that will not protect them from error and ignorance, although it might persuade them to make amends where necessary. A further complication, however, is that people acting in a public capacity often feel less personally responsible – they feel they are acting "under orders".

This last point leads on to something Nozick makes much use of, especially when explaining why social contracts and general assent are not needed for the growth of the state: "invisible hand" processes, a term he borrows from Adam Smith. The idea is that actions by many people can lead to a result which looks as if it was intended, but in fact wasn't. (Compare the subtitle of Part One of *ASU*: "How to Back into a State without Really Trying".) He gives as an example the invention of money (*ASU*: 18), and we might compare the more recent example of the alleged role of cigarettes in the army (or occupied Europe): I have some philosophy books I want to swap for a Walkman, but the Walkman-owners don't want philosophy books. Eventually I find someone who does, but he can only give me cigarettes. Although a non-smoker, I take these, because I know the Walkman-owners like them, and so I get my Walkman. Others some-times do the same. Cigarettes (like gold) must have some intrinsic value for the process to start, but even smokers may accumulate more than they need, and eventually smoking might die out (e.g. for medical reasons) but cigarettes remain as currency. In this example people do horde cigarettes for what they can swap them for, but no-one need intend that they become a general currency, or even realize at first that others are hoarding similarly. (I am not clear why Steiner (1977b: 122) says, "this has never been a satisfactory expla-nation of the invention of money [because] it leaves us no more enlightened as to how all individuals will thus be saved any bother in seeking out purchasers of their goods and vendors of their require-ments; nor is it clear how each exchanger can have goods less gener-ally wanted than the goods of others which, after all, are what money represents on this construction".) Nozick compares invisible hand explanations to fundamental explanations, which explain a whole realm without using the terms of that realm, but the significance of all this for us here is that those responsible for producing the dominant agency, and those acting for it, may not intend the ultimate results of their actions, nor realize their significance. This is all that is needed for an invisible hand to replace a social contract, explicit or implicit, in accounting for the development of a state. (*SP*, Ch. 9, discusses invisible hand explanations further, linking them to evolutionary explanations of rationality, on which see Ch. 6 below.)

Objections of principle I: transitivity and compensation

So far we have been concerned with practical objections to the envisaged growth of the state, which mainly concern its earlier stages. The most important objections ask whether the account offered is consistent, especially in view of the requirement that no morally impermissible steps be involved. These mainly concern the later stages, but R. P. Wolff offers one which is partly practical and partly moral, and concerns all the stages in the process (see Paul 1981: 93–5). If I have a right I can, for Nozick, transfer that right to someone else who will now have the right and so in turn can transfer it on. This seems to imply that the transfer of rights is transitive, and in particular that if I transfer a right (e.g. to punish anyone attacking me) to a protection agency, it can in turn transfer it to its own officers, who may again delegate or subcontract it indefinitely. But Wolff sees "a minute slippage or blockage in the rights transfer", because the agent may always misuse the powers he inherits, or misunderstand them, or misapply them in error, and these possibilities will accumulate as the transfers go on, so that the responsibility I have to see that my rights are not misused, by myself or anyone I transfer them to, will become progressively harder to carry out. This is in fact another aspect of the problem we met above: who will control the protective agencies? This forms the practical aspect of the problem, while the moral aspect lies in the question: what is involved in the transfer of rights?

In Chapter 2 we discussed compensation and some of the difficulties attached to its use. There we were mainly concerned with how the amount of compensation due was measured, and whether the justification for it was deontic or teleological. R. P. Wolff points out

(Paul 1981: 82–3) that Nozick first introduces a principle of compensation as a mere suggestion (*ASU*: 82–3) but then treats it as established despite cheerfully admitting that he has neither formulated nor justified it properly (*ASU*: 110–11, 87). Wolff then asks whether Nozick should, consistently with his strong theory of rights, never allow unconsented rights violations, even when they are compensated – a "crazy conclusion", as Nozick realizes (Paul 1981: 87). A related criticism is made by Young (1986), who accuses Nozick of not distinguishing compensation which is accepted by the independent (as Nozick calls non-clients of the agency) from restitution which is imposed by a third party without being accepted. Why, he asks, should the agency need to force a person fully compensated to accept? Young, however, does not seem to distinguish defining (full) compensation as what the independent would voluntarily accept and defining it (with Nozick) as what would leave the independent as well off, in his own estimation, within the whole package as without it. An independent offered compensation in the second (i.e. Nozick's) sense might refuse it, i.e. refuse the package of which it was part. Would such an independent be irrational? If the compensation left him indifferent, all things considered, between accepting and rejecting, although forced to do one or the other, why should rejecting be any more irrational (even if a bit cussed) than accepting? But even if his choice is irrational, he surely has a right to make it, in terms of Nozick's general philosophy (cf. Wolff in Paul 1981: 87, referred to above). Young goes on to suggest in effect (Corlett 1991: 273–4) that the agency could simply offer the increased compensation that *would* persuade the independent to accept. But if Nozick accepted this, while keeping his own definition of compensation, he would be open to the charge that the agency would be unjustly taxing its own clients to pay the increased amount (cf. Paul 1981: 75). Nozick could switch to the other definition of full compensation (as what the independent would accept), but as well as making him reformulate his version of the Lockean proviso, this would let tough-minded independents do some pretty hard bargaining.

Young further asks (Corlett 1991: 272) how Nozick-style compensation could apply to cases like rape without implying that "everyone has their price". This is indeed a problem – not just for Nozick but for everyone. What could someone who has suffered violation of their honour, or loss of a child, accept either as restoring them to their previous welfare level or as what they would take in a market exchange? Young makes the charge in terms of compensation. If we use his own notion of restitution we could at least escape the need for the victim to accept it voluntarily, in the sense of acknowledging its adequacy, although we would still face the problem of balancing values that seem incommensurable – a task, however, that courts seem able to make some headway with. (Young in fact accuses Nozick of confusing the possibility of rightful compensation with the possibility of non-market restitution.)

The general approach underlying these criticisms asks whether compensation can properly appear in Nozick's account at all (except presumably for purely accidental violations), for either the agency acts without violating any rights, so that no compensation is needed, or it does violate some rights, so that its development involves a morally impermissible step, whether or not this is compensated. Holmes (1977) uses this to criticize the step from the ultraminimal state, which has a monopoly of force but does not protect everyone in its territory, to the minimal state, which does. (Nozick and his critics assume throughout that the state has a geographical basis, although other possibilities exist. An autonomous church replete with ecclesiastical courts might govern some aspects of our lives while a similarly autonomous trade union might govern other aspects. If the same person belonged to both, their prescriptions might clash, but they might have non-overlapping memberships which were still territorially intermingled. The search for examples is left to the reader.) The ultraminimal state is an essential stage in the development Nozick assigns to the state, and for Holmes its distinguishing feature is that it exercises a monopoly of force without compensation, which only comes when we get to the minimal state itself (Paul 1981: 61). Since for Holmes the ultraminimal state's only motivation for becoming a minimal state by compensating is a moral one (Paul 1981: 62), he concludes that either the ultraminimal state is an immoral stage in the state's development, contrary to Nozick's claim, or if not, the minimal state will never develop out of it, because unmotivated (Paul 1981: 63).

Perhaps Nozick could answer this last point by making the ultraminimal state a purely hypothetical or conceptual stage in the development, so that the dominant agency offered compensation throughout its process of becoming a monopoly. But this does not answer the general problems about compensation, which involve also the notions of risk and procedural rights. Holmes, J. Paul and R. P. Wolff in particular, develop criticisms based on these; compare J. Wolff (1991: especially 64–5).

Objections of principle II: procedural rights and incomplete knowledge

Nozick allows agents, and therefore agencies, to have procedural rights, i.e. rights to use certain procedures and in particular to have only certain procedures, notably reliable ones, used against them by those claiming to punish them for violating rights. J. Paul (1981: 72) asks where these rights come from, as they don't seem to derive from the rules of entitlement, and Steiner (1977b: 122–3) similarly asks whence we get the rights, which seem to ground them, to emotional states such as security and freedom from fear, as against simply rights to non-interference in our legitimate activities. However, Nozick's general grounding of our rights in the notion of a meaningful life does not seem to limit them to rights to unfettered (legitimate) activity.

More serious is the danger of a regress of procedural rights. If in setting up a minimal state an agency questions an independent's procedure against one of its clients, can the independent demand a second procedure to judge this questioning, and then the agency demand a third to judge the second, and so on? If so, the minimal state will either never be reached, given a persistent independent, or only reached immorally by the agency arbitrarily cutting off the appeals process (Paul 1981: 72–3). This will presumably apply to any system unless an unappealable supreme court can be legitimated, and Nozick needs to show how in his own system this could happen. The argument is again a version of the "Who controls the agencies?" one.

An agency, like any agent, can only know so much. This is why an agency may find itself prohibiting actions that would not in fact have violated any rights, although they risked doing so, or prohibiting as unreliable procedures that were not in fact unreliable. Compensation can hardly be required for prohibiting an act that would have violated a right, on the grounds that because of the prohibition itself no violation occurred. My right to defend myself surely includes a right to attack pre-emptively anyone clearly about to murder me. It is with prohibiting merely risky actions or procedures that complications arise. Perhaps the agency should simply negotiate a deal with the independent. Nozick thinks this might be too difficult or costly sometimes. But as Paul points out (1981: 71), this should be irrelevant on Nozick's principles.

People or agencies who have to act with incomplete knowledge will find themselves acting either under risk or under uncertainty (a

distinction Nozick made much use of in his 1963 Ph.D. thesis). The
difference is that when acting under risks one knows enough to assign
probabilities to various outcomes and therefore assess benefits and
probabilities together to form a rational plan of action, but when acting
under uncertainty there are insufficient grounds to do this. R. P. Wolff
claims (Paul 1981: 86–7) that Nozick treats the state as growing by a
series of actions under risk, with measurements of, and calculations
based on, utility, etc. (he refers in particular to *ASU*: 58). He then
makes three criticisms: that what drives individuals to form associations in the first place is clearly uncertainty; that the gathering and
use of information needed for calculating compensations will often
presuppose sophisticated state machinery; and finally (actually he
puts this second) that a traditional social contract could be seen as
partly aiming, in effect, to transform situations of choice under
uncertainty into situations of choice under risk, so that Nozick's
account is circular, "for it assumes the prior existence of the very state
of affairs it is supposed to produce". One could comment that the
growth of knowledge is gradual, so that the conditions for action under
risk (as well as those for assessing complex compensations) would
grow up *pari passu* with the Nozickian process rather than being
presupposed by it; but this would only partly answer the objection,
which would apply especially to the earlier stages.

Many other criticisms have been made of *Anarchy, State, and
Utopia*; see, for instance, in addition to the literature I have
discussed, Sampson (1978), with Danley's (1979) discussion, the end
of R. P. Wolff's article (Paul 1981: 96–101) for some more general
considerations, and also of course J. Wolff (1991) especially Chapter
3, and Hailwood (1996), Chapter 3. But let us finally look briefly at
the third part of *Anarchy, State, and Utopia*.

Utopia I: the framework

Most writers on *Anarchy, State, and Utopia* treat its third part,
which is about a quarter the length of either of the first two parts, to
at most a few casual remarks, but there are two quite full discussions
of it by Hailwood (especially Ch. 8) and Fowler (1980). J. Wolff (1991)
allows it a few pages (see his index), and Singer gives it a brief but
incisive critique (Paul 1981: 38–9).

Nozick's conception of utopia is striking and original, and he introduces it as a hopefully inspiring dessert after the rather bleak and

unappetizing main libertarian menu. Its main feature is that there are two tiers. He is convinced, plausibly enough, that no one society could be the ideal choice for Wittgenstein, Elizabeth Taylor, Thoreau, Moses and Henry Ford, to select a few from the long list he gives (*ASU*: 310). So why not let everyone construct their own utopia, provided they can find enough others to make it possible, under the aegis of a highly permissive "framework" (the second tier) to see fair play (no inter-utopian aggression)? "Let a hundred flowers bloom", with a benign and *verklärte* Mao to provide the garden.

Applying his earlier interest in game theory, Nozick constructs a theoretical model wherein each of us can imagine our own utopia (presumably without breaching scientific laws), populating it as richly or sparsely as we like, but with the constraint that all its inhabitants are rational beings with the same rights as ourselves who can imagine their own utopias and migrate to them if they don't like ours, and none of whom are deliberately constructed so that it follows, either logically or causally, that they will prefer ours. The same constraints apply to the worlds they imagine, and to the inhabitants of those worlds, and so on. Anyone can migrate from the world he is in to another he imagines, provided only that that world will accept him (presumably by a majority vote of its members, dissenting minorities being free to leave if they wish). There is no guarantee that stable associations (as he calls them) would result, but he offers some empirical reasons, based on human nature, to think they well might (*ASU*: 306).

Applying this model to the real world, i.e. treating the associations as real and not just constructed by people's imaginations, we get the set-up Nozick envisages. Unsurprisingly the general framework turns out to be the minimal state, reached here by arguments independent of those given earlier. The framework differs from the abstract model because we cannot create people at will, and associations will impinge on each other, not merely by attracting members from each other, and there will be difficulties both practical and of principle in transferring from one to another. The framework settles disputes between the constituent associations or communities, but although itself libertarian it will allow each community to be as authoritarian as it wishes; only "imperialistic" ones, which seek to take over others by force, are banned.

Rather than being designed by the state, communities will grow, change and wither by an evolutionary selection process he calls "filtering", an approach Nozick himself compares to the scientific

methodology of Popper (*ASU*: 352 n.7), and which fits well the growing preference for intellectual flexibility we discussed in Chapter 1.
When a community changes, the central agency may make it compensate some of its members, but this could be avoided (*ASU*: 324) if
members joining a community explicitly contract to be compensated
in such circumstances – although this would lead to the problems the
entitlement theory shared with social contract theories about
children born into the community. Even the framework itself admits
of some flexibility, although it must remain voluntary, and could
even disappear if everyone contracted out of it.

Utopia II: objections

As with his account of the growth of the minimal state, the present
account faces objections both practical and of principle, some of which
Nozick foresees – and sometimes cheerfully defers, in accordance
with his habit of plotting his way around minefields without clearing
them or guaranteeing himself a path to his destination.

Anyone can set up a community, if he can find enough like-minded
others, and they have enough resources, and can find and travel to
enough vacant or purchasable land, and avoid interfering with other
communities. (Hailwood (1996: 88) comments that, "Nozick's utopian
programme seems to involve a rerun of the history of the United
States, but without the more unfortunate aspects".) A redistributive
community might have difficulty attracting and keeping members
with enough wealth to redistribute, while not being swamped with
applications to join from the poor of neighbouring capitalist communities (Singer 1975). One of the framework rules is that anyone may
leave their community, but whether they can if they have debts, and
what they can take with them, are among the mines left undefused
(*ASU*: 330–31). What, if anything, is the central agency supposed to
do about those who cannot find any community to accept them? And
for that matter what guarantee is there in this world where everyone
does their own thing that enough suitable people will be found to man
the agency itself (presumably financed by taxing the communities, on
a basis they all agree on)?

These practical problems are perhaps less fundamentally important, especially for philosophy, although they do take the edge off the
inspiration we are supposed to receive (but cf. *ASU*: 308–9, with
Hailwood's comments (1996: 89–90)). But there are also problems of

principle. Another mine left undefused concerns information. "In some way it must be ensured that [children] are *informed* of the range of alternatives in the world. But the home community might view it as important that their youngsters not be exposed to the knowledge that one hundred miles away is a community of great sexual freedom" (*ASU*: 330). "Though the framework is libertarian and laissez-faire, *individual communities within it need not be*" (*ASU*: 320), and "paternalistic restrictions geared to nullify supposed defects in people's decision processes [may not] be imposed – for example, compulsory information programs" (*ASU*: 324).

This last quote brings us to an issue raised at some length by Hailwood. Unlike Rawls's abstract and bloodless original choosers, those making choices in Nozick's world are full-blooded human beings. But how did they become what they are? Where did they get their conception of the good, in the light of which they choose? Hailwood insists that it is not so much a matter of "a lack of proper context for choice, or of selves shorn of social attachments", but that Nozick simply assumes that people in the model "can and do choose, in the light of conceptions of the good which they possess fully formed, to set up and live in stable associations" (Hailwood 1996: 86). He ends (1996: 90) by appealing for support to Singer (1975), who asks whether "the free flow of information [is] sufficient to wash away the encrusted muck of billions of dollars worth of advertising for a style of life devoted to the acquisition of consumer goods and the elimination of stains and odors". Admitting that his view "smacks of paternalism" he adds: "But what if the choice lies not between paternalism and freedom, but between making a deliberate attempt to control the circumstances under which we live and allowing these circumstances to develop haphazardly, permitting only an illusory sense of individual liberty" (Paul 1981: 38–9). One trouble with this communitarian approach is that it raises again the question: who controls the controllers, who make the above "deliberate attempt"?

The same approach underlies another of Hailwood's criticisms. Nozick allows any ways of life to be followed except "imperialistic" ones: the relations between communities must be one of live and let live. But Hailwood thinks he has not justified his rejection of "imperialism". Nozick's whole approach to utopias rests on his conviction that there is no objectively ideal way of life for everyone. Hailwood claims that he never defends this, and accuses him of arguing that because there is no general agreement about ideals, the best possible world overall is neutral between the different ideals, and is therefore a neutral framework of stable associations (Hailwood 1996: 76). Later he criticizes Nozick's appeal to voluntariness: "Nozick's claim in effect is that if after a voluntary filter operation one level of stable association is left standing, then that can be taken to be the objectively best community" (Hailwood 1996: 79). One might be inclined to comment that this ignores the deontological rather than teleological bent of Nozick's whole philosophy; he is not looking for the objectively best set-up but for one that does not violate rights. This comment is admittedly rather offset by Nozick's defence of his framework (*ASU*: 309) in terms of maximizing preference satisfaction, which Hailwood points to as "at odds with the anti consequentialism of the rest of *Anarchy, State, and Utopia*" (Hailwood 1996: 77). But this very remark treats the consequentialism (of *ASU*: 309) as untypical (as Hailwood is aware), and Nozick could in any case reply that whatever maximising of preference satisfaction, or of any other ideal, takes place, it must be compatible with his strong theory of human rights. However, Hailwood's point (1996: 79) is rather that there is no reason to think such a filtering would lead to an *objectively* best community unless one simply assumes that an objectively best one just *is* one that survives such filtering.

Hailwood also claims (1996: 84) that the framework is not, as Nozick thinks (*ASU*: 333), equivalent to the minimal state, because it is neutral between different ideals and does not, like the minimal state, promote the libertarian ideal of justice or property. It is not concerned with the policing of fraud, theft, and the honouring of contracts (except presumably between associations and their members; it does protect some right of emigration). This is fair enough, although the framework is still libertarian at the second level, as it were; its fundamental *raison d'étre* is Nozick's theory of rights, and its main role is to protect the individual's right to choose his own way of life, subject no doubt to practical difficulties but not to deliberate interference by others, even when he chooses, as for Nozick he can (*ASU*: 331), to sell himself into slavery. But Hailwood's point is that this discrepancy is important, because it raises a doubt about what the outcome of *Anarchy, State, and Utopia* really is – the libertarianism of parts One and Two or this neutralism, the minimal state or the framework for utopia.

Fowler's (1980) critique of Nozick on utopia is harsh. He starts by saying that what is new in Nozick's account is not good, while what is good is not new, and ends by saying that he "has still to catch up with his [liberal] predecessors" (Corlett 1991: 259). He points out that religious and similar duties may clash with the entitlement theory, but seems to forget that Nozick never makes his entitlement theory the whole of morality; and he seems to think that Nozick's toleration of authoritarian communities implies tolerating imperialistic ones, although perhaps he means that they will tend to *become* imperialistic.

But Fowler's main criticism is that Nozick relies on an assumption about the extreme diversity of human nature to support his claim about the need for a plurality of utopias. This assumption, however, would also mean that there would never emerge a sufficient consensus to establish the framework and keep it going. He thinks Nozick is wrong to appeal, as he does (*ASU*: 328) to Toqueville to support the idea that liberty leads to the development of virtues; and although Fowler allows that for Madisonian liberals some balanced factionalism was necessary for stability and the prevention of tyranny, he adds that for them the divisions were along lines of race, religion, class, etc., rather than, as for Nozick, ideological. But one might wonder whether societies divided by Islamic fundamentalism or Marxian class warfare have really any better prospects of ideological unity.

Summary

Moving from the moral basis of the system to the resulting system itself takes us from Part Two of *Anarchy, State, and Utopia* back to Part One, the growth of the minimal state by a process involving no morally impermissible steps. Nozick's theory is a contract theory of sorts, although the contracts are a disparate mass of individual ones. Such a state will be justified if it is an improvement on what went before, which introduces a surprisingly teleological element. Also standard contract theories can rely on merely hypothetical contracts, but the contracts in Nozick's entitlement theory must be actual, and since clearly no actual state arose without morally impermissible steps, how can any of them be justified? Nozick's aim is in fact unclear. Perhaps he is trying not to justify the state but merely to explain it, but since his overall aim is clearly to justify a certain political outlook, he must think that explaining the state is somehow relevant to justifying it. He seems, although not always unambiguously, to be saying what would, rather than merely could, arise from a state of nature, whose inhabitants usually acted morally, as he thinks they would, and the relevance of this is perhaps that were a minimal state to arise, from whatever source, it could be regarded as though it had arisen inevitably, and without morally impermissible steps, from a state of nature whose inhabitants usually acted morally. By a state of nature Nozick, following Locke, means individuals socialized but without political institutions, but it is hard in fact to mark off sharply the sort of state of nature Nozick wants.

After outlining the growth of the ultraminimal and minimal states we turned to practical and theoretical objections. Practical objections mainly concerned the behaviour of the agencies and the need to control them, which led to a brief account of Nozick's appeal to "invisible hand" explanations. An objection with both practical and theoretical aspects concerned delegation of authority to subcontractors, while the theoretical objections started with ones about compensation. If the agencies never act immorally (or those that do are weeded out by natural selection), how is compensation by them ever needed, except for purely accidental violations of rights, and how can the minimal develop from the ultraminimal state? Also how about "uncompensatable" violations like rape (although Young's own notion of restitution might help here)? Further objections concerned the basis of the procedural rights the agencies use, and the effects of their inevitable ignorance, which involves problems about relating risk and uncertainty.

The final discussion of utopia, although relatively ignored by commentators, is striking and original. A central agency provides a framework wherein people can get together and form their own communities, as libertarian or authoritarian as they like except that they must respect each other's independence. Such communities will develop by a "filtering" process of natural selection. Objections raised have been practical and especially theoretical. Will authoritarian communities let their children know about libertarian ones? How do people get the values governing their choice of community? Hailwood doubts that the filtering would produce an objectively best community, as he thinks Nozick wants it to, and sees an important tension between the libertarianism of earlier in *Anarchy, State, and Utopia* and the neutrality of the framework between different ideologies. Fowler doubts in particular whether the diversity of human nature Nozick relies on would succeed in establishing and maintaining the framework.

Chapter 4

The later ethics and politics

Introduction

After *Anarchy, State, and Utopia* Nozick's ethical and political views
underwent both development and modification, leading him away
from his original libertarianism. *Philosophical Explanations*, his
next work, is an immense sprawl of a book, covering three main areas
(metaphysics, epistemology and value) in six chapters, of which the
main one relevant here is Chapter 5, "Foundations of Ethics", itself
divided into six substantial sections.

We saw in Chapter 1 how Nozick's approach to philosophy
changed from trying to secure conviction by proof to explaining how
something is possible, and *Philosophical Explanations*, as its title
suggests, follows this line explicitly. On ethics he says that, although
he hopes his view "contains much that is actually true and illuminating about ethics, the project is to sketch what an objective ethics
might look like, to understand how there (so much as) could be such a
thing" (*PE*: 400), and he ends Chapter 5 by saying: "We opened this
chapter with the question of how ethics is even possible. I have
sketched one possible answer . . . . I would not have pursued this way
in such detail if I did not think it largely right, yet . . . it can yield an
understanding of how ethics is possible even if the explanation it
provides is incorrect" (*PE*: 570; cf. also *PE*: 498, 512, 559). We might
wonder how an incorrect explanation of how something is possible
could produce understanding, since for all it tells us the thing might
really be impossible. But since he thinks his view is "largely right" he
presumably means that any incorrectness in it will be in the details,
and not such as to leave open the possibility that those details could

73

not be corrected. The logic of the argument is that the explanation is possible, even if false, and the thing to be explained follows from the explanation, and so is itself possible.

As well as this emphasis on the new approach Nozick also uses from time to time notions developed earlier in *Philosophical Explanations*, such as those of tracking and the closest continuer theory (which we shall come to in later chapters), and in this way he gives *Philosophical Explanations* and his later philosophy in general a unity it might seem at first sight to lack. (See, e.g. *PE*: 411, 412, 442, 443, 524, 550.)

This change in approach from proof to persuasion (to put it roughly) is also reflected in a change in the content of the treatment of ethics and a certain softening of some of the harsher features of *Anarchy, State, and Utopia*, a process which is taken further in his later books *The Examined Life* and *The Nature of Rationality*; see in particular for material relevant to ethics and politics *The Examined Life*, Chapters 3, 18, 25, and *The Nature of Rationality*, Chapter 1. We find now a far greater emphasis on value than on rights, and the discussion is structured in terms of "pushes" and "pulls" (notions absent from *ASU*, although he says he had them in mind (*PE*: 748 n.19)), where pushes represent the constraints on my behaviour that ought to apply because of what I am myself, while pulls represent the constraints derived from you, the person affected by my action, because of what you are. "My value fixes what behaviour should flow from me; your value fixes which behaviour should flow toward you" (*PE*: 401). Moral push and pull are described as forces, but their magnitude is not their actual effects but those they should have. Ethics then has the tasks of specifying and explaining these forces, and also of showing "that the push is greater than or equal to the pull: that for any two persons, the moral push of one toward the other is greater than or equal to the pull of the second upon the first" (*PE*: 401). Finally, ethics must explain the connection between moral behaviour and the fact that it is pulled. The relations between these tasks are not entirely clear, but we need only look at how the discussions develop as we go on.

Ethics and motivation

Morality in one of its guises – and many, like Kant, would say its main guise – appears to us as a call or pull from outside, something to be contrasted with self-interest, which it claims to override when they clash, and throughout the ages moralists have had a recurrent nightmare that if they emphasize this feature they will end up making morality so alien to us that we shall ask "What is that to us?" and set it aside in our acting. Glaucon and Adimantus in Book 2 of Plato's *Republic* challenge Socrates to show that acting morally is in our interest intrinsically and not just for its consequences, and the rest of the *Republic* is a not too obviously successful attempt to answer this challenge. In modern times Sidgwick notoriously ended his *Methods of Ethics* by talking of "the vital need that our Practical Reason feels of proving or postulating this [previously described] connexion of Virtue and self-interest, if it is to be made consistent with itself" (1907: 508), and earlier quoted passages to the same effect from Joseph Butler's eleventh sermon (Butler 1914) and Samuel Clarke (1978). Philippa Foot goes so far as to say that "if justice is not a good to the just man, moralists who recommend it as a virtue are perpetrating a fraud" (1958–9: 100), while Griffin in his *Well-Being* introduces rather more vaguely a "Requirement of Psychological Realism", which he thinks "[w]e all accept" (1986: 134), to the effect that "the source of morality can never stray far from the natural sources of action" (1986: 127); "moral restrictions" must "fit the human psyche" (1986: 163).

It is this challenge with which Nozick starts his discussion of the ethical push; the task is to show "that and how we are better off being moral. Being moral is not simply a sacrifice, there is something in it for us" (*PE*: 403). The challenge itself has not gone unchallenged, and many would call it, with Kant again, unduly cynical: to claim that morality must be in our own interest is to claim that morality is not really morality at all. Nozick's own attitude is to accept the challenge – although we should remember his reaction to Adler which I mentioned in Chapter 2 (end of the "Introduction") – but his answer to it is not entirely unambiguous, and involves an affinity to Aristotle, as he realizes, despite his criticism of one feature of Aristotle's position (*PE*: 515–17).

The problem in the first place is to decide what counts as an answer to the challenge. The obvious way of taking the challenge is as asking to be shown that morality is in our self-interest, but what counts as self-interest? Is this to be defined independently of morality, or can it only be understood after we have included a reference to the moral life? (Cf. the four ways of relating morality and self-interest (*PE*: 505) that Nozick sketches.)

Nozick's treatment of self-interest, sometimes varied to rational self-interest, especially when talking of Plato (e.g. *PE*: 405), has a certain ambivalence, which reflects a distinction he makes between a sanction on certain behaviour and a motivation to avoid that behaviour – even though ultimately he wants these to coincide. He sees something "deeply correct" in Plato's claim that morality and rational self-interest coincide, but adds that this cannot be captured "by attempting to correlate morality with self-interest or happiness" (*PE*: 405–6). Is there an implied contrast here between self-interest and rational self-interest? Probably not, and it would not really help, since rational self-interest presumably means no more than real as against merely apparent self-interest, and anyone concerned with self-interest at all would agree in demanding the former.

What Nozick does in fact say is that the cost to the agent of immoral behaviour is a value cost, although he agrees with the Kantian that the force of the obligation does not depend on this cost (*PE*: 409). The immoral person leads a less valuable life and is a less valuable person. He may not know this, or care about it, but he pays the penalty nonetheless. "Not all penalties are felt" (*PE*: 409).

This is all very well, but to what extent can we talk of a penalty or sanction that is not felt, and so presumably cannot motivate behaviour? Well, we might of course miss out on something without realizing we were doing so. In that case as soon as we did realize it we would presumably alter our behaviour. This is because we normally only talk of "missing out" on something we would prefer to have if we knew about it. But why should anyone bother about whether he or his life is valuable? It is true that "valuable" here is evidently intended to mean "intrinsically valuable", not just valuable to other people, i.e. useful (although this will raise a problem later). But it does not mean "in the agent's interest", in the sense that it would satisfy him if he knew about it. Is education in the interest of a child who knows about it all too well through his hateful lessons? We might say yes, because the child may know about it but does not yet appreciate its point. Perhaps then we can still say that being a valuable person is in the interest of someone even though he does not yet appreciate it? But the point about education is that it *will* let us satisfy desires later. Does this apply to the valuable life? If we come to appreciate what a valuable life is, does it follow that we shall desire to live it (without trivializing the issue by making this a condition of appreciating it)? Aristotle, who thought people were only virtuous if virtue came naturally to them, after relevant training, and gave them pleasure, might object to this bracket and ask what else appreciation might amount to. Here we seem to come down to the view that the cost of immorality is only *felt* by those who can appreciate, and therefore would find satisfactory, a valuable moral life, and only is a cost to the others because they would get greater satisfaction if they could appreciate this value. It is not a cost to them *merely* because an immoral life is a less valuable one, except in the sense that they will be less valuable people; but this will not be a cost *to them*. A. I. Goldman, in fact, in his review (1983: 88) claims that acting immorally may make us less morally valuable, but not necessarily less valuable in any other way, so that it amounts simply to saying that virtue is its own reward. However, I am not sure that Nozick, any more than Plato or Aristotle, would take this as a criticism. Goldman then asks whether the moral push would require us to act immorally if we could achieve more overall value that way, to which Nozick might perhaps reply: "Yes, *if* we could – but we couldn't". More generally Goldman sees "a severe problem for Nozick's whole approach" (1983: 88) in his attempt to solve problems about morality by appealing to value in general. A similar criticism is made very briefly by another reviewer, Fogelin (1983: 825).

The line Nozick in fact takes is to say that the value sanction "need not actually motivate the person or connect with any motives he (actually) has", but that there is a less direct connection because "value would inspire and motivate us under valuable conditions" (*PE*: 438). He implicitly follows Aristotle in saying that we should learn to take pleasure from the right things, such as developing certain talents and helping others (*PE*: 508), and to do this is "to solve for oneself the conflict between self-interest and morality" (*PE*: 515). His case would be helped by the sort of qualitative hedonism that Mill (1863) advocates in Chapter 2 of his *Utilitarianism*, if that could be established. Incidentally he makes a good use of this point to answer the sort of cynic who decries altruistic action as really selfish because we only do it because we get pleasure from it (*PE*: 508).

This is not quite all there is to be said about motivation, however, because this emphasis on "higher" pleasures and a more valuable existence does not specify moral as against aesthetic or any other value as our legitimate target. It does not exclude a Gauguin who abandoned his family to develop his artistic talents – with happy results for the artistic community, as it happened, but how far this justified his action is another and controversial question. (Hailwood makes a similar criticism (1996: 174–8), claiming that Nozick cannot explain the "lexical priority" of ethics, its ability to trump other values. One feature Hailwood brings out is how this ultimately frustrates Nozick's attempt to decry recourse to the "experience machine" (*ASU*: 42–5), which could allow us all our experiences, and even actions, except for those which presuppose the reality of other people.) Nozick raises this general issue (*PE*: 531–4), but postpones his discussion of it until Chapter 6 (on "Philosophy and the Meaning of Life"; cf. also Hailwood 1996: 177–8). The treatment there is complex and involves a notion of "worth" (introduced at *PE*: 612), which goes beyond value. But it seems, and Nozick evidently hopes (*PE*: 534), that the basic issue about motivation that we have been discussing will not be affected.

Value as organic unity

It is time that we turned to the nature of value itself, and in particular of intrinsic value. This seems to be presupposed as a foundation by other types, such as instrumental value (but on this see Korsgaard 1983), although Nozick points out (*PE*: 414) that foundationalism, the view that a certain subject matter must have foundations if we are to avoid a regress, may not apply in all areas and is controversial concerning, say, certainty and probability, where it says that something must be certain if anything is to be probable. (*PE*: Ch. 6 joins value with "meaning" to form "worth". See *PE*: 610–19 and also *EL*: Ch. 15.)

What Nozick actually suggests is that value is primarily given by degree of organic unity, a notion most at home in aesthetics. Organic unity consists in a unity in diversity. It increases in proportion both to the degree of unity induced in a given amount of diverse material and to the degree of diversity of the material in which a given amount of unity is induced. Obviously strict measurement is out of place here, but a painting in which each colour patch and line is as it is because of its relations to all the others, so that one cannot alter any part without harming the whole, is better than one where it seems arbitrary that any given patch or line is as it is; and, more controversially, one where many such patches and lines are successfully unified in complex patterns is to that extent better than one where this is not so. More controversially because great art surely does not always involve complexity: could not a Mozart miniature be just as high in quality as a Mozart symphony, although we might admittedly be less willing to apply the term "great art" to a small-scale piece?

This last point is of some significance concerning Nozick, since he treats organic unity as by far the most important "dimension" of value, but he never equates the two, and allows that there might be values, e.g. simple pleasures, to which it does not apply, and perhaps also quite different dimensions of value that he hasn't thought of (*PE*: 441–2, 418, 449–50). We cannot then simply *analyze* value in terms of organic unity, and he in fact treats the relation between them as one arrived at inductively (*PE*: 413–14), and allowing of exceptions, despite such categorical remarks as, "[v]alues are organic unities; something is intrinsically valuable in accordance with its degree of organic unity" (*PE*: 446).

To be, or constitute, value organic unity must satisfy various conditions, and be the only thing that does so. First it must be an ordering relation, since some things are more valuable than others. This is a very weak condition, and Nozick allows that the ordering may be only partial (*PE*: 429): we could hardly insist that there must be an answer to whether the St Matthew Passion is more valuable than Mozart's Requiem or Michelangelo's David, to say nothing of a non-aesthetic value, like the distribution of happiness according to desert; and there may be incompatible values so that the realm of value itself need not exhibit high organic unity – a "strong pluralism" that he claims "eliminate[s] the threat that the objectivity of values might appear to pose to individuality" (*PE*: 446–8). He then lists a lot of notions such as "valuing", "seeking", "contemplating", "support-ing", and calls them generically "V-ing", and claims that value has a function, that we should V it, and that V-ing value is itself valuable, and so is the existence of values. But these "external" conditions (*PE*: 436) are not enough; value must also inspire and attract us.

How well does organic unity fare under these requirements? They are necessary, if it is to constitute value, but Nozick makes rather heavy weather of saying they are not sufficient for it to be the unique dimension of value, for, as Goldman complains, "[s]eeming counter-examples rush to mind" (1983: 87). He does not list any, but as well as the simple pleasures mentioned earlier one might think of things valuable for their rarity or uniqueness (of course they won't be valuable *just* for that, or Hitler would be valuable for being uniquely murderous; but that may increase their value). Compare also Swinburne (1983: 306), who mentions feeding the poor and telling the truth. The eradication of smallpox was presumably valuable, but it is not clear where organic unity comes in there; Goldman in fact doubts whether any unified account of value in general can be given

(1983: 88). It has been suggested (by Hailwood) that these last three examples could fall under the organic unity account as exemplifying ethically responsive behaviour, linking moral agents and patients in an appropriate way. In this case the organic unity would presuppose rather than grounding the appropriateness of the linking.

One trouble with organic unity, as we have just seen, is its vagueness. How do we decide when we have a case of it, without begging the question by choosing cases we already think valuable on other grounds and then interpreting them as showing organic unity, while refusing so to interpret other cases that might seem equally plausible candidates but which we do not think valuable? The fact that different cases of it are often not comparable may not matter if the same applies to value itself. But when is a unity organic as against being a mere aggregate? Moore (1903: §§ 18–20) treats a unity as organic when the whole has a value greater than the sum of the values of its parts taken separately, but we can hardly use this as a definition when value itself is to be defined, or at least primarily specified, in terms of organic unity. The nearest Nozick seems to come to an explicit definition is when he says in a much earlier chapter: "Something is a unity, whether by its metaphysical nature or as carved out, if its identity over time is not equivalent to the sum of the identities over time of proper parts it may have" (*PE*: 100). He adds, thinking of biological entities, that "[a]n organic unity *does something* to maintaining the integrity and continuance of the whole, unlike a heap which just lies there like a lump" (*PE*: 100, my emphasis), although this last point would hardly apply to many of the cases he considers when discussing value.

How can we tell an organic unity from a merely organized unity, such as a concentration camp (Nozick's own example at *PE*: 419), which is highly organized? Nozick appeals to their purpose, which is "an important component of their unity, indeed it is their central unifying factor", and in this case is "destructive of organic unity" (*PE*: 419). Presumably the point is that their purpose was to destroy (some) people who are organic unities. But they were also intended, however misguidedly, to preserve (some) people, the Herrenvolk. Even if the Herrenvolk were really superior, and their preservation therefore good, we would still condemn the camps, and Nozick surely would too, because the end would not justify the means, but where at this point would organic unities come in? It would beg the question to say that the end and the means do not (morally) "fit".

Value and disvalue

Nozick claims it as a merit of his theory of value as organic unity that it allows for the positive nature of disvalue, which will involve not a mere absence of unity but an opposite to it, "something that can be viewed as underlying disvalue, having a character of its own" (*PE*: 420). When he comes to discuss this he relies heavily on the point that V-ing value is itself valuable. This lets him say that disvalues are things we should not merely refrain from V-ing but should anti-V (destroy, reject, hate, etc.). Not all V-ing is valuable, just as not all pleasure, including sadistic pleasure, is good (he claims: *PE*: 431). Anti-V-ing has a disunifying character (presumably because it either destroys the object, and so its unity, or puts a gap between the anti-V-er and the object). It thus matches or fits the disunifying character of the object, and this matching constitutes an organic unity – although Nozick has some qualms and says, "it may seem paradoxical that a disunifying relation or stance can establish any sort of unity with anything, even with a disunity. Perhaps we shall have to say that this (type of) unity is established one level up, at the metalevel" (*PE*: 433). The point presumably is that it unifies disunities, or disunifications; but it is confined to human attitudes. How about other things? An earthquake or a massacre destroys people and thus organic unities. But does a very poor painting, or a graffiti scrawl, have the opposite of organic unity as opposed to its mere absence? Are we justified in anti-V-ing it rather than merely not V-ing it? Perhaps we should not destroy it, if it does not itself spoil an attractive environment, but we should surely ignore, shun, reject or avoid it, all of which are among Nozick's anti-V verbs (*PE*: 430).

How about the allure of disvalue itself? Nozick refers to unspecified "antinomian sects" as evidence that this exists (*PE*: 437), but thinks it is parasitic on the allure of value, because it depends on envy, felt by those frustrated in their own search for value. Nozick has a strong tendency to attribute things he disapproves of to envy (cf. his article "Why Do Intellectuals Oppose Capitalism?" in *SP*, and the entries under "envy" in the index to *ASU*). One might think that plenty of other things, such as resentment of insults, come into play, although actually the pursuit of evil as such is rare at best, and possibly confined to fiction (Iago perhaps, and Milton's Satan (*Paradise Lost* 4.110)). Even Hitler did not pursue evil for its own sake; he thought the Jews were an evil that needed eliminating. In fact there is something paradoxical because self-defeating about pursuing evil qua evil, since in one sense to pursue anything at all is to treat it as good. A sadist might pursue cruelty for its own sake, and cruelty is presumably evil, but if he said to himself, "Cruelty is evil but therefore for me it is good and to be pursued" we might wonder whether he was fully committed to the view that it was evil. Would he not be rather like someone who said, "It is false that grass is blue, but therefore for me it is true and I believe it"? The analogy is admittedly not perfect, because the grass case, but *perhaps* not the cruelty case, remains paradoxical if "therefore" is replaced by "in spite of that"; but it is close enough to be suggestive. Satan may have said "Evil be thou my good", but apart from being fictional neither he nor his author was concerned with philosophical precision.

Nozick's own answer is an expansion of the remark I quoted earlier that "value would inspire and motivate us under valuable conditions" (*PE*: 438). If value is to be organic unity it must inspire and motivate us, at least in general. When it does not we may put this down to distorting factors, but to avoid trivializing the case we must limit these to factors that are themselves low on organic unity. He presumably intends us to conclude, although he does not explicitly say so (see *PE*: 438), that envy is so, because it aims at destroying, and so distancing itself from, the value of that which is envied.

Organic unity as value

So value is (at least primarily) organic unity. But Nozick is not content, and goes on to ask whether organic unity is (i.e. amounts to) value, and if so why *(PE*: 441–50). Drawing on a theory he developed in Chapter 1, and which we shall meet later, the closest continuer theory of identity, he insists that organic unity must be not just the only candidate but close enough, if it is to constitute value. "Why isn't the universe just dark", as he puts it (*PE*: 441), containing lots of organic unity but no value? This is a question we might well want to ask. Why should organic unity be *good* in particular? If we say, *pace* Nozick, it is *because* it inspires or motivates us, this suggests that what is really valuable is some state of ourselves. In the version that the state must be one of feeling or experience this has been a common assumption of many philosophers, especially of those called hedonists. But there are powerful objections to it, since so many of our values are "intentional", i.e. directed to something: we find it valuable *that something (often outside ourselves) be the case*, and the value we find in our own states (of satisfaction etc.) often depends on this. Here, however, Nozick contents himself with pointing to the possibility we have already noted that there might be some quite different criterion of value, which dwarfed organic unity to insignificance, or even to zero, and was appreciated by "superior beings". This recalls the reference to such possible beings in *Anarchy, State, and Utopia*, where I suggested his view of them was not radical enough, as they might think in categories that superseded not just organic unity but value itself; perhaps those now adumbrated would have just an intermediate degree of superiority.

Some criticisms

Nozick's account of organic unity emphasizes both the unity induced and the diversity of the material in which it is induced. Hailwood criticizes this account because of its vagueness (1996: 171–4). One sign of this, he thinks, is that Nozick tends to emphasize the unity at the expense of the diversity, for instance when isomorphism (sameness of structure) is a source of organic unity. Such unity arises here when an abstract structure is realized in material, which therefore becomes isomorphic to the structure, and when several realizations of the same value occur ("value", because values are treated as abstract structures: *PE*: 424). Hailwood (1996: 172) asks where uniqueness comes in, for the uniqueness of the individual is important for Nozick; his view implies that a collection of exact reproductions of a Rembrandt should have more value than the single original. Nozick explicitly denies that the *intrinsic* value would be affected in this case (*PE*: 425), while adding that a "whole that includes other new types of valuable things will have greater value [than the set of exact copies], because of the increased diversity this involves". Hailwood could well ask how this fits with the "tightness" (something Nozick approves of) given by isomorphism. The vagueness here comes in the fact that Nozick has given two criteria for organic unity – unity induced and diversity of the material – but has not said how they relate together. (Compare the notorious vagueness of the catch-phrase of utilitarianism: "The *greatest happiness* of the *greatest number*".)

Hailwood's other main criticism of the vagueness of how Nozick treats organic unity, and of his emphasis on unification, concerns its effect on his political theory of utopia. A pervading theme of

Hailwood's book is to discuss how far Nozick can achieve the political neutralism that seems to be called for by the "live and let live" philosophy of *Anarchy, State, and Utopia*. He sees it as a "fundamental mistake" of *Anarchy, State, and Utopia* that its attack on patterns "is expressed in terms of a defence of libertarian voluntarism . . .. If the aim is supposed to be to avoid the suppression of real plurality involved in the demand for a final solution, or tidy harmony, then the way to do this is not to assert, in the teeth of controversy, a set of universal natural rights" (Hailwood 1996: 158). One might at first wonder why not. One reason would presumably be that one man's rights are another man's duties, and so can be constricting, but Hailwood has more important reasons. (His argument is somewhat difficult and diffuse, and interpreting it is not helped by the book's infuriating lack of any kind of index, but I have been considerably helped by private correspondence, although obviously I am responsible for the use I have made of this.) Organic unity can be seen as "an account of value which supports imperialism via expressivism" (Hailwood 1996: 158), i.e. supports the attempt to impose a single best way of life on everyone via "the view which says that the state should promote a particular conception of the good" (Hailwood 1996: 3; cf. also 172). Nozick's emphasis on unity rather than diversity makes against the proper appreciation, which Nozick wants, of the value of individual uniqueness; there is a tension between organic unity and individual uniqueness. So we need an account of real neutralism, the problem of justifying which "without presupposing a substantive ideal, and thereby sacrificing neutrality with respect to rival ideals" Hailwood calls a "unifying theme" of his book (1996: 179). A view neutral between *all* views would have to be neutral between itself and its own denial, an obvious absurdity which Hailwood does not intend, so how shall we construct a neutralism that avoids this absurd extreme? In Chapter 3 ("Utopia II: objections"), I spoke of the framework for utopia as "still libertarian at the second level, as it were", and it is this distinction between levels that I think we need here. Libertarianism at the first level involves the apparatus of the minimal state, for Nozick, which we have discussed previously. But this libertarianism at the first level is only one factor to be counted along with others in the libertarianism at the second level. It is the tension between these levels that leads to the difficulty Hailwood emphasizes (as we saw in Chapter 3) in deciding what is the real outcome of *Anarchy, State, and Utopia*. As an example we can note, on the question of imperialism, that when Nozick comes to discuss rights later he explicitly defends a right to personal liberty and to not being paternalistically forced towards the good (*PE* 500–501).

Another critic of Nozick's treatment of value in general and organic unity in particular is Ellis (1984: 452–4), who asks why we should expect *any* unitary account of value, whether of its structure or of its content. Nozick discusses the structure of value (*PE*: 422ff.), suggesting that values can be regarded as abstract structures, valuable things being realizations of those structures – but we will return to the ontology of value later. Taking values to be organically unified structures then lets him in this case avoid a foundationalist view of values, whereby there must be atoms of value from which all other values are constructed. This might well be an advantage since in epistemology foundationalism, common in the days of logical positivism, is now rather out of fashion (cf. *PE*: 414). The point would be that if an organic unity is one which has a value greater than the sum of the values of its parts taken separately, it could have value even if none of its parts had any at all. This point is suggestive, but of course not conclusive, and Ellis does not discuss it. What he does do is claim that Nozick ignores our need, and ability, to say *why* organic unity confers value in cases where it does. In aesthetics it does so because "our attitude to a work of art is that of a spectator", which would not explain why, say, acts of heroism are valuable. In society, organic unity has been thought valuable "because it was thought that living in an organic society was the truest expression of man's nature"; and in general organic unity "makes different things valuable for different reasons". We cannot therefore assume, he thinks, that organic unity will produce value elsewhere, even when it is present. Ellis's criticism here seems to come to this: there are all sorts of values of quite different kinds, and it may be rather an accident that organic unity appears as often as it does in the account of them. There does seem something in the charge that Nozick puts values into a straitjacket; he passes, for instance, from talking of the value of experiences to talking of that of persons without batting an eyelid.

The basis of value

Why is there any value at all, or rather, how can there be? We have already briefly met the question why the universe is not "dark" (see above, "Organic unity as value"), but Nozick develops his answer

(§ vi), where he offers what he calls "realizationism", that values exist because we choose that they should, although their nature is independent of us; en passant he compares the dependent existence but independent character of children (*PE*: 556), and draws comfort, if no more, from the idea that on some views mathematical entities and Popper's "third world" of abstract entities similarly depend on us for their existence but not their nature (*PE*: 556–7).

The prospects for this are not promising. Nozick leaves unclear whether the existence of values is chosen by God or us or both, and whether the choices we individually make commit others or only ourselves (which Hailwood (1996: 171), who makes these and other criticisms, calls "barely distinguishable in principle from choosing to live in an illusion"). Apart from anything else, if we choose that values exist, although not their nature, *what* exactly are we choosing? And does not our very act of choosing presuppose some value? Otherwise why do we bother? A more plausible view, although not obviously Nozick's, is that only if creatures capable of choice exist can values exist (but one would surely not say there was no value or disvalue at all in a world populated only by animals). Moore (1903: § 50) held that a beautiful desert would have value even if no-one ever saw it or could see it. This is usually considered a rather extreme view. We saw above ("Organic unity as value") that there are reasons against confining value to experiences. But more plausibly, other things that have value only have it because of some relation to experiences, whether because there are creatures that can appreciate them, or because they consist of (e.g.) happiness being distributed according to merit, or someone making a right choice – since only those who can experience can choose, one would think; if there were no experiences there would be no value. What might depend on choice is moral value: if there were no choices (or the capability of choice – but could this exist without *any* choices?) there would be no moral value perhaps. But we are getting too far from Nozick. I am tempted to conclude with Hailwood (1996: 171): "The less said about realizationism . . . the better for Nozick"; but before going on I will simply refer to the way Nozick brings in the idea of self-subsumingness, an idea that recurs as a motif in many parts of his philosophy. Here it applies to the way we pursue value by choosing to pursue value, because that very choice is itself valuable, something he then illustrates by comparing the way a placebo will cure us if, but only if, we believe it will (*PE*: 560–62).

Our question at the start of this section – why is there, or how can there be, any value at all? – suggests another: what is it for there to "be" value? More grandly, what is the ontological status of value? Nozick raises the question in this form (*PE*: 424), meaning not "whether organic unities [i.e. values] are imposed on an inchoate and structureless world, or are discovered residing there", but whether they are adjectival (things are valuable in having organic unity) or entities that we treat as existing parts of reality. Nozick's answer, mentioned briefly above, is that values are abstract structures, a notion borrowed from model theory. But that still leaves the former question – what is the status of these structures? – and he returns to this question, at least implicitly (*PE*: 562): organic unities are "what value would be if there *were* value". On the same page he treats the question whether there is value as amounting to, or at least on the same level with, whether there are ethical truths.

This suggests the question of objectivism: are ethical truths true, and are values real, in their own right independently of our attitudes (and of the differing mores of different societies, although this is more properly called absolutism, as against relativism)? To say that they are, denying subjectivism, is compatible with saying that they depend on our existence, in the sense that if we (or beings of some relevant kind) did not exist, neither would values or ethical truths – that is, nothing would be valuable and no ethical propositions would have any application. But Hailwood accuses Nozick of making two confusions, or at least conflations. The first is between objective value (independent of our attitudes) and intrinsic (as opposed to instrumental) value, and here Hailwood allows that Nozick may be simply following a tradition which assimilates claims about these two notions (1996: 130). (Hailwood also refers, privately, to Korsgaard (1983) for a further distinction Nozick, and Hailwood in his book, ignore, between intrinsic and non-instrumental.) More serious, he thinks, is a confusion between objectivism in this sense about values and platonism (the view that values are substantial though non-material entities, rather like Plato's Forms) (Hailwood 1996: 167–71). This is not implied by objectivism and Nozick does not need it, Hailwood thinks, and perhaps adopts it only because he thinks, wrongly in Hailwood's view, that it is implicit normally in ordinary thought; it leads to difficulties for his view that we choose the existence of values. There is indeed a certain tension between Nozick's treatment of values as "things" whose existence is itself valuable and his view of them as chosen by us, and the discussion of objectivity (*PE*: 728–9 n.45) treats it in terms of knowledge and agreement in a way totally independent of any platonist considerations.

The ethical pull

So far we have discussed the ethical push, which is the dominant element in *Philosophical Explanations*. The ethical pull is the moral claim that others exert on us in so far as they have a certain feature that he calls the "basic moral characteristic" (*PE*: 451). There may be more than one such characteristic – animals may have a different one from ourselves and still exert some claim on us – and Nozick allows a certain flexibility about sentience (*PE*: 730 n.51), but he concentrates on the main one. Three questions arise about it (*PE*: 451–2): what is it, what constraints on our behaviour does it imply, and why? Nozick proceeds to discuss these in order (although the third comes rather later).

The characteristic Nozick settles for is being a value-seeking self or I, which he thinks can embody the uniqueness that we seem to require when considering people; the characteristic is not just multiply instantiated, like having two legs, or even having desires; each person is not just *an* I, nor even just a unique I, but the particular I that he is. This is important when we want (as we presumably do) to avoid treating people as interchangeable. It is not enough to say, without further ado, "This policy will harm X, but it will benefit Y and Z"; we need to know that it will, in some other way perhaps, also benefit X. We cannot compensate Y for X's loss (a point that was relevant in our discussion of compensation in Chapter 2). To ignore this, which *might* be justifiable when dealing with animals (although this could be disputed, with possible repercussions for Nozick's choice of characteristic) would be to fall into a crude version of utilitarianism.

To seek value, however, is not for Nozick the same as merely seeking the satisfaction of desire, as an animal might do. To distinguish the two he borrows Moore's "open question" argument (see Moore 1903: §§ 18–20), although using it slightly differently from Moore (*PE*: 731 n.57). It always makes sense to ask of something I desire for some feature it has, "But is it valuable? Ought I to pursue it?" Only if I ask this question, or rather if it is possible "to make the question seem real and salient" to me, even if I do not in fact ask it, am I a value-seeker.

On the basis of this Nozick claims that the basic ethical principle is to treat value-seeking I's *as* value-seeking I's, which he compares to Kant's injunction to treat people as ends, never merely as means (*PE*: 462). But what does so treating them consist in? We could treat people as intelligent and having desires by hunting them and pitting our wits against theirs as they try to escape. But Nozick thinks that this sort of behaviour (covered by game theory) would not really treat them as value-seekers in the above sense rather than as mere desirers (see *PE* 463 and 731n. 60). Perhaps not; but could we not refine our pursuit to take full account of them as value-seekers? Could not a certain kind of sadist (or as Nozick might say, of envious man) deliberately try to morally corrupt someone, just for the sake of doing so? Nozick's own example is of killing value-seeking I's, whether to get them out of the way or simply because you like doing so; here "the victim's being a value-seeking I [still] does, qua value-seeking I, move and guide your actions as pursuer" (*PE*: 464). He therefore insists that we are only treating value-seeking I's as value-seeking I's if the content of our behaviour is shaped or controlled by their being so. This deals with the killing case but it is not obvious that it deals with the corruption case. Later (*PE*: 466) he distinguishes between treating the characteristic of being a value-seeking I as that characteristic and treating it as valuable. This might seem to deal with the corruption case. But one can anti-V value as well as V-ing it, and here it is the value that one is anti-V-ing, not just the characteristic that makes for value (although *PE*: 467, end of first paragraph, doesn't bring this out very clearly). However, we saw above ("Value and disvalue") that anti-valuing value as such has a certain incoherence about it, and Nozick says that anti-responding to a valuable characteristic "rubs against the grain of the characteristic" (*PE*: 467). Perhaps the best way of presenting a Nozickian position then would be to rely on the incoherence point to deal with anti-V-ing value as such, and treat anti-V-ing a valuable characteristic as involving a moral error, justifying this by saying that the characteristic would be valued in valuable conditions, of which the psychological state of the sadist is presumably not one.

Deontology and teleology: rights

So the basic content of the ethical pull is responsiveness to value-seeking I's, with some allowance made for secondary cases such as the treatment of animals – an allowance, we may note in passing, which displays a welcome flexibility, but like that concerning value and organic unity means that we have not been given a strict analysis of the notion under discussion.

But anyway there are obviously plenty of questions left about how to act in particular cases. Nozick discusses what he calls the "structure" of the ethical pull mainly by drawing on his early (pre-*ASU*) article on "Moral Complications and Moral Structures" (in *SP*). We need not pursue the details of this, beyond noting that he dismisses two structures, those of maximizing something (which got such a bad press in *ASU*) and deduction from first principles, since they tend to ride roughshod over the particularity and complexity of moral situations, and ends up with a complex structure balancing the right and wrong features of any proposed action and taking account of available alternatives (Principle III at *PE*: 488); this he thinks also takes account of the asymmetry of right and wrong shown by the need to compensate or apologize for wrong done even when that wrong is justified by an overriding right.

One feature of ethical calculations is their inconclusiveness, and here Nozick makes two points. First, "[T]he lack of procedure guaranteed to answer a question does not show the question has no correct answer" (*PE*: 482). He appeals to the results of Gödel and Church in number theory, that there are truths of any given system that cannot be proved within it, which does not make the notion of theoremhood indeterminate. The point has some force, but there is no clear line in ethics as there is in logic between what can and cannot be proved, if indeed the notion of proof applies at all in ethics. The second point is that in respect of requiring intuitive judgement ethics is no worse off than philosophy of science, where different theories must be compared in respect of "explanatory power, goodness of fit with the data, breadth and diversity of evidential support, degree of testability, range and diversity of the phenomena [the theory] covers, simplicity, fit with other accepted theories, and so on" (*PE*: 483). This seems much stronger, and we can no doubt agree with Nozick that ethics need not be denied all objectivity.

The account referred to above of the structure of the ethical pull goes back to pre-*Anarchy, State, and Utopia* days. But there is nevertheless a shift of emphasis between *Anarchy, State, and Utopia* and *Philosophical Explanations*, which is carried further in *The Examined Life*, as we shall see a little later. *Anarchy, State, and Utopia* was decidedly deontological in outlook, despite the reservations of Chapter 2 above ("Blurring the distinction"), but Nozick's present view has softened enough to be presented "*despite* [his] obvious leaning toward deontology" (*PE*: 498; my emphasis). Referring to a notorious passage (*ASU*: 30n.) about violating side constraints to avoid "catastrophic moral horror" – notorious because of the casual way in which it is introduced in a footnote – he now says (*PE*: 495) he had imagined teleology would take over there, but without any smooth transition to it or rationale for just when teleology became relevant.

After discussing various ways in which deontology and teleology might split the work between them of contributing to an ethical view, Nozick now constructs a view that combines them both, distinguishing two versions of teleology according as what is aimed at is the best consequence or the best action, but where the best action is no longer automatically defined as the one with the best consequences (*PE*: 497). Two actions with the same consequences may differ in value according to whether those consequences are all aimed at. Nozick gives the example of the "double effect" doctrine where an action that involves some evil differs in value according to whether the evil is intended as a means to some ultimate good or is merely a foreseen but unintended step towards achieving that good. Consider the difference between bombing civilians as a means toward terrorizing an enemy into surrender, where their deaths are essential to the aim, and bombing them as a foreseen but unwanted consequence of destroying an arms factory – one would be happy enough if they escaped first. Ironically what makes the former case morally worse is the greater organic unity it involves between the means and the end (cf. *PE*: 497–8). Could Nozick say that the overall organic unity was greater in the latter case (compare his treatment of the concentration camp example at *PE*: 419)? Perhaps, but it does not seem obvious and would require some arguing to show it. He does talk (*PE*: 498) of the "more intimate connections to value in action" as against that in pursuing valuable results. But will this necessarily exceed the organic unity in the terror-bombing case?

This allows Nozick to subsume certain deontological views under a maximization strategy, and thus under teleology, by extending that strategy to cover maximizing the value of one's actions as well as, and sometimes instead of, that of the world. (The earlier discussion (*PE*: 475) where the maximization structure was dismissed already spoke of maximizing the score of an act as well as of the world in respect of some natural property (organic unity perhaps?), but presumably there the score of the act was still being calculated in terms of the result it produced.)

How does this compare with Nozick's dismissal in *Anarchy, State, and Utopia* (28–9) of what he called a "utilitarianism of rights"? There he pointed to cases where one should not necessarily maximize the avoidance of violating rights, presumably even by oneself, which would seem to mean, in his later terminology, that one should not necessarily maximize even the value of one's own actions. This need not, I think, be inconsistent with his *Philosophical Explanations* view because the point is that one should not necessarily act now so as to maximize one's own future avoidance of violating rights (e.g. by putting the development of one's future character before fulfilling some important claim on one, where they clash). In fact, the point is brought out again with explicit reference to one's own avoidance of violating rights (*PE*: 547–8), where he treats it as a side constraints rather than a maximization view, adding that "ethics binds us in the first person". But it can still be a maximization view in the sense of the last paragraph.

Closely linked with deontology is the notion of rights, which formed the central notion for *Anarchy, State, and Utopia*. They are still important, and we saw above ("Some criticisms") that Nozick defends a right to personal liberty against paternalism, as he did in *Anarchy, State, and Utopia*. But he emphasizes perhaps rather more the distinction between how others ought to treat us in responding to our status as value-seekers and what we can demand from them (and enforce) as of right without ceasing to respond to *their* similar status. It is important that we have a sphere of autonomy where we can exercise our personal liberty, but the limits to the extent of that sphere are now given greater emphasis, but with no discussion of what happens when rights clash in the way that in *Anarchy, State, and Utopia* led to the awkward difficulties about compensation. The general attitude to rights is now more relaxed. It is still true that they form a framework within the interstices of which other moral oughts must flourish, but it is now possible that they can be transcended, although Nozick seems to have primarily in mind the sort of spiritual development that makes some of a person's previous rights no longer relevant as a response to what the person now is (*PE*: 503–4). This may seem a rather abstruse point, but it does illustrate that rights no longer have the prominence they had in *Anarchy, State, and Utopia*.

The is/ought question

Ever since Hume, philosophers have puzzled over how statements about what we ought to do, or what ought to be the case, are related to statements about what is the case, or how we can get from an is to an ought without committing what Moore (1903: §§ 5–14) called the "naturalistic fallacy" of assuming that an is could logically entail an ought. A similar puzzle, in fact Moore's form of the puzzle, concerns how to get from statements about what is the case to statements about what is valuable or good, and these two forms of the puzzle are commonly lumped together, a practice I will follow when convenient and not misleading, as Nozick himself does. Some writers have simply denied that the "fallacy" is a fallacy at all, but most seem to agree at least that the situation is not quite as simple as that.

Nozick does not enter the arena of the debate about the fallacy as such. After discussing briefly but inconclusively three possible relations between is and ought, he turns to a fourth, which accepts the gap, or chasm, as he calls it, but tries to explain it by seeking some property that belongs to one of the terms but not the other. The discussion is difficult because Nozick does not make very clear whether he is looking for something that holds of and so explains ought-statements as such (as *PE*: 538 suggests), or something that explains one ought-statement rather than a rival to it (as *PE*: 545 suggests). The difficulty is perhaps that what looks as if it will be a complete explanation in the first passage becomes only a partial explanation in the second. A further important point is that the feature we are looking for will only explain why something is true if it *is* true; it will not serve to prove *that* it is true. This emphasis on explaining rather than proving is in line with Nozick's new approach to philosophy that we discussed in Chapter 1, although he does eventually go on to what does underpin his favoured ethical principle, responsiveness to a value-seeking I (the realizationism we discussed above).

Before introducing the feature that is to do the explaining, Nozick gives an interesting list of nine other cases where one kind of statement cannot be derived from another; one example is metaphor and another the synthetic necessary identity that Kripke sees between light and electromagnetic radiation. He leaves open whether this latter holds between value and organic unity, but claims that none of his nine applies to is and ought.

The feature Nozick chooses is self-subsumption, of which we shall see more later. A principle subsumes itself if it falls under or is an instance of itself, but this gives no guarantee of its truth. Nozick gives "Every principle containing seven words is true" as an example of a false self-subsuming principle (*PE*: 541). Having Rawls in mind, he then offers as at least plausible that any principle that would be agreed on by a majority in certain conditions ought to be followed. This principle itself might be agreed by a majority in the same conditions, although this does not follow automatically, since people might fear the tyranny of the majority, for instance (Nozick originally writes "unanimously" for "by a majority", but then softens it to "by a majority" (*PE*: 541–2), presumably to make this last point easier).

How does this serve to do any explaining? Nozick points out that a moral principle that subsumes itself in this way follows deductively from that fact together with itself. But it also follows, of course, from itself alone (it is a triviality of logic that any proposition can be deduced from itself), so why should adding a superfluous premise help? Nozick elaborates an example, which we can omit, before saying more (at *PE*: 543–4). It now turns out that the explaining principle must also be "sufficiently deep". This is evidently in part because it will then explain "many other more particular principles", in the straightforward sense that they can be deduced from it, but also presumably because only then is it likely to subsume itself. "Pay your debts" does not subsume itself (it is a principle, not a debt). But what we are concerned with is explaining the self-subsuming principle itself, not the subordinate principles it straightforwardly explains. Nozick insists that the explaining principle must be not only "sufficiently deep" but "correct", which as we have seen introduces a quite independent point. We cannot know whether a principle explains itself, by subsuming itself, until we already know that it is correct. If it is not, it will not explain itself or anything else although it will still subsume itself. So subsuming itself is not sufficient for explaining itself, any more than for its being correct. So why does it help? Nozick talks of it as stopping the principle in question from being a merely brute moral fact, where "brute" seems to mean just "unexplained". But although subsuming itself does mark a principle out as being of a certain sort and not just any old principle, it does not seem clear that any explaining has been done.

However, Nozick is anyway not satisfied, because rival moral principles too, such as egoistic ones, might be self-subsuming, and for all we have said so far the correct moral principle, even though not merely a brute fact, has not been shown to be necessary, which it surely must be. Before going on to his realizationism Nozick toys with a possible Kantian structuring of ethics whereby "we structure the world so that the [ethical] statements come out true" (*PE*: 546; cf. 547). If this could work it would be a highly important development in ethics, but we need not discuss it further because Nozick rejects it for three reasons. First, it is not easy to see how it works exactly. Secondly, it angles ethics too much towards the moral push rather than the moral pull. It makes our duties depend too much on the nature of ourselves rather than of the value-seeking I we are supposed to be responding to. This is hard to assess. Is the point that the pull should pull us however we structure the world? But it does not pull just anything (animals, for instance). But to say more would involve a long excursus into the details of the theory. Thirdly, it militates against our desire to track independently existing values (see Chapters 5 and 9 below), even though it lends some support to our desire for autonomy. Again it would take us too far afield to discuss this in detail, or ask how it relates to Nozick's own view, whereon the nature of values but not their existence is independent of us, beyond saying that Nozick is well enough aware of the narrowness of the gap between being unwilling to pursue ends we have created ourselves and preserving our autonomy, yet he thinks we must still try to slip through it (*PE*: foot of 551).

Political implications: symbolic utility

What are the effects of all this on the political philosophy of *Anarchy, State, and Utopia*? We have already seen that Nozick has moved a great distance from there. The major role played by value is a large element in this change, and so is the partial reconciliation of deontology and teleology in the policy of maximizing the value of actions. Side constraints are still there in *Philosophical Explanations* (although not in the index, which should refer to pages 495, 497, 548, 734 n.74 at least); but they are less prominent and there is less emphasis on their exceptionless nature. Similarly rights play a lesser role and can sometimes be transcended. The emphasis now is more on responsiveness than on the mere avoidance of anti-responsiveness, so that the hard shell surrounding negative rights (rights in particular to non-interference) tends to dissolve. We saw above ("Deontology and teleology: rights") how one's spiritual development may affect the way others ought to treat one, so that one's previous rights are no longer so relevant and can to some extent be transcended. One might wonder whether this could be expressed by saying that one simply acquires new rights based on responsiveness, but this might distort the development of Nozick's thought if the rights are thought of as hard-shelled and absolute, as they were earlier. The effect of the push and pull account of morality on Nozick's views about rights is discussed at some length by Hailwood (1996: 120–24, 178).

The political implications of this are far-reaching. The inheritance laws are modified (*EL*: Ch. 3), and the dreaded word "taxation" has now become respectable (*EL*: 288; in *Philosophical Explanations* he was still refusing to accept research grants funded by public taxation (*PE*: 523), and called such acceptances "wrongs", even if "committed for a good purpose" (*PE*: 507)). In fact his defence of compulsory taxation (albeit allowing conscientious objection) as constituting society's "solemn marking and symbolic validation of the importance and centrality of . . . ties of concern and solidarity" (*EL*: 289) might have been intended, whether or not it was, to answer R. P. Wolff, who had said of the Nozick of *Anarchy, State, and Utopia*: "He portrays social interactions as marginal to the existence, integrity, and coherent identity of the individuals who participate in them" (Paul 1981: 95). "The bonds of concern for others", Nozick goes on, "may involve not simply symbolically expressive and (it is hoped) effective policies through the general tax system, but also particular limitations of liberty concerning kinds of action" (*EL*: 291) (a most un-*ASU*-ish remark!) (The kinds in question are illustrated by discrimination.)

This reference to the symbolic marks a new entrant on the scene in the later ethics and politics, symbolic utility, which is only hinted at in *Philosophical Explanations* but is appealed to in the political revisions in Nozick's next book, *The Examined Life*, and discussed at some length in his last main book so far, *The Nature of Rationality* (*NR*) (especially 26–35). As the name suggests, something has symbolic utility not in virtue of its intrinsic nature, nor of what it causes, but of what it symbolizes. The most obvious examples are perhaps Freudian. If handwashing symbolizes freedom from guilt then an act of handwashing takes on the utility not of making physically clean but of making free from guilt (*NR*: 28). A more everyday example might be when on receiving some frightful white elephant from great-aunt Bertha at Christmas we say, "Oh well, it's the thought that counts"; and similarly there is the sentimental value we often attach to otherwise useless objects. Nozick also points to the importance of symbolic meanings in anthropological contexts (*NR*: 32).

The obvious question that arises about symbolic utility concerns its rationality: surely in some sense it is not "real" utility? Certainly symbolic and causal utility may clash to the disadvantage of the latter. It is irrational to insult one's employer to symbolically get at one's father. The family affection displayed by great-aunt Bertha's white elephant may outweigh the small cost she paid at the jumble sale where she got it. Nozick in fact goes further: "A large part of the richness of our lives consists in symbolic meanings and their expression, the symbolic meanings our culture attributes to things or the ones we ourselves bestow" (*NR*: 30), and he goes on to add that because certainty often has a different symbolic meaning for us from mere high probability, symbolic utilities should be treated as a separate component in a decision theory (*NR*: 34).

We may perhaps conclude that symbolic utility has no direct causal effects in the physical world but it may well have causal effects in the psychological world, and we are psychological creatures as well as physical creatures, and inevitably so. However, there is one further question: if symbolic utility has purely psychological value, but still is an important part of our total value-scheme, how does this fit with Nozick's rejection, never retracted, of the experience machine and its virtual reality sophistications? (Nozick does indeed allow a limited recourse to the machine (*EL*: 108), as Hailwood has pointed out to me; but this seems a far more trivial matter than the large role allotted to symbolic utility in his later philosophy, perhaps, as I will say again shortly, for reasons connected with organic unity.) Nozick never discusses this, I think, but perhaps one answer would be that although symbolic utility directly has only psychological effects these are not confined to a single mind. One's symbolic actions can, qua symbolic, have real if only psychological effects on other people; and so far as the sophistications of the experience machine go (which allow one to have real effects on other people but only by cheating, as it were, in acquiring one's achievements) the objections to this, that it makes one's actions somehow inauthentic, have no bearing on the present questions about symbolic action.

Symbolic utility is one of the things Nozick says he had ignored in *Anarchy, State, and Utopia* when announcing the death of his libertarianism (*EL*: Ch. 25): "It neglected the symbolic importance of an official political concern with issues or problems, as a way of marking their importance or urgency, and hence of expressing, intensifying, channelling, encouraging, and validating our private actions and concerns toward them" (*EL*: 287). Although symbolic utility as such does appear to be a new entrant, as I have said, it may well be, as Hailwood has suggested to me, that Nozick intends it to fall under the rubric of organic unity, in that the relation of symbol to symbolized is a case of the sort of linkage Nozick requires. If this is true, although Nozick never says it explicitly, I think, it would provide another instance of the role of organic unity as a unifying theme in Nozick's philosophy itself.

In the ten pages of *The Examined Life*, Chapter 25, Nozick does not of course develop the details of an alternative political system. But this lurch from libertarianism in the direction of communitarianism, despite its dismissal as "vague and ill-defined" (*PE*: 631n.), or perhaps even the dreaded socialism, shows how far Nozick has travelled from the *Anarchy, State, and Utopia* for which he is so famous.

Summary

Nozick's next book, *Philosophical Explanations*, exemplifies his philosophical switch from proof to persuasion, and asks, in the relevant chapter, how ethics is possible, shifting away from *Anarchy, State, and Utopia* in content as well as method, and introducing the notions of moral push and pull. Starting with the moral push Nozick asks what motivates morality, answering that the immoral person lives a less valuable life, and even if he does not in fact value living morally he would in valuable conditions. But it is not clear that this distinguishes moral from other values, and Nozick has been criticized for appealing to value to solve problems about morality.

Value itself Nozick thinks is primarily organic unity, i.e. unity in diversity – an important theme running through much of his work. Value has the function that we should "V" it (a generic term for various pro-attitudes), and V-ing value is itself valuable, a point he relies on in claiming to account for the positive nature of disvalue, which he admits has its own allure, but this he thinks is parasitic on that of value. He elaborates to some extent on the nature of organic unity, but how adequate it is for the role he gives it has proved controversial at best.

Critics have seen a tension between unity and diversity in Nozick's appeal to organic unity, e.g. concerning the value of uniqueness in a painting. Hailwood also sees Nozick's emphasis on unification as giving rise to the tension he sees (as we saw in Chapter 3) between libertarianism and the framework for utopia in *Anarchy, State, and Utopia*. Ellis asks why value should have any unitary account, and why organic unity confers value. He thinks Nozick unduly straitjackets value in his appeal to organic unity.

To the question how values can exist Nozick offers his "realization-ism", that we choose their existence but not their nature, a doctrine left in some obscurity. What values are is abstract structures, although Hailwood sees a confusion of objectivism and platonism.

Turning to the moral pull, Nozick introduces the "basic moral characteristic" of "being a value-seeking I", which must be treated as such. This leads to a certain softening of his deontology and the admittance of some teleology, and even a maximization strategy, when we distinguish the value of actions from that of their conse-quences. His emphasis on rights is also somewhat relaxed.

After some preliminaries Nozick accepts the famous gap between "is" and "ought", and uses one of his favourite tools, self-subsumption, to help explain (not prove) moral principles (whether some as against others or morality as such is unclear), but admits this is not satisfac-tory, because it will not show that the principle is correct, let alone necessary (which it should be), and rival principles too might subsume themselves. Nor will a "Kantian structuring" of ethics satisfy him.

Our last section summarized Nozick's new approach, emphasizing responsiveness rather than rights, and discussed some of its political implications. It also discussed a new and important idea that will reappear in epistemology (see Chapter 6), symbolic utility. All in all, let us add, Nozick's ethics and politics have been more influential for his early challenging and detailed advocacy of libertarianism than for either his novel application of it to utopias or the notion of organic unity that so governed his later and both methodologically and ethically more relaxed approach.

Chapter 5

Epistemology

Introduction: internalism and externalism

It is generally agreed among reviewers that Chapter 3, on epistemology, is the best chapter in *Philosophical Explanations*. It is not very original. Its leading ideas were already put forward by Dretske in particular a decade or more earlier, as Nozick acknowledges in some detail (*PE*: 689 n.53). But it is with Nozick that the ideas really come to the fore, perhaps because he has developed them more extensively. The chapter has three sections, on knowledge, scepticism and evidence, of which the first two are very closely bound together.

We can set the stage by introducing a contrast – prominent in recent discussions of epistemology – between internalism and externalism. How does knowledge go beyond mere belief? (I say "mere" belief because nearly everyone agrees that knowledge, at least of facts as opposed to people, places, etc., does involve belief, although there are exceptions (see McGinn 1984, especially 547ff.). Clearly to be knowledge a belief must be true. We may think we know, or feel absolutely certain about, something false, but once we agree it is false we must withdraw any claim to know or have known it. (This is sometimes expressed by saying that "know" is a "factive" verb.) But more interesting is the question: what must be true about the knower himself? This raises issues about the role of knowledge in our lives. Why do we have the concept of knowledge at all? Do we want knowledge primarily for our own sakes or for the sakes of our relations with others? When we ask whether someone has knowledge, are we assessing him and asking whether he is a knowledgeable person, or are we mainly concerned with whether he is a reliable source of information for ourselves?

Internalists can be thought of as concentrating on the first question and externalists on the second. For the internalist what matters is the state of mind of the knower. If I am to know something I must be able to produce a justification for my belief. This justification must either logically entail what I am believing or else support it in some weaker although still pretty strong way, and it must itself be true. But the important point for the internalist is that it must be accessible to me – I must be able to produce it. Otherwise what would be the point of attributing the knowledge to *me*?

Externalists on the other hand, to put the point rhetorically, might rather phrase the question like this: what would be the point of attributing the *knowledge* to me? What matters, if my belief is to be knowledge, is that it be linked in some suitable way to what it is about. Whether I am aware that it is so linked is a secondary matter. The link may be of various kinds. An obvious case is causation. If my belief is caused by its object, or what it asserts to be the case, one might expect it to represent the object accurately – indeed how could it fail to do so, since a belief's object must exist or be the case if it is to cause the belief? A causal link is not the only link the externalists may choose, however, for the object may cause the belief in a roundabout way and rely on various extraneous circumstances that might not be on hand in other similar cases, so that the belief, although true, was only so by good fortune and could not be taken as reliable. The idea that what makes a belief knowledge is that the process by which it is arrived at is one that reliably results in true beliefs is called reliabilism. The process need not be causal, and the mechanism underlying it, if any, may be quite unknown. Consulting tea-leaves would do, if beliefs formed in this way turned out regularly to be true. (A case often referred to in the literature derives from a story by D. H. Lawrence about a boy who always managed to predict the results of races when he was sitting on his rocking horse. If you knew such a boy with an established track record, would you not consult him before placing your bets?) We shall see later that reliabilism itself may not entirely escape the chance of relying on good fortune. But whatever knowledge turns out to be, Nozick brings in organic unity again (*PE*: 417, 524), suggesting that knowledge has value because it unifies a person with a fact.

Many objections have been raised to each of these two approaches, some of which we shall meet as we go along, and various compromises between them can be constructed; but let us now turn to Nozick.

Robert Nozick

Outline of Nozick's theory

Nozick is an externalist. There is one passage (*PE*: 267; we shall see more later) that might be thought to show some hesitation on this, where he says, "it seems plausible that justified true belief is a necessary condition for knowledge; but I prefer to leave this question unsettled". He has just said that it is not a sufficient condition, because of the notorious counterexamples produced by Gettier to the effect that what makes it justifiable for someone to believe something may be quite different from what makes the belief true, so that, as we saw with the externalist causal theory, the belief might happen to be true but could not be relied on. But the reason why he thinks justification may be a necessary, even though not a sufficient, condition for knowledge seems to be (*PE*: 267 is not very clear here) that whenever one knows one will be using a reliable method of one sort or another, and this will carry justification with it as a sort of byproduct. This is different from the sort of motivation I attributed to internalism above, and he has just said (*PE*: 265) that he will follow "the externalized treatment of justification as reliability" (but cf. also *PE*: 281).

The theory Nozick offers was originally developed, he tells us (*PE*: 169), in connection with action rather than knowledge, a topic we shall meet in a later chapter. A causal account of knowledge sounds plausible, but in the sphere of action causation has been thought to threaten responsibility, and he seeks "a way for action to parallel belief, to be so connected to the world, even causally, in a way that is desirable", adding that if we succeed in this "determinism would be defanged" (*PE*: 170–71).

As we have seen, it has generally been agreed that for a subject S to know a proposition *p*, *p* must be true and S must believe *p*. Nozick agrees too, but he realizes that we cannot simply add a role for causation, because of the problem of deviant causal chains we saw earlier. His solution is to appeal to counterfactual conditionals, or counterfactuals, so called because the antecedent is presented as though it were false, whether or not it is so, and the consequent tells us what *would* then be, or have been, the case. The difference between counterfactuals and ordinary indicative conditions can be brought out by appealing to a famous example: "If Oswald did not kill Kennedy someone else did"; "If Oswald had not killed Kennedy someone else would have". Plainly these are not equivalent. The two conditions that S must satisfy if he is to know *p* are that were *p* not true S would not believe *p*, and were *p* still (in somewhat changed circumstances) true S would still believe p (and would not also believe that not-p, i.e. would not contradict himself). These conditions Nozick calls the "variation" and "adherence" conditions respectively (let us label them "Variation" and "Adherence".) When a belief satisfies these conditions Nozick says it "tracks" the truth, a metaphor that has become a hallmark of this theory.

Such is the theory in bare outline, but before discussing it we had better introduce one or two complications. Variation is often regarded as the more prominent and important of the last two conditions, but there are at least two cases where Nozick thinks it is insufficient on its own. One he illustrates with an example from Harman (*PE*: 177). A dictator is killed and the media at first report this but then are made by the Government to deny it, so that people think the dictator is still alive. Smith, however, does not hear the later reports and so continues to believe, truly, that the dictator is dead. But does he know this? He satisfies Variation, for had the dictator not been killed he, like everyone else, would believe he was alive. But can he really be credited with knowledge merely because he failed to hear the later reports? In the changed situation where he did hear them he would have believed them (we assume), and so would have believed, falsely, that the dictator was still alive. He does not satisfy Adherence, and that is why he does not know.

The other case concerns necessary propositions, e.g. that twice two is four (*PE*: 186–7; I am simplifying slightly to avoid the next complication to be mentioned). Variation does not apply here, Nozick thinks, for it hardly makes sense to ask what would happen were twice two not four. But Adherence comes to the rescue. A child who believes that twice two is four merely because his teacher says so, but would not believe it were his teacher to say otherwise, does not have knowledge.

We have said nothing so far about how we come by our knowledge. Sometimes this does not matter, and our two main conditions as stated can represent the theory well enough. But sometimes they can lead to odd results if left unadorned. Nozick gives this example (*PE*: 179): "A grandmother sees her grandson is well when he comes to visit; but if he were sick or dead, others would tell her he was well to spare her upset". So she violates Variation, yet surely she knows he is well. So Nozick adds that we must take account of how she knows, namely by seeing, for in the case where she forms the belief that he is well even though he isn't, she would be using the method of relying on others, not that of seeing. If p is true then and S believes it via method M, Variation should be rephrased to say that were *p* not true S wouldn't believe, via M, that *p*, while Adherence will say that were *p* still true (in somewhat changed circumstances) S would believe, via M, that *p* (I have adopted a small modification of Variation suggested by Luper-Foy in a difficult discussion (Luper-Foy 1987a: 225) where line 14 seems to misprint "not-*p*" for "*p*"; see also 1984b: 28–9). Luper-Foy sees problems with Adherence whichever formulation is adopted.

Nozick adds various other complications and refinements to deal with cases such as where S uses several methods at once to form a belief, and then runs through a set of problem cases from the literature which he claims his approach will solve. But we have now got a sufficient view of the theory to let us start discussing some of the issues it raises.

Counterfactuals

The notion of tracking the truth depends essentially on that of counterfactuals, which claim that something would be (or have been) the case if something else were (or had been). But what are we to make of such claims? The model Nozick appeals to is that of possible worlds, due mainly to R. Stalnaker and D. K. Lewis (although going back ultimately to Leibniz). Imagine all the logically possible scenarios laid out in a great array round the actual world, with similarities between them represented by closeness in the array and similarity to the actual world by closeness to it. Then the general idea is that a counterfactual such as "If *p* were the case, then *q* would be" (or for short, "Were *p*, then *q*") will be true if the nearest worlds or scenarios to the actual one in which *p* is true (the nearest "*p*-worlds") are also *q*-worlds. The situation is more complicated than this mainly because there are infinitely many possible worlds and they probably form a "dense" set, i.e. between any two of them, however close, there are infinitely many others.

Nozick considers some of these complications (*PE*: 680–81 n.8), but mostly they do not affect the basic idea. One point is worth noticing however, namely the use of the plural ("worlds or scenarios") in the above statement of the general idea. Here Nozick differs from Lewis, for whom the nearest world to the actual world is the actual world itself, so that "Were *p*, then *q*" will always be true when *p* and *q* themselves are both true. But this trivializes the issue; we want there to be some connection between *p* and *q*, be it causal or of some other kind. We don't want "Were grass green, snow would be white" to be true merely because grass *is* green and snow white. Again suppose that I am standing at the roadside when a bus sweeps past – I might say, "Had I stepped out then, I would be dead now". This will be true, on the theory, if in the scenario which is as close, i.e. similar, as possible to the actual world except that I step out, I promptly die. But it surely ought to be true in other scenarios too, such as where everything is the same and I step out but am wearing socks of a different colour. I would hardly comfort myself after my narrow escape by the thought that had I been wearing different socks I'd have been OK.

In the footnote just mentioned (*PE*: 680–81) Nozick deals with this sort of problem by appealing to a set of scenarios close to the actual world and having in common that *p*, or whatever is at stake, is true in these. This set is then called a "neighbourhood" – in this example the *p*-neighbourhood of the actual world – and "Were *p*, then *q*" is true just when *q* is true throughout this *p*-neighbourhood. The notion of a neighbourhood is given a somewhat intricate, but clear enough, definition and is then developed still further to deal with some of the complications mentioned above. These details need not concern us as Nozick himself feels "little inclination to pursue" them, and does not insist on a rigorous and polished account.

Counterfactuals are slippery customers. We all assert them cheerfully enough in our daily lives, but we would probably be embarrassed if asked to say just what made them true when they were true. They don't seem in any direct sense to describe the world as it is; indeed hence the talk of merely possible worlds. McGinn (1984: 535–6) thinks Nozick treats them as simply true (or false), without being grounded in anything, although Nozick (*PE*: 266) seems to presuppose an underlying, if unknown, "mechanism". Any appeal to counterfactuals to support a philosophical theory faces objections of two kinds: general ones like these about their nature and ones about the actual use made of them in supporting the theory. Let us start with the former (we will come to the latter in "Some criticisms of Nozick" below).

A rather scathing attack on the appeal to possible worlds is made by Fumerton (Luper-Foy 1987a: 167–9), who says, "the attempt to 'explicate' subjunctive conditionals [i.e. counterfactuals] using the possible worlds metaphor is at best disingenuous". He doesn't say what it is at worst. Nozick himself, as Fumerton goes on to point out, is well aware that we cannot, without circularity, analyze counterfactuals in terms of the closeness or similarity of possible worlds and then analyze this closeness in terms of what "would" happen in certain circumstances (*PE*: 174n.). We cannot use possible worlds to explain counterfactuals then, but we can, Nozick thinks, use them to "represent" them, a term that Fumerton professes not to understand, although Nozick does try to elucidate it by comparing the way utility theory represents preferences without explaining them. He illustrates this by comparing how a librarian might shelve his books either by numbering them in some order, e.g. alphabetical, and using the numbers to shelve them, or shelving them directly in alphabetical order and numbering them afterwards for reference; in the first case the numbers explain the positioning of the books, while in the second they merely represent it. The illustration is not perfect, though. The numbers, even in the second case, have a clear role when it comes to finding a book or briefly referring to it, but it is not clear what role the possible worlds have or what the "representing" amounts to unless it is simply an alternative way of expressing the counterfactuals.

Perhaps the closeness of the worlds maps the probabilities of various hypotheses. Perhaps the world where when I step under the bus I die is closer than the world where I am merely bruised because it is more probable that I would die than merely suffer bruises. What happens if we read this sentence the other way round: it is more probable that I die because the world where I do is closer to the actual world? In the first sentence the "because" seems to be clarificatory: we are more familiar with probabilities than we are with the closeness of possible worlds. The second sentence, however, seems to be doing some real explanatory work, or claiming to. This sounds more plausible if we replace the spatial metaphor "closer" by its intended sense: "more similar". To say that something would have happened because the world where it does is as similar as possible to the actual world seems promising at first, but the trouble comes when we ask what counts as similarity here. An example sometimes taken is this: (i) If Nixon had pressed the button there would have been a nuclear war. (ii) If Nixon had pressed the button the connecting wire would have broken. Example (ii) describes a world that seems much more similar to the actual world (where there was no nuclear war) than (i) is, but (i) seems to be the acceptable counterfactual, with (ii) being arbitrarily optimistic. If we say that (i) is really more similar to the actual world because that's what would have happened, we are back in the circle that Nozick rightly rejects.

One thing Nozick does not commit himself to is the strong modal realism of Lewis (see *PE*: 174, 681 end of n.8). This is why I have sometimes used "scenario" instead of "world". On that view possible worlds are just as real as the actual world, and for themselves *are* actual, although not for us. They are spatiotemporal (or many of them are) but they have their own spaces and times and are spatiotemporally disconnected from the actual world, rather as places on the moon may have their own latitudes and longitudes but are neither north, south, east nor west of places on the earth. There are many difficulties with such a view, but here we need only note that Nozick is not missing out on anything in rejecting it, since even if we could give a clear account of when one such world is closer or more similar to ours than another, it is not clear why the fact that something would be the case in a close world should have any bearing on the actions that we use counterfactuals to guide us to in the actual world (not stepping out in front of buses, etc.). What we want is some sort of link between the worlds to explain why we should bother about what merely would have happened, but didn't. We might try appealing to some generalization such as "All (or maybe just: nearly all) those who step out under fast-moving buses die". This won't help if it merely tells us about what has actually happened in past cases, since I am no more one of those past cases than I am a case in a merely possible world. We need something stronger, such as a causal generalization or something that introduces the notion of necessity, although, as we have seen, a mere appeal to causation will not do because of deviant causal chains.

As he says himself when acknowledging the priority of Dretske (*PE*: 689 n.53), Nozick's view is of the kind known as a "relevant alternatives" view (despite the apparent distancing at *PE*: 174–5), a kind that Dretske introduced. Dretske defines a relevant alternative as "an alternative that might have been realized in the existing circumstances if the actual state of affairs had not materialized" (1970: 1021). The idea is that in order to justify a belief I need only consider those alternatives to it that are relevant in this sense. I need not consider the possibility that I would have escaped falling under the bus because an eagle would have swooped down and plucked me out of harm's way, since this is not something that might have happened (unless of course a benevolent eagle actually was hovering overhead at that moment). This appeal to relevant alternatives itself involves an appeal to counterfactuals and is not a way of solving problems concerning them of course, but simply classifies the kind of use of them that is being made.

Scepticism and closure

So far we have discussed questions about the general nature of counterfactuals and limitations on what we can expect from them. I deferred discussion of objections based on Nozick's use of them, but before getting onto that we ought to look further at how he does use them.

Scepticism is officially treated in the second section of *Philosophical Explanations*, Chapter 3, but as with so much modern epistemology it underlies the whole discussion, starting with the opening sentences of the chapter (*PE*: 167). In keeping with the methodological outlook we discussed in Chapter 1, Nozick insists that he is not seeking to convince the sceptic but only to "show how knowledge can exist even given the skeptic's possibilities" (*PE*: 167). At the start of the second section he talks of seeking "to explain to ourselves how knowledge is possible, not to prove to someone else that knowledge is possible" (*PE*: 198), but here he has been accused (by Shatz in Luper-Foy 1987a: 255) of misstating his own point, for he *can* prove that knowledge is possible, if knowledge is tracking and it is *possible* that we track, but what he can't prove is that we do track.

Nozick starts by saying: "The skeptical possibilities, and the threat they pose to our knowledge, depend upon our knowing things (if we do) mediately, through or by way of something else", which "leaves room for the possibility of these intermediate stages holding and producing our belief that *p*, without the fact that *p* being at the other end" (*PE*: 168). A page later he talks of scepticism as "in tension with the existence of (almost all) knowledge". The first passage, and the bracket in the second, suggest that some knowledge, being immediate, is immune to the sceptic's attack. This suggests, but does not entail, foundationalism, the view that if, but only if, we start from some knowledge that is absolutely certain and incorrigible we can build up the rest of our knowledge from there. It does not entail foundationalism because it could be that we do have some immediate knowledge but cannot use it to build up any further knowledge. Nozick does not, I think, ever explicitly repudiate foundationalism as such, but in various passages he seems to deny it (see *PE*: 275, 414), and it is quite out of keeping with the general spirit of his philosophy. An obvious candidate for immediate knowledge is the statement "I exist", beloved by the doyen of all foundationalists, Descartes, who thought he could escape the clutches of his demon by appealing to it. It is true that anyone who utters it cannot be mistaken, but any self-respecting demon (or modern brainwasher) ought to be able to persuade Descartes, possibly using a bit of hypnotism etc., to hold the false view that he didn't exist. The demon could not create a contradiction, but he could make Descartes believe anything, including a contradiction, and so think it true. So *whatever* Descartes believes *he* cannot guarantee that it is not a contradiction (see Watling 1964).

Another question famously associated with Descartes, although it goes back to Plato, asks how I can know, if I can, that I am not now dreaming. Recent discussions of scepticism tend to replace this with an idea deriving from Putnam and known as the brain-in-a-vat (or BIV) possibility (but for a claim that the dreaming and BIV cases have very different effects on Nozick's position see Lipson 1987). Some mad scientists take a brain, either from a newborn infant or from an adult, detach it from its body, and attach electrodes to it through which they first (if necessary) wipe out any memories etc. that it has and then send into it electrochemical impulses of the same kind as it would normally receive from its nervous system (together with suitable nutrients). They also let it send out signals of the kind the brain normally would to its nerves and muscles, although these may be stopped as soon as they get outside the brain. Such a brain would presumably have conscious experiences like those of a normal brain receiving the same impulses from its normal nervous system, but instead of representing an outside world its experiences would be determined by the mad scientists. The question then is: how do you know you are not such a brain?

It is this BIV question that Nozick takes as representing extreme (exotic or global) scepticism, as opposed to local scepticism about some particular matter (he refers to the vat as a tank) (for some other versions of scepticism see *NR*: 196 n.36). His reaction to this is simply to admit it. I cannot know that I am not a BIV, because I cannot track the truth on this question. If it were false that I am not a BIV (i.e. if I were a BIV) I would still believe (as I do) that I was not a BIV, because the mad scientists would be ensuring that I did so. Variation would not be satisfied. If I cannot know that I am not a BIV it seems to follow that I cannot know that I am in fact at home.

It is here that, as Fumerton puts it (Luper-Foy 1987a: 170), "probably the most startling, original, and dialectically ingenious move that Nozick makes is to take the most devastating objection to his view and embrace it as one of its advantages". The originality might be questioned in view of Dretske's anticipations, but let that pass; Nozick does bring out the issue rather more saliently. Similarly Sosa in the same volume (Luper-Foy 1987a: 320) says that at this point

Robert Nozick

Nozick "tries to turn critical weakness into spectacular strength".

The "devastating objection" and "critical weakness" is this. Nozick thinks that I can know that I am at home, and also that if I am at home I am not BIV, yet cannot know that I am not a BIV. How can this be? Surely if I know that p, and know that p entails q, I must know that q? This principle is standardly expressed by saying that knowledge is "closed under known entailment". This means that if you start with the class of propositions that some subject S knows, you will never get outside that class and reach something S does not know by moving from any member of that class (any proposition S knows) to another that S knows is entailed by the first one. In the present context this can be called for short the "closure principle", or just "Closure" ("closure" for the notion and "Closure" for the principle), and its denial "Nonclosure" (although the general idea of closure in this sense has many applications outside the spheres of knowledge and entailment; you could say for instance that responsibility is "closed under causation" if whenever one is responsible for something one is also responsible for whatever that thing causes). The closure principle we are concerned with is sometimes called by other names, such as the "entailment principle" or the "transmission principle".

Note that saying that knowledge is closed under known entailment is not the same as saying that knowledge is closed under entailment (although Hetherington (1992: 43 n.3) claims that if Nozick's argument for the former proves anything it proves the latter). One can know the five Peano axioms, which in fact entail the whole of arithmetic, without knowing the whole of arithmetic. But a word of caution is needed here: I know the Peano axioms, and know that they entail the whole of arithmetic, so why don't I know the whole of arithmetic? For the axioms to entail the whole of arithmetic is for them to entail each true arithmetical statement, and indeed I know that they do, but what I don't know is which statements those are. If I knew just which statements the axioms entailed then I would indeed know those statements. So this example need not stop us from saying that knowledge is closed under known entailment.

The "startling" and "ingenious" move that Nozick makes is to treat it as a merit of his tracking theory that it involves denying Closure and to use this to deal with the sceptic. Then he can indeed say that I know I'm at home, and know that if I'm at home I'm not a BIV, and yet don't know that I'm not a BIV. The point depends on the closeness of the various possible worlds. To track the fact that I'm at home I must satisfy Variation, which demands that if I were not at home I would not believe I was. But the closest worlds in which I am not at home are those where I go shopping or into college etc., and in those worlds I do not believe I'm at home. Similarly for me to track the fact that I am not a BIV, Variation demands that in the closest worlds where I am a BIV I do not believe I am not. But the closest worlds in which I am a BIV are those where the mad scientists ensure that my experiences are exactly the same as they are at the moment, so that I do believe, as I do at the moment, that I am not a BIV. Therefore I do not track, and so do not know, that I am not a BIV.

The price that Nozick pays

The appeal to different degrees of closeness of possible worlds to solve philosophical problems is not new. Lewis, for instance, had used it to deal with the problem of pre-emption in his account of causation. But Nozick uses it not, like Lewis, to iron out a possible counterexample to his theory, but to persuade us to accept something that seems counterintuitive – the denial of Closure. It is true that this is done in the interests of something intuitively desirable, to escape the clutches of the sceptic and be able to know that we are at home, or wherever. As Nozick agrees, however, the genie that he has let out of the bottle may have some further and less attractive results as well, although he himself seems to accept these results with a cheerfulness that not all his readers will share. He does allow that knowledge is closed under known logical equivalence (as against mere entailment), or at least that we have seen no reason to think it is not (*PE*: 229). That I am at home and not a BIV entails that I am at home, and that I am at home entails that I am not a BIV, and so also entails that I am at home and not a BIV. Therefore that I am at home is logically equivalent to the conjunction that I am at home and not a BIV. On Nozick's account if I know, and therefore track, that I am at home I also know and track the conjunction. This is because the nearest worlds in which the conjunction is false are those where I am not at home (but in college, etc.), and in those worlds I do not believe that I am at home, and so do not believe the conjunction. So I satisfy Variation regarding the conjunction. Assuming, as Nozick tacitly does, that I also satisfy Adherence, I know the conjunction. But, as we have seen, I do not know that I am not a BIV. So I can not only know that I am at home without knowing that I am not a BIV, I can also know that I am at home and not a BIV without knowing that I am not a BIV. I can know a conjunction without knowing each of its conjuncts (*PE*: 228).

It is important to note that we are talking of knowledge, not of belief – we are not attributing any psychological acrobatics to people. If I believe a conjunction I must believe each conjunct. Otherwise Nozick could not argue, as he needs to above, that in worlds where I do not believe I am at home, I do not believe that I am at home and not a BIV. Similarly if I believe that p and believe that p entails q I believe that q, at least in the sense that I shall if the question arises – I might not bother to draw the influence explicitly for myself. (If the way the question arises itself makes me doubt q, perhaps because I now see its further implications, then provided I still remember them I shall doubt one of the two premises, that p and that p entails q.) Nozick does not spell all this out, but he does refuse to deny that were I to know that p and that p entails q I would believe that q (*PE*: 688 n.49).

That a conjunction entails its conjuncts is related to the logical law of universal instantiation, that what holds of all so-and-sos hold of any given so-and-so, and here too for Nozick knowledge may not be trans-mitted. Suppose I know that all cats purr and that Tiddles is a cat: must I know that Tiddles purrs? No, for if she did not I might still think she did. (She's such a fat and contented creature.) But I might still know that all cats purr because the closest worlds where not all cats purr might be those where scrawny and mangy ones don't, and in those worlds I realize they don't, while still thinking Tiddles does. So I track that all cats purr (and that Tiddles is a cat) but don't track that Tiddles purrs. (In all this I am for simplicity ignoring Adherence.)

Parallel, as it seems, to universal instantiation is the law of existential generalization, that what holds of a certain so-and-so holds of at least one so-and-so, and as before a conjunction entails its conjuncts so now a disjunct entails its disjunction: p entails p-or-q, i.e. if p is true then at least one of p and q is true. (Readers who feel unhappy about this should note that, as "or" is used in logic, p-or-q entails that if p is false, q is true; it does not entail that if p were false, q would be true.)

I called these laws parallel "as it seems", since they seem to be on a level in logical systems. But for Nozick they are not parallel, at least as far as Closure goes. As we have seen, he denies that closure holds for universal instantiation; but he insists that it does hold for existential generalization and the entailment of its disjunction by a disjunct. He constructs an apparent counterexample, but leaves it hanging, saying simply that "this apparent nonclosure result surely carries things too far", and that such results "cut things too finely. Surely our knowledge that p does not stand in such splendid isolation from knowledge of other things so closely connected to p" (*PE*: 230). Later he allows the counterexample, saying that knowledge is "almost always" closed under existential generalization (*PE*: 236 with *PE*: 293 n.68). However, it is not clear that the disjunctive and conjunctive cases are really different here. Suppose p is true and I believe p, while the closest not-p worlds are not-q worlds, where I do not believe p, so that I track p (given Adherence). Suppose also that I track that p entails p-or-q (for which only Adherence is needed), and that the closest not-(p-or-q) worlds are all worlds where I still believe p-or-q. Then I do not track p-or-q, and Closure does not hold here.

One might anyway think there was also a certain "splendid isolation" about knowledge that p-and-q and that p-and-q entails q which does not carry with it knowledge that q. In his acknowledgement of Dretske (*PE*: 689 n.53) Nozick wonders why Dretske's views have not had "the proper impact", and hopes that his own independent statement of the position "will make clear its many merits". Perhaps he should have added something about his statement also making clear some of its demerits.

It might seem that Nozick makes his position even less plausible by treating the two cases, conjunction and disjunction, differently. But this would be not quite true. He does allow that Closure holds in the disjunction case only "almost always", as we have seen, and he does not claim that we never know a conjunct on the basis of knowing a conjunction, but only that we don't automatically do so (and in particular don't in the sceptical case about the BIV possibility). In fact in general he does not think that Closure never holds, but only that it doesn't always do so, and this is important because otherwise, as he points out (*PE*: 230), we could never come to know anything from a deduction or proof.

When then *does* Closure hold, so that we can come to know things by deducing them from other things? Nozick's answer is that if I am to come to know q by deducing it from p, which I know, then my belief that p must track not only p itself but q too, so that were q false I would not merely not *know* p (since if p entails q, p itself would be false, so I could not know it), but would not believe p. He does not say this is the only case where Closure holds, however. Another is where I know p and know q and infer that p-and-q (*PE*: 236).

An incidental merit Nozick claims for his theory is that it helps to solve a puzzle he attributes to Kripke about evidence (*PE*: 236–8). If I know p, p must be true, so any evidence against it must be misleading. Why then can I not simply ignore such evidence, which would normally be thought dogmatic and irrational of me? Nozick's answer is that p is logically equivalent to all evidence against p being misleading, and since knowledge *is* closed under known logical equivalence (as against mere known logical implication, or entailment (*PE*: 229)), if I know p and know this equivalence I shall know that any counterevidence is misleading. But since Closure does not apply to universal instantiation I may not know that any particular piece of counterevidence I meet is misleading, and so I cannot ignore it.

Does this beg the question? To know that p I must satisfy Adherence, i.e. still believe that p in close worlds where p is true but some other things are different. But these close worlds surely include some where I meet some such misleading counterevidence, and it may be that I not only ought to but do take it seriously and so fail to believe p; but then I don't know p in the first place. Saying I do know p seems to require, for Nozick, saying there are no such close worlds but only those where I ought to take the counterevidence seriously but don't, which puts a premium on being dogmatic or uncritical. Compare also Nozick's discussion of the example of Tom and the library book (*PE*: 191–2).

However, Nozick might claim that this ignores the need to take account of the method used. In the world where I fail to believe p because I meet and take seriously the counterevidence, I use a different method from what I use in the actual world. As many critics have pointed out, Nozick is avowedly vague about how to individuate methods. But in the present example, unlike that of the grandmother, who *sees* that her grandson is healthy (*PE*: 179), no method is specified for why I believe p in the actual world. If we call my method in the counterevidence world "using the counterevidence" I shall have a different method, but if we call it "using the available evidence" (or just "using my senses", or "using my reason", according to the faculty I use in each case) I shall have the same method. Could Nozick rely on his suggestion (*PE*: 684 n.21) that one could always invent some gimmicky method to cover whatever one wants, but that this would trivialize the question?

Some criticisms of Nozick

So far we have mainly been concerned with the price that Nozick is aware of paying. But he has attracted much criticism from outside, both of his general position and the principles underlying it, and of the detailed working out of the theory. It will fit in best with what we have just been saying to start with something on the latter.

Various critics have accused the tracking analysis of being too weak because it lets through various cases that intuitively would not count as knowledge, or too strong because it excludes some genuine cases of knowledge, or of having both these faults. We have just seen that there are problems concerning what counts as using the same method. There is also a question what counts as satisfying Variation and Adherence. Barker (Luper-Foy 1987a: 291–2) insists that the conditionals must be contingent and empirical if they are to make their proper contribution, which excludes my knowing, as I surely do, that I have at least one belief; for if I did not, I would indeed not believe I did, but this would be a necessary, not contingent, fact. The same presumably applies to my knowledge that I exist, for if I did not I would hardly believe I did, and again this would not be contingent.

We have already seen that for knowledge of necessary truths Nozick allows that Variation does not apply. That I exist and have beliefs are not necessary truths, but there is something akin to necessary truths about them when looked at from my point of view. Could Nozick then widen his view and say that here too Variation drops out? Adherence would still be satisfied here, for in the closest worlds where I exist and where I both exist and have beliefs I surely believe I do. However, Nozick's treatment of knowing necessary truths has been criticized by McGinn (1984: 533–5), who argues that Adherence may not be enough, for cases might arise of the kind made famous by Gettier in his brief but fundamental attack on the notion that knowledge is justified true belief. Suppose I believe a mathematical truth, using a method that is usually reliable, so that my belief is justified, although I made a slip which as it happened did not affect the result. In close possible worlds I still believe the truth because I use the same method but always making the slip (it's one I'm prone to), so that Adherence is satisfied, yet I don't have knowledge, McGinn thinks. He adds that Nozick makes an unwanted asymmetry between knowledge of contingent and of necessary truths, because epistemological questions about the nature of knowledge ought not to depend on metaphysical questions about the status of its objects. To this, though, Nozick might reply from his externalist point of view that this dependence is fair enough if the status of what is known is such as to affect whether our beliefs are likely to be led astray: any errors in our beliefs will not be due to variations in their objects.

Garrett (1983) too, however, complains that we might believe a necessary truth, such as Fermat's last theorem (that $x^n + y^n = z^n$ is never satisfied for positive integers where $n > 2$), merely because no counterexamples have been found. Even though we tracked the truth by satisfying Adherence we would not have knowledge here because the method of relying on not finding counterexamples is not a reliable one in general. Gordon (1984) objects that relying on finding no counterexamples *is* a reliable method if it involves searching long and hard, although Garrett (1984) is not convinced.

Dropping Variation in the case of necessary propositions has led one critic, Hughes (1996) to accuse Nozick of giving the sceptics too little. Suppose aliens construct an atom-by-atom duplicate of me and lay it in bed beside me one night. On waking, each of us is convinced he is the real Lacey, yet even an arch anti-sceptic like Moore would agree, Hughes thinks, that neither of us can *know* he is. But for Nozick I do know, since I am Lacey, I believe I am, and in close worlds where I am I still believe it (i.e. Adherence is satisfied). Either Variation must be reinstated, whatever the difficulties, or another analysis of knowledge is needed.

Actually Hughes sees a possible, although technical and not very obvious, escape for Nozick here, but he adds the opposite charge that in certain other cases Nozick gives the sceptic too much. Suppose I know, via the method of apparently remembering, that I remember lunching yesterday (I do remember, I believe I do, and Variation and Adherence are satisfied). Can I also know that I don't misremember lunching yesterday? No, because were it false that I don't misremember (i.e. true that I do misremember), I would still believe, via the same method of apparently remembering, that I don't misremember, and so would not track the truth. This time it is Variation, rather than its absence that causes the trouble.

Whatever we think about all this, Nozick's treatment of knowing necessary truths, where tracking is reduced to Adherence, will suffer a further blow if BonJour (Luper-Foy 1987a: 301) is right in saying Adherence is out of place because a poor-sighted person who is careful only to form beliefs through vision when he does see clearly, surely has knowledge then, although he does not satisfy Adherence, because in close worlds where what is there is the same but, say, the light is dimmer he does not form the relevant belief.

Here tracking is under attack, but Barker (Luper-Foy 1987a: 292–5) thinks that tracking might be rescued, and Nozick shown to be contributing to our understanding of the issues, if it is taken in an extended and more flexible manner. When we ask whether S knows that *p* we should consider not just what S believes about *p* but what S believes about situations similar to *p* when they are the case: does S's belief vary in line with variations in *p,* not just in the all-or-nothing cases where *p* is true or false? Nozick does say that tracking involves "some generality to other (subjective) situations" (*PE*: 267), but he is evidently not thinking of the kind of generality Barker demands. Barker applies this to Nozick's claim that I cannot know I am not a BIV, which Barker allies with the earlier cases because when we say that were this not true (i.e. were I a BIV) I would still believe it, and so not satisfy Variation, this conditional is not empirical or contingent but follows from the way the set-up is defined. If we consider a range of situations where we are "more nearly disembodied in various ways" (which he doesn't specify) and receive deceptive sensory information, it is contingent whether anyone would be shrewd enough to see through such deceptions, "even when they become extreme", and so "Nozick is making more of a concession to scepticism than is called for". But Barker is not entirely clear here. Even the "extreme" cases seem to involve only "near-disembodiment", and even the shrewdest person could not see through the full BIV case (because of its definition, as Barker says). However shrewd I am then in seeing through partial deceptions, how can I know I am not a BIV?

One charge made by critics of Nozick's use of tracking is that he applies it inconsistently in different cases. Shope for instance (1984: 35–6) argues that Nozick treats inconsistently two of the examples he considers (cases (e) and (h) at *PE*: 191 and *PE*: 193). Nozick introduces (e) as follows: "Faced by one of two identical twins, Judy and Trudy, a person believes it is Judy before him, but only because he has bumped his head which (somehow) gave him the idea that Judy has a mole; coincidentally, Judy has just developed a mole. He doesn't know it is Judy who is before him. [Adherence] is not satisfied; if Judy was before him, but in the very close situation of not having developed the mole, he wouldn't believe it was she." Here the method the person uses is that of relying on whatever it is he sees; had he seen someone moleless he would not have thought it was Judy. In (h) the person sees a masked robber, but the mask slips and he sees, and surely knows, it is Jesse James. Here the method is that of "seeing certain things", as Nozick puts it, i.e. the unmasked robber. In close worlds where the mask stays on the person would indeed not know it was James, but this doesn't violate Adherence because he wouldn't be using the same method (seeing an unmasked robber).

Had his method been that of relying on whatever it was he saw, as in (e), he *would* have violated Adherence. Actually Nozick's phrase "seeing certain things" is unclear. I have assumed it means seeing the unmasked James. But if it means having visual experiences indistinguishable from that, then in the world where another robber impersonates James to frame him the witness would still think it was him, and so would violate Variation; whether such a world is closer to the actual world than that where the mask stays on is doubtful, but we are getting into the complications Nozick discusses (*PE*: 680–81 n.8). As BonJour points out (Luper-Foy 1987a: 299–300), such an appeal to visual experiences as such would sit unhappily with Nozick's externalism, although Nozick (*PE*: 184–5) does suggest it (without reference to this example). Furthermore if the method is that of seeing an unmasked James, then as Mazoué (1986) points out in another context, this would ignore Nozick's insistence that the method must not itself be identified by reference to the actual truth.

An even clearer case perhaps of opportunistic knowledge like that in the James case is where I return home unexpectedly and find you in bed with my wife. The fact that my return was unexpected, perhaps even by me, in no way lessens my claim to know and here the method must be seeing *you*, not just relying on sight, despite Mazoué's point, or in the close worlds where I do not so return I would not believe in your sins, thus violating Adherence.

Another discussion pointing out the inconsistency of Nozick's treatment of the James and Judy cases is that of Forbes (1984, especially §III), who thinks the solution lies in abandoning the counterfactual account of knowledge altogether and relying on the "Transmission Principle" (i.e. Closure), which Nozick of course has rejected. Forbes also uses this to solve the vase case (Nozick's (c) at *PE*: 190), which Nozick treats in a way that even he himself regards as "somewhat counterintuitive". Forbes defends the Transmission Principle in §IV.

One of the strongest reasons for thinking that Nozick's tracking requirement is too strong is just that it does imply that I do not know that I am not a BIV, and then can only save my knowing that I am at home by the implausible and ad hoc device of Nonclosure – ad hoc because the only reason for accepting it seems to be that the theory requires it; although to be fair, Nonclosure does have its defenders, e.g. McGinn (1984: 542–6), whose rather different theory also leads to it, and tentatively A. H. Goldman (1981: 107). The correct approach here is by no means obvious. Surely I do know that I am at home, but know also that were I a BIV my experiences would be precisely as they are. How then can we avoid either scepticism about whether I am at home or a dogmatism that says, as Dr Johnson might have put it, "Sir, I know I am not a BIV, and there's an end on't!"? I also believe I live under the influence of gravity. The closest world where this is false is a very distant one, so why not say that when the closest world where our belief is false is very distant we can ignore it? Nozick does toy with this idea but rejects it: see Shatz's discussion with references (Luper-Foy 1987a: 249–50). One objection to it is that, as Goldman puts it (Luper-Foy 1987a: 188), "[i]f we cannot know that the sceptic's worlds are not actual . . . , then we surely cannot know that they are distant from the actual world"; a similar point is made in passing by BonJour (Luper-Foy 1987a: 307. This is indeed an important point concerning radical scepticisms of the "we might be dreaming" variety. It is tempting simply to dismiss them as so extremely improbable that we can ignore them. But the trouble comes when we try to attach any probability to them, great or small.

One of Shatz's claims is that Nozick does not, as he appears to do, take a tracking theory he had developed independently (in thinking about free will: *PE*: 169) and then use it to justify his sceptical conclusions (that I can't know I am not a BIV), but rather tailors the theory to justify sceptical conclusions that he holds already. Only so, Shatz thinks, can we see why Nozick rejects various emendations that would block the sceptical results, such as allowing "inferring *q* from *known p*" (not just from *p*) as a method; then I could claim to know I am not a BIV by inferring it from my knowing that I am at home. He concludes that it is this antecedent commitment to partial scepticism (I do know I'm at home but not that I'm not a BIV) that leads Nozick to the "crazy quilt" of unsystematized bits of knowledge that we have already seen in discussing Closure, a conclusion perhaps supported by such remarks as: "It is a virtue of our account that it yields, and explains, this [the sceptical] result" (*PE*: 201). Of course to say all this is not to solve the problem of scepticism itself. To attempt that is beyond our present scope.

Shatz (Luper-Foy 1987a: 246) thinks that tracking can be amended but not saved. Others are more optimistic. A. I. Goldman (1983), reviewing *PE* generally with sympathy, suggests that "knowledge is defeated if there are *any* serious or relevant counterpossibilities in which the belief would be held, even if these aren't (among) the very closest counterpossibilities to the actual situation". This has an appealing flexibility, although of course we need to decide which counterpossibilities are serious. (Goldman develops his view elsewhere.)

This is a version of the "relevant alternatives" approach, as we saw (end of "Counterfactuals" above) that Nozick's own view is. Shatz, who treats Nozick as merely having "strong affinities" to that approach (Luper-Foy 1987a: 250), criticizes it on various grounds, one of which is that to know that p I must know that irrelevant alternatives too are excluded, which I can only do either by deducing this from p or on independent grounds. The argument is rather complex but I will make just one comment: to know that I have a computer before me (to take his example) I must know it is not an aardvark (an irrelevant alternative). But why can't I know this *in* knowing it's a computer? Why can't I see that it's a computer *and* (*not*: therefore) not an aardvark? This won't solve the sceptical problem, though, for I know what it would be like to see an aardvark, but not what it would be like to be a BIV (as *opposed* to being normal). (For criticism of Nozick as taking too narrow a view of what *is* relevant see Greco 1993, especially 11–13.)

Scepticism may be global or exotic, as in the BIV or dreaming cases, or it may be merely local, e.g. that a natural law has been breached. Vogel (Luper-Foy 1987a: 206) sees further trouble for the tracking analysis in this latter case concerning inductive knowledge. Suppose I left some ice cubes in a hot sun some hours ago: do I know they have melted? If they had not, I would still believe they had, and so violate Variation. Nozick escapes this by appealing to "backtracking" conditionals, of the form that had the cubes not melted this would have been because of some earlier differences in the situation, so that my evidence (and so method) would have been different, and so I don't violate Variation (*PE*: 223n.). This ignores the breach of natural law possibility by making the close worlds ones where that is not required, but Vogel points out that appealing to backtracking conditionals leads to a morass of indeterminacy, and concludes that: "an inconsistency results from combining Nozick's tracking requirement, our intuitions about counterfactuals, and our intuitions about inductive knowledge" (Luper-Foy 1987a: 208). We do, Vogel thinks, know that unobserved breaches of natural law don't occur, although we don't track here (Luper-Foy 1987a: 209). This distinction between exotic and local scepticism is also appealed to by Shatz (Luper-Foy 1987a: 262). Of course it is assumed that we do indeed have knowledge in the local cases.

A criticism of the tracking analysis from a different angle is made by Ziff (1984: 103). "Know", as we saw, is a factive verb. Suppose (to use my own example) that $E = mc^2$ and that I say that Einstein tracked this. Do I too therefore know it? As a non-physicist, Ziff would say, I would no doubt still believe it were it false, and so do not know it. If so, I am not qualified to say that Einstein knew it. Yet I can surely say he tracked it, since "track" is not obviously a factive verb. Two comments seem possible, the first a technical one: to say that tracking analyzes knowledge is not to say they can be intersubstituted in intentional contexts, such as my beliefs or attributions; but this does not seem to get to the heart of the matter. Secondly, were the equation false Einstein, if he tracked it, would have rejected it; so in the close possible worlds where I still have access to Einstein's thoughts I presumably reject it too.

A more positive proposal is made by Wright (1983). "Had there been avalanches there would have been snow in the valley" and "had there been snow in the valley I would have skied" both seem reasonable but seem to imply the suicidal "Had there been avalanches I would have skied." Nozick, like Lewis, would block this inference by saying that the premises, although both true, depend on different sets of possible worlds. Wright thinks this solution implausible, and that if both the premises are true, so should the conclusion be. But, he thinks, when the premises are taken together like this, they should be assessed by reference to a single set of possible worlds; we should look to context as well as content. In that case the second premise is presumably false; I would not have skied in avalanche snow. So the inference need not worry us.

To treat the counterfactual relation as nontransitive, as Nozick does, or would, here, is akin to the Nonclosure he uses to deal with the sceptic, and Dancy (1984) offers independent support for Wright's criticism of Nozick on scepticism. The sceptic need not rely on Nonclosure to claim you don't now know you're not a BIV. Using an argument analogous to one common in ethics, he can argue that if you don't know you're not a BIV in one situation (where you are one), you can't know it in any other unless you can point to some recognizable difference between them, and so can't know it when you're in fact at home. This seems to presuppose internalism, as it relies on how the situations seem to you from the inside. But Nozick couldn't reject the argument on this ground, Dancy claims, because he needs it himself to give a premise (that you don't know you're not a BIV) for his argument *for* Nonclosure. (Cf. Shatz above on Nozick's antecedent commitment to scepticism.)

Dancy himself, however, is criticized by Brueckner (1985), who doubts that the externalist Nozick does need this internalist support rather than just using his own tracking argument, and claims that Dancy's argument must be defective and could be used in reverse. It must be defective, at least if, as internalists hold, when I have justified true belief I have knowledge, for on Dancy's argument I must also have knowledge in the (to me) indistinguishable situation where my belief is false, which is absurd. It can be reversed because if I can't know I'm not a BIV (because I can't distinguish being and not being one), I also can't know I'm at home, because I can't distinguish being at home and being not at home but a BIV.

Dancy's universalizability argument sounds plausible, but it does, as he seems to admit, presuppose internalism, so Brueckner's attack on it leads us naturally to the next section.

Internalism and externalism again

One approach to the question of knowledge in the face of both exotic and local scepticism is that of Luper-Foy (1987b: 238–40). He appeals to usage, although not in the crude sense of the paradigm case argument that Nozick rejects at the start of his discussion (*PE*: 168n.), while Wright (1983: 140) accuses Nozick's treatment of the sceptic as reducing to just that. Luper-Foy's position is that "[f]acts about usage neither prove nor presuppose that we know anything. [But] when people are actually in situations *in which they take themselves to be when collectively believing that they possess knowledge,* they *do* possess knowledge" (Luper-Foy 1987b: 238). To apply this he suggests replacing tracking by "contratracking" (short for "the contrapositive of tracking"), which requires replacing Variation by its contrapositive: "[i]f I believed that p via method M, then p would be true" (Luper-Foy 1987a: 9; cf. 234); the other three conditions remain. We no longer need abandon Closure, he thinks (he calls it the Principle of Entailment), because contratracking sustains it, since if p is true so are its logical consequences. In close worlds where I believe, by sensory evidence, say, that I'm at home I am at home, and so not a BIV, and we can now allow that if I infer that I'm not a BIV, I know this too. The sceptical scenario has not been refuted – we don't have a proof that I'm not a BIV. But the sceptic has been refuted in the sense that he cannot argue that because I have no such proof I cannot know that I'm not a BIV, and he has been refuted without appeal to the implausible Nonclosure (cf. Luper-Foy 1987b: 240). Luper-Foy repeats this point about the need for the sceptic to have an argument in his other writings (for a rather similar point see Klein in Luper-Foy 1987b: 273–5).

The quotation just above (from Luper-Foy 1987b: 238) suggests that what makes the difference between knowledge and its absence may be just the situation itself, which returns us to the internalism/externalism issue. Philosophers seem to be divided fairly evenly into internalists and externalists, although not exclusively (see Fumerton in Luper-Foy 1987a: 178–9, and also BonJour in Luper-Foy 1987a: 310), but since Nozick is avowedly an externalist it is not surprising that many of his critics focus on the need for internalism. We have already seen that Nozick sometimes embodies internalist features in his own account (as at *PE*: 184–5; cf. 232–3), and has been criticized for inconsistency in doing so (BonJour in Luper-Foy 1987a: 299–300). In another such passage (*PE*: 196), he asks whether it is enough that the knower tracks the truth: what if he believes that he does not? Presumably Nozick has in mind the case of someone who lacks confidence, but of whom people often say, "He does know really". Nozick concludes tentatively that the knower must not believe that he does not track the truth but need not positively believe that he does. He takes things a bit further (*PE*: 686 n.41) by asking whether these second-order beliefs themselves should be justified or not justified. Here he is touching on a point often made against internalists, that they face a regress; if to know I must be able to justify my belief, must I also be able to justify my belief that I can justify it, and so on? (Cf. also *PE*: 281).

The risk of a regress can also face the externalist, at least as seen by the internalist. Fumerton (Luper-Foy 1987a: 177–8) sees the roots of externalism in the naturalizing of epistemology. Externalists try to reduce epistemic terms such as "knowledge" to non-epistemic ones. Fumerton, who compares the "naturalistic fallacy" in ethics, claims that the question "How do you know that you know?" can always be pressed against the externalist and against each answer that he gives to it – although Nozick himself explicitly says that "[y]ou can know that *p* without knowing that you know that *p*" (*PE*: 280), something he thinks the internalist denies (*PE*: 281). Of course this whole attack does presuppose an internalist point of view, and returns us to the question I mentioned above ("Introduction: internalism and externalism") about why we have the concept of knowledge in the first place (on which see also *PE*: 283–8).

One point in favour of the internalist is that externalism seems compatible with irrationality (see Luper-Foy 1984b: 38–40, reading "not" for "now" at 40 line 28). Swinburne (1983) gives an example where I believe something on the basis of consulting tea-leaves, where it happens that on this one occasion they are causally related to what I am believing. (Philosophers, including Nozick, are good at thinking up bizarre connections between things.) Here I shall track the truth, but have no justification for my belief. Similarly Shatz (Luper-Foy 1987a: 246) insists that, if I am to know q by inferring it from p, I must have good reason for thinking that p does indeed entail q. And BonJour (Luper-Foy 1987a: 310) thinks that many of the interesting issues about scepticism concern the rationality of our beliefs rather than whether they can properly be called "knowledge". (Incidentally at Luper-Foy 1987a: 310 line 28 the context suggests that "externalist" is surely a slip for "internalist".) Nozick (*PE*: 267) seems to anticipate some such example as Swinburne's. Swinburne expresses the internalist's complaint well when he says that Nozick tries to give objective connections to underpin subjective notions such as justification, evidence and probability, but that this ignores that justification is a matter of connections the knower is aware of, not those which actually hold. The issue is somewhat muddied, however, because "justification", although basically an internalist word, is sometimes used in an externalist sense, as when Fumerton (Luper-Foy 1987a: 179) talks of "*externally* defined justification", and apparently when Garrett (1983: 184) talks of beliefs as needing to be "justified or reached via a reliable method", where the "or" seems to mean "i.e." (cf. also BonJour in Luper-Foy 1987a: 312 n.8, and Nozick himself at *PE*: 267 and 264–5).

One form of externalism is reliabilism, as we saw earlier. Critics differ on whether Nozick is a reliabilist. Klein (Luper-Foy 1987a: 268) says his account "can be seen as a variety of reliabilism" and Luper-Foy (1987a: 9) describes his own contratracking as "loosely a version of reliabilism". But BonJour (Luper-Foy 1987a: 300–302) sees various differences between Nozick's position and reliabilism, partly because of Nozick's internalist appeal to the nature of the experience when individuating methods, but mainly because reliabilism does not involve Adherence, and so can cater for cases like BonJour's poor-sighted person who does have knowledge in the few cases where he sees clearly. He also adds a more subtle difference, which arises because the reliabilist condition for knowledge is roughly the contrapositive of Variation, and contraposition does not in general hold for counterfactuals. (Perhaps this is why Luper-Foy describes his own position as only "loosely" reliabilist.) Nozick himself more or less aligns his position with reliabilism (*PE*: 265), although he sees differences between them and problems about defining reliabilism (e.g. *PE*: 264n.), as does Martin (1983: 32). Nozick adds (*PE*: 267) that a reliable method may reach the truth without tracking it.

Many other criticisms of Nozick have been made, but it is time to turn to our final topic of this chapter.

Evidence

The last of the three sections of Chapter 3, on evidence, has received much less discussion than the other two, although the first two items in Luper-Foy (1987a) are devoted mainly to it. Nozick is an objectivist concerning both knowledge and evidence. Knowledge is a "real subjunctive relation between belief and fact, holding in the world" (*PE*: 248), and he thinks the same of the evidential relation, holding between evidence and a hypothesis. Like knowledge, evidence turns out to involve tracking, but Nozick insists that his treatment of evidence is distinct from that of knowledge and is "one way of elaborating" the discussion of knowledge and scepticism but does not "underlie" them (*PE*: 248). Later (*NR*: 108) he is open-minded about the particular account of the evidential relation he gives here.

As a belief, to be knowledge, must track the truth, so if something e is to be evidence for a hypothesis h it must track h. This gives two conditions parallel to Adherence and Variation respectively: Were h, then e, and: Were not-h, then not-e. This gives what Nozick calls strong evidence. In fact he says that, given e and that e is strong evidence for h, we can "deduce" h, and "the truth of the hypothesis (logically) follows" (*PE*: 249). This seems excessive. If h *logically* follows, one would think that e is not just strong but conclusive evidence – or indeed not really *evidence* at all but a verification of h. The tracking relation demands that e holds in close worlds where h holds, and fails to hold in close worlds where h fails to hold. But if we are confronted with e, might it not be, as far as logic goes, that we are in a distant world where not-h holds?

The second condition, that "Were not-h, then not-e", is needed because if "Were h, then e" and "Were not-h, then e" are both true, then e is simply a standing background condition, and not evidence either way. But Nozick does allow a weakening of this condition, from "Were not-h, then not-e" to "Not-(were not-h, then e)". When this occurs *e* is weak evidence for *h*. (He points out at *PE*: 695 n.77 that in the case of knowledge the analogous weakening of Variation could not be allowed. There is no such thing as "weak knowledge", for knowledge is not indeed entirely analogous to evidence, but is an all-or-nothing notion, while evidence allows of degrees. Actually Nozick does later (*PE*: 259) allow something called "almost- knowledge", which occurs when truth is replaced by very high probability. But the very fact that he introduces a technical term shows that it is at best a marginal case; note the hyphen, which remains in the verb, "almost-knows".)

Strangely, Nozick does not allow any weakening of the first condition ("Were *h*, then *e*"), or only a minimal one (*PE*: 253). One might think *e* could still be evidence for *h* even if *h* could occur without it. Footprints on the flowerbed can surely be evidence that the burglar entered by the window, even though a careful burglar would have erased them before entering. In fact this brings out a feature of the account that perhaps Nozick would not mind, given the price he was willing to pay for introducing Nonclosure in his treatment of knowledge. On Nozick's account the footprints will not be evidence that the burglar entered by the window, for he might have done so without leaving them, but they will be evidence (we may assume) that he both entered by the window and was a careless burglar. In other words, it will be evidence for a conjunction without being evidence for one of its conjuncts. To be fair, however, a similar feature affects other notions in this area. Take an American election where one party is doing very badly and may well win no states at all, although their best hope of winning is in a certain small state. Now suppose some of its supporters move from that state to a larger state. Their move will slightly increase the party's chances of winning the large state, but decrease more strongly its chances of winning the small state, its only real hope. Winning the large state would entail winning at least one state, but the overall effect of the move is to increase the chances of the party winning the large state, but decrease its chances of doing something entailed by that, namely winning at least one state. (Cf. Foley on confirmation in Luper-Foy 1987a: 135–6 n.9.)

There seems perhaps to be something strangely back-to-front about this whole approach to evidence. What we want to know is whether, given the evidence, we can infer the hypothesis. Why should we have to approach it indirectly by asking whether, given the hypothesis, we could infer the evidence? Sometimes that might be a useful strategy, but why should it be written into the very specification of what evidence is? The conditional we seem to need is "Were *e*, then *h*" rather than "Were *h*, then *e*". Do we also need "Were not-*e*, then not-*h*", to parallel Nozick's "Were not-*h*, then not-*e*"? It is not clear that we do. As we have just seen, the burglar might have entered by the window even in the absence of footprints, had he been careful. How about the weaker form, "Not- (were not-*e*, then *h*)"? If this is false, while "Were *e* then *h*" is true, then *h* will hold regardless of *e*. In that case *e* will be irrelevant to *h*, and so hardly evidence for it, any more than, say, my being at home is evidence that France is a republic, which it is even when I'm not at home (but see next paragraph). Suppose we are interested in *h*, that *e* is easier to verify than *h*, and that we believe (perhaps because someone has told us) that were *e*, then *h*. Then it might be worth verifying *e* in order to infer *h*. We need not worry about whether *e* has any real connection with *h* – it is evidence *for us*, since it gives us a way onto verifying *h*. But *e* need not be evidence in Nozick's objective sense. For it to be that, we need not just "Were *e*, then *h*" but at least "Not-(were not-*e*, then *h*)". We may not need the strong "Were not-*e*, then not-*h*", for the footprints surely are, or at least may be (unless they were left by the gardener), evidence that the burglar entered by the window, even though he could have erased them. If, unknown to us, the gardener left them, they will not be objective evidence, but may still be evidence *for us*, until we find who did leave them.

But there are complications. Suppose I had eggs for breakfast today. Is that evidence that the sun rose today? Had I not had eggs it would still have risen, but had it not risen I would not have had eggs or anything else (the earth's ceasing to rotate would surely have killed me). This seems to return us towards Nozick's view, but not all the way, for in close worlds where the sun did rise I do not always have eggs, but maybe tomatoes etc. What this suggests is that it would be an oversimplification simply to reverse Nozick's direction of tracking, whatever account of evidence we may ultimately want to give.

However, the idea that Nozick's tracking here goes in the wrong direction is defended at length by Foley (1987). Nozick develops his view by introducing probability and remarking that "Were *h*, then *e*" can be represented by saying that the probability of *e*, given *h*, is one (or very high: *PE*: 253), while "Were not-*h*, then not-*e*" says that the probability of *e*, given not-*h*, is (nearly) zero. He then introduces a notion of support, where "[t]he support of *e* for *h* is the difference between the probability of *e* given *h* and the probability of *e* given

not-*h*" (*PE*: 252). The degree of support *e* gives *h* can vary between
plus one and minus one, figures below zero representing negative
support, where *e* supports not-*h* rather than *h*. Foley points out that
as so defined *e* can give strong support to *h* without being even weak
evidence for it, because even weak evidence only occurs when the
probability of *e*, given *h*, is (almost) one, which it need not be in cases
of support. Foley goes on (Luper-Foy 1987a: 123–5) to give an example of a lie-detector that never reads "guilty" for an innocent subject,
but only very rarely reads "guilty" anyway, even for a guilty subject.
Although a "guilty" reading invariably indicates guilt, such a reading
gives only very weak support for thinking the person guilty, since the
support will be a very low probability (that of a "guilty" reading if the
person is guilty) minus a zero probability (that of a guilty reading if
the person is innocent). It will also, for Nozick, be no evidence at all,
not even weak, since the former probability is very far from one.

Foley then goes on to invert the order of Nozick's tracking, as said
above, and claims that this resolves the puzzles for Nozick that he
has introduced.

"The evidential connection is a subjunctive one, a real factual
relationship which holds in the world" (*PE*: 261). Two features of this
are pointed up by the words "real" and "factual". Whether something
is evidence is objective and not a matter of our situation, knowledge,
intelligence, etc., but it is also not a matter of logic but of the actual
contingent nature of the world. What is evidence for something in
this world, need not be so in other possible worlds – despite the fact
that in tracking we take account of other possible worlds, albeit if
only of relatively close worlds.

Foley's inversion of the tracking relation is similarly a "real
factual relation" (Luper-Foy 1987a: 131), but he sees a problem about
its being real, i.e. objective, when we try to connect it to rationality
(Luper-Foy 1987a: 133–4). The problem is that we cannot, as we
would like to, call people rational just so far as they base their beliefs
on evidence, for they may be so placed that however rational they are
they have not got access to this evidence relation in a particular case,
just as they may not have access to ordinary facts. Foley attributes
the problem to the evidence relation being objective, but it surely
depends really on its being empirical and contingent; a rational
person *qua* rational ought to have access to logical facts and
relations. Anyway this is clearly a problem for Foley as much as for
Nozick, and he solves it by introducing a "nonobjective" notion of
evidence whereby for S *p* counts as good evidence for *q* just in case "S

would regard p as good objective evidence for q were he to be carefully reflective". He adds an alternative "social" conception that we can ignore.

This sounds like the distinction I made earlier between objective evidence and evidence "for us", which goes back in spirit if not in letter to Aristotle. But Foley's way of making it, in terms of what S would do if he were "carefully reflective", may not be enough. S after all may be rather stupid, however careful, and we should surely demand that his reflectiveness obey canons of the type which *are* accessible to people *qua* rational. It is well to remember, though, that there are various notions in this area (cf. again Foley's note in Luper-Foy 1987a: 135–6).

Paxson too (1987) criticizes Nozick on evidence, although somewhat less radically than Foley since he keeps Nozick's order of tracking. He constructs examples to show that Nozick's first condition ("Were h, then e") is too strong and his second condition ("Not-(were not-h, then e") is too weak. Taking advantage of Nozick's alternative account in terms of probabilities, he suggests that e is evidence for h when the probability of e, given h, exceeds that of e, given not-h, or equivalently (he proves this equivalence in a technical appendix) when e increases the initial probability of h. This he thinks is adequate, in that it overcomes the objections he has raised, but trivial, apparently because of Foley's objection, which we discussed two paragraphs ago, about the externalist nature of an objective view of evidence in Nozick's sense, and because of the danger of ignoring the need for rationality.

Much of the rest of Nozick's chapter consists of a 12-page discussion of whether there can be evidence for the evidential relation itself (*PE*: 268–80), a discussion he claims is independent of the preceding discussions of knowledge and evidence (and which is omitted in the reprint of this chapter in Luper-Foy 1987a, as is also the final subsection, *PE*: 283–8). The details are somewhat complex and intricate, but suppose someone asks whether we ever have effective evidence for something, i.e. whether there are any cases where something is true, stands in the evidential relation to something else, and thereby shows that this something else has a certain desirable feature (truth, probable truth, etc.). Call the statement that we do S (cf. *PE*: 273). Then can there be such evidence for S without making us ask about the evidence for there being such evidence, and so leading to a regress?

The evidential relation is contingent for Nozick and our access to it empirical. He does not claim to show that the regress *can* be halted, but only to show what *would* halt it, and the nub of his answer is (*PE*: 276): "The regress can be brought to a halt if there is reached some evidence which is evidence for two contingent statements: a particular statement, and also the statement that this evidence stands in [the evidential relation] to that particular statement". He does not attempt to show us what such evidence might look like, let alone to provide it. What he does do is show that such evidence, if it exists, will be a case of self-subsumption, which he discussed at length in the previous chapter, and which we will meet again later. Although the evidential relation is contingent, he compares this regress to that concerning deductive reasoning introduced by Lewis Carroll, and gives the same answer for it; however, one might wonder how far these cases really are parallel, since Carroll's problem is plainly a priori and to be solved by a priori methods, which are accessible to reason. He also claims that the same approach can be applied to the traditional problem of induction, a reasonable enough claim if it can be applied at all. Finally he makes a point in favour of his own externalist approach by saying that on it we can have knowledge or evidence without knowing or having evidence that we do so (*PE*: 280), so that we do not have to solve the above problems before getting on with our ordinary business; for the internalist, on the other hand, "we know each and every precondition of our knowing – whenever we know we also know that we know, and so on" (*PE*: 281), so that unless we get this second-order knowledge we cannot know anything at all.

The final subsection of the chapter (especially *PE*: 283–6) offers an evolutionary account of why we need knowledge as well as true belief, but we will see more about Nozick's appeal to evolution in our own next chapter.

Summary

Nozick's analysis of knowledge, although anticipated by Dretske, has been by far the most widely praised and influential of his later writings. After distinguishing internalism from externalism (including reliabilism) we found that Nozick is primarily an externalist (with occasional touches of internalism). His basic idea (developed from one he originally thought of in treating action) is that to know is to track the truth, i.e. roughly, to believe it, to have not believed it had it been false (Variation), and to still believe it were it true in somewhat changed circumstances (Adherence). Variation and

Adherence vary in relative importance, but in either case a reference to the method underlying the belief is often essential (although he has been criticized for vagueness in distinguishing methods).

The notion of tracking presupposes counterfactuals, which lead to problems about their nature and about the use made of them. They differ in closeness or similarity, but criteria for degrees of these are problematic. Critics have pointed out that they cannot explain counterfactuals without circularity (so that Nozick says they merely "represent" them), and *why* their closeness or similarity should be relevant is unclear. Nozick does, however, reject Lewis's strong modal realism, and seems to regard himself generally as following Dretske's "relevant alternatives" approach.

Scepticism is the bugbear of epistemology, and leads some, like Descartes, to foundationalism, the view that to know anything at all we must know something for absolutely certain. Following his new philosophical approach Nozick seeks not to refute but to disarm scepticism, represented by the brain-in-a-vat (BIV) hypothesis. He introduces perhaps the most "startling" and "ingenious" (Fumerton) move of his whole philosophy by denying Closure, the principle that I cannot know p and that p entails q without knowing q. For Nozick, I can know I am at home, and that if I am at home I am not a BIV, without knowing I am not a BIV. This is because analyzing counterfactuals involves considering close possible worlds, and worlds close for the antecedent may not be close for the consequent. Nozick's startlingness lies in using this well known fact to disarm scepticism.

But this disarming comes at a price, notably that I can know a conjunction without knowing (as against believing) each conjunct. (Nozick claims incidentally that refinements of his theory will solve a puzzle of Kripke's.)

Critics of the tracking account have attacked it for being too weak, allowing cases of knowledge that are plainly not so, or too strong, excluding cases that plainly are. Necessary propositions cannot be false, and Nozick tries to dispense with Variation there, but examples have been found that make this difficult, while other critics claim that tracking gives inconsistent results for different examples. Others try to modify tracking, or dispense with it and reinstate Closure, because Nozick only denied it because his theory required him to (although Nonclosure has its defenders). Shatz doubts the independence of the tracking account, thinking Nozick tailor-made it to suit sceptical conclusions he already held. Problems have also been seen in assessing the closeness of possible worlds, for how can one assign *any* probability to scepticism? Luper-Foy tries an amended version for tracking that raises again the internalism/externalism issue, and we discussed some further aspects of this, and how far Nozick is really a reliabilist. But despite these and many other criticisms, some of which we discussed, Nozick's tracking theory has had a major influence in epistemology, and indeed outside it.

Finally, Nozick treats evidence as partly, but only partly, analogous to knowledge. It is objective, factual (not logical) and involves tracking the target hypothesis, but has degrees and can be strong or weak. But Nozick ignores a subjective notion of evidence *for us*, and Foley, who thinks the tracking should go from hypothesis to evidence rather than vice versa, similarly introduces a "nonobjective" notion of evidence, and also distinguishes evidence from support. But Nozick on evidence has received far less attention than Nozick on knowledge. Nozick ends by using one of his favourite weapons, self-subsumption, to deal with a regress generated by asking whether there can be evidence for the evidential relation itself.

Chapter 6
Rationality

Introduction: rationality in general

Philosophical Explanations is a long book, and there is much in it that we have not discussed and must defer until later chapters, but the topics that fill Nozick's later book *The Nature of Rationality* are connected so closely in subject matter to the epistemology of *Philosophical Explanations* that it clearly makes sense to bring them in now. The two books are separated by a volume of essays, *The Examined Life*, that takes much further than *Philosophical Explanations* the informal style and new outlook on philosophy that we discussed in our first chapter. *The Nature of Rationality* refers back several times to items in this, but itself returns to a more rigorous style, and promises to be "awash in technical details" (*NR*: xiv), but not, the reader may note perhaps with relief, to anything like the extent of many contemporary philosophical articles.

While *Philosophical Explanations* in its third chapter was concerned with what knowledge is and what sort of things we can know, especially in relation to scepticism, *The Nature of Rationality* asks what strategies our thinking can adopt and how we should assess them, as well as seeking the historical origins of our present overall ways of thinking and the significance of those origins. It perhaps ties up most closely with *Philosophical Explanations'* discussion of evidence. We found that in *Philosophical Explanations* Nozick saw himself as primarily an externalist although with some internalist leanings. *The Nature of Rationality* does not discuss the issue in those terms, but it treats rationality as embodying the two elements on an equal level, since a rational belief involves "support by reasons that make the belief credible, and generation by a process that reliably produces true beliefs" (*NR*: xiv, expanded at *NR*: 64). Rationality does indeed seem to be a rather more internalist notion than knowledge, at least to this extent: when I ask whether you know something I may well be wondering whether I can use you as a source of information on something not accessible to me by other means (see Craig 1990), but whether you are rational is something I can at least in principle assess for myself without examining anything but you. That rationality produces reliable results seems to follow from its nature rather than constituting it.

But right at the start Nozick deals briefly (*NR*: xii–xiii) with a challenge to the whole notion of rationality: perhaps rationality as such is biased by being "class-based or male or Western" etc. After pointing out that if bias is ineliminable, being subject to it can hardly be criticized, he insists that charges of bias must be supported by rational argument, and so would themselves be in the dock, and that more seriously the accuser must specify just what bias exists and where. Later (*NR*: 100–106) he gives a useful discussion of the nature and effects, not always very obvious, of different kinds of bias, and ends by returning to whether rationality itself is biased, in particular by excluding emotion and spontaneity. He points out reasonably enough that reason need not always prescribe its own use. It may often be justified in taking a holiday, although under its own watchful eye at the second level, as it were. Second-order reason can consistently tell us to abandon first-order calculations in favour of spontaneity when dealing with friends, for instance.

Here rationality has been split into two levels or orders of which one can be used to justify the use or non-use of the other. But what if the challenge is directed at reason as a whole? How can rationality or reason justify itself, without circularity or a never-ending regress of levels? This is a big question, but let me here just appeal to Nozick's remark in the last paragraph above that if bias is ineliminable we cannot be criticized for being biased. If we cannot avoid using reason then we cannot be accused of irrationality (and of what else could we be accused in this context?) in continuing to use it. This sort of argument, known since its use in Kant as a transcendental argument, derives ultimately from Aristotle and is probably the best we can do in this area. But with this sketch of an approach let us return to the course of *The Nature of Rationality*.

In the program and summary (*NR*: xiv) Nozick proposes to cover and contribute to two main areas: rationality of decision and of belief.

He offers a new proposal for decision theory, which emerges in part from a discussion of two by now traditional problems – Newcomb's Problem and the Prisoner's Dilemma (see below) – but also from an idea we have met before, symbolic utility. On the rationality of belief he insists on the need to cater for both theoretical and practical considerations, and indeed the book as a whole is as much concerned with practical as with theoretical reason. The search for the historical origins of rationality leads him to a substantial and controversial discussion of the role of evolution, and then the final chapter asks whether, as is often thought, rationality is confined to the instrumental or can also prescribe goals for us, and it also offers some heuristic suggestions.

Principles and their uses

One of the main things we associate with reason is acting on principle. This is particularly so in ethics, although that has led to quite a bit of controversy in recent years. We often ask "What would happen if everyone did that?", and Kant famously insisted that a moral act, or more strictly a moral maxim, was one we could consistently will that everyone should act on in the relevant circumstances. This general idea has been a prominent feature of modern ethics, despite an opposite line of thought as well, associated with existentialists among others, which says that real-life moral situations are too complex and subtle to be straitjacketed within principles; each situation is unique and must be treated as such.

The Nature of Rationality does not discuss this directly and as such, but Nozick does touch on it in the first chapter, which opens by discussing the uses of principles and compares legal, scientific and ethical ones. He points out that scientific laws are always underdetermined by their instances, partly at least (although not wholly, if Quine is right: *NR*: 7 and 183 n.7) because these are finite – the "curve-fitting problem", that if you represent data by points on a graph there are in theory infinitely many curves that can connect the points, each curve representing a "law"; other criteria, like simplicity or explanatory power, must be used to decide between them. Nozick simply raises the question, "Are correct ethical principles uniquely determined by the totality of correct judgements about particular cases, actual and hypothetical, or does underdetermination reign here?" (*NR*: 7) He does not discuss it further, but it is a point *against* the usefulness of principles that casuistry has got a bad name because of its apparent readiness to provide a principle to cover practically any course of action in the interests of some point of view, be it personal or ideological.

Much of what Nozick says about the use of principles in general intellectual (scientific, legal, etc.) contexts and in interpersonal relations is useful and uncontroversial. He also discusses their use for persons themselves, which he thinks is presupposed by their interpersonal uses (*NR*: 12). Obviously consistency of character is useful to the individual, and among other things may give one's life greater organic unity, which for Nozick may be valuable in itself and superior to the mere avoidance of inconsistency that one might achieve by simply having no principles at all – at least, so Nozick assumes (*NR*: 13), although one might wonder whether the refusal to have principles was not itself a (second-order) principle, and whether the complete avoidance of principles is any more possible than the complete rejection of reason we touched on earlier; but Nozick's remark is only en passant.

An obvious use of principles in people's lives is to help them overcome temptations. But why overcome them? Leaving aside temptations to immoral actions etc., the answer is presumably that we shall gain greater good for ourselves by doing so, and we prefer a greater total of good to a lesser one. But why in that case do we feel tempted in the first place? At least one main reason is what has been called time preference or discounting the future: we prefer present goods to future ones, other things being equal, but the problem arises because we tend to do so even when the present or near good is less than the more distant one. Can it ever be rational to prefer a lesser good to a greater merely because of the time when it is due to occur? Nozick follows a psychologist, Ainslie, in representing our attitudes by a graph involving two intersecting hyperbolic curves. That detail (for which see *NR*: 15, with 185 n.19) need not delay us, but the point is this. Suppose we must choose between an earlier but lesser good X and a later but greater good Y. The period between now and the time for Y can be divided into three consecutive periods that we can call (following Nozick's diagram) A, B and C, and in which we may well feel as follows. During A both X and Y are fairly distant and we prefer Y. (A may be of zero length, but ignore that.) During B, which ends at the time for X, X looms large and we prefer it. During C, the period between the times for X and Y, we prefer Y as being greater, whether or not it is still available.

Why is it rational, or as Nozick puts it "appropriate" (*NR*: 16), to follow our preference for Y and resist that for X? First we should dismiss, as Nozick in effect does (*NR*: 14–15), appeal to the idea that Y is less certain than X because more distant and so more likely to be forestalled by outside causes, or even lose its value because our preferences change. This is no doubt often true. Many young people probably prefer a cancer-free old age to the mild pleasures of smoking, but go on smoking because they may die of something else before cancer hits them, or a cure may be found by then. But this is still something of a red herring, and in many cases such probability considerations are relevant only marginally if at all. Nozick suggests that "often" what makes resisting temptation the "preferred" (*NR*: 16; I presume he means "preferable") option is that it is preferred over a longer period (A + C, and presumably after C), and so is a stable preference, while X is only preferred during the unrepresentative period B. He adds in brackets that if B is longer than A + C (and we ignore times after C) perhaps the temptation to take X should *not* be resisted.

Perhaps we could develop this a bit, although Nozick doesn't, by taking account of the amount by which the attractiveness of Y exceeds that of X, as well as the durations for which they are respectively preferred. Then we might think it rational to choose X only if X times B is greater than Y times A + C. Suppose that if offered an immediate choice I would always prefer visiting India to visiting China (they cost the same and I can't afford both), although only by a modest amount, but that I know that the only chance to visit China will come before the only chance to visit India, which will only come when I have not long to live, so that I spend a long time preferring the China visit because it is nearer and more vivid. Then perhaps I may rationally choose the China visit. A complication, however, is that the pleasure of anticipating the China visit during period B might itself need to be added to the total, and so distort the original comparison.

Another question involving time, which Nozick does not discuss here, is why, when having to undergo two experiences, one good and one bad, we usually prefer, as I think we do, to have the bad one first, and whether it is rational to do so. In a way this goes against what we have just said: perhaps if the good one loomed near we would grab it. Anyway we must discount not only the probability argument (the later one might never happen) but also the fear that might spoil the good one were the bad one to follow. Would we – should we – mind about the order if we knew that during each we would neither anticipate nor remember the other?

But be that as it may, it is to deal with resisting temptation that Nozick brings in acting on principle here. The point is to link the action you are trying to persuade yourself to do (resisting the temptation) to a whole class of similar actions so that your present action stands for or symbolizes all such actions, and if you fail on this action you see yourself as failing on the whole class – a much higher psychological penalty to pay. You will see yourself as not only more likely to succumb to future temptations but also as a weak-willed person, a blow to your self-image. But if you cannot resist the temptation how can you manage to adopt the principle? Well, you might have already adopted it in calmer times, or you might as it were *find* yourself adopting it as it simply occurs to you that your present action belongs to the class in question.

An issue arising here is that of the relevance of sunk costs, resources already irrecoverably spent on one option; we must be careful here though – if in my holiday example I have spent much time learning Hindi, this is not just a sunk cost, wasted if I go to China, but will affect the options themselves by making a visit to India more enjoyable. There are two cases here. In one, reflection on sunk costs spent on option Y may help to tide me over the temptation during period B to choose X. In the other, they may affect me when I am genuinely re-evaluating X and Y, or perhaps considering a new alternative, Z. Nozick does not explicitly distinguish the cases, but treats them together. Economists tell us to ignore sunk costs, since we can do nothing about them, but this, he says, may be correct for maximizing monetary profits, but not as a general policy. We clearly cannot ignore our commitments to others, and ignoring those to ourselves may make it harder for us to rely on our own future consistency and reliability, as well as depriving us of an aid in resisting temptation as explained above. But how far sunk costs are really involved here has been disputed (Steele 1996).

A case Nozick does not mention is that of sunk costs incurred by others and to be honoured by others. It is sometimes argued that to make peace with the enemy would be to ignore the sacrifices made by our soldiers so far. This raises the question: is it rational or justifiable to send further soldiers into battle to honour these sunk costs?

There is another topic here which Nozick does not discuss, but which has been discussed by others. Questions about how desirable it is to resist temptations, and about whether it matters which order our experiences come in, are questions about whether it is rational to treat all parts of our life equally. It seems plausible, if no more, to say yes. But can we extend the argument and say that it is rational, and not merely moral, to treat ourselves and others equally? Is selfishness irrational as well as immoral? The question is not whether selfishness is likely to be self-defeating in practice, as it probably is, nor even whether impartial reason tells me that I am no more important than anyone else, as it no doubt does, but whether privileging myself over others can be shown to be irrational in the same sort of way that it is (it seems plausible to say) to privilege one part of my life, such as the present, over other parts. One question arising here is whether impartiality is really an ethical notion at all rather than a logical one. (Some years ago an article was published with the unlovely title "The Trivializability of Universalizability".)

At this point Nozick introduces the discussion of symbolic utility which we saw something of in Chapter 4 and which will become relevant later, so let us defer it.

The last section of *The Nature of Rationality*'s first chapter has the title "Teleological Devices", and starts by telling us that: "Principles are transmission devices for probability and for utility" (*NR*: 35). Scientific principles "help you to discover the truth by transmitting evidential support or probability from some cases to others", while moral or prudential principles "help you to overcome temptation by transmitting utility from some actions to others" (ibid.). Later Nozick adds that principles may "deepen and unify and make explicit our understanding of what the principles concern" (*NR*: 38).

What we might note here is a possible difference, not in content perhaps but in attitude, between this and *Anarchy, State, and Utopia*. Correct moral principles are still truths, and perhaps even truths inaccessible to us, since it is an empirical matter whether we can best realize them by acting on "the principles we are able to formulate and follow", which may be "far from" the correct ones (*NR*: 39). (Nozick does not expand this surely rather strange claim: how to achieve a known result may be an empirical question, but how can which moral principles are correct be so? If he has in mind, as Hailwood has suggested, "basic moral characteristics" (cf. *PE*: 451), identifying whether a creature has such a characteristic may be empirical, but deciding that it *is* such a characteristic, and so morally relevant, is surely not.) But one can hardly imagine *Anarchy, State, and Utopia*, with its emphasis on side constraints, treating moral principles, at least, as "teleological devices" or talking about their "functions" in the way Nozick does here. I call this a possible difference in attitude rather than content because Nozick ends the

chapter rather ambiguously. He remarks that even for Kant principles have a function, but adds that for Kant they are also "an expression of our rational nature, constitutive of rationality" (*NR*: 40). He
appears to endorse this himself and uses it to introduce the rest of the
book by switching the topic from principles to rationality itself, which
he will eventually argue (in the final chapter) is not solely teleological
or instrumental. Hailwood in fact suggests (cf. Hailwood 1996: 54, 65)
that the constraints of *Anarchy, State, and Utopia* may have had the
"function" that respect for them is necessary for a meaningful, self-
shaping, life (although he goes on to argue that they are not in fact
necessary for this). There may be some truth in this, and Nozick (*NR*:
40) talks of the utility for us of moral principles as lying in what they
symbolize and express rather than in what they lead to.

Practical rationality in the dissertation

The Nature of Rationality is Nozick's last main book so far, but
rationality was the subject of his first philosophical writing, his
Ph.D. dissertation on "The Normative Theory of Individual Choice",
eventually published in (not very legible) typescript form in 1990.
Much of this consists of technical discussions of decision theory and
game theory that will not concern us, although we shall meet his
later treatment of one or two issues soon. (Game theory is the
theory of decisions taken against a rational opponent.) But *The
Normative Theory of Individual Choice* (*NTIC*) begins with some
general questions about rational action and preference. In general
an action is rational if it is likely to lead to its intended end, but it
must not have too many bad side effects nor get in the way of an
alternative action which would be even better for reaching the end
and would have no worse side effects, nor must it have unduly bad
effects if it fails to achieve the end. Presumably, but Nozick doesn't
say so, we should also consider the initial costs of the action, unless
these are to be subsumed under side effects – although they are
hardly *effects*.

One thing Nozick does say, which will become relevant when we
discuss belief and acceptance, is that "[t]hough [action] A is not
believed likely to achieve what would be intended in doing it, it might
be believed to be more likely to achieve it than any other action available, each of which yields bad consequences, and would be the
rational thing to do" (*NTIC*: 7).

A further point Nozick makes is that the action should not preclude some other action that would achieve another end which the agent would prefer to the original end. Here he leaves the point at that (*NTIC*: 7–8), but it foreshadows the last chapter of *The Nature of Rationality*, which asks whether rationality can go beyond the instrumental.

This point also raises a question about symbolic utility, a notion of course that Nozick did not envisage for many years to come. Presumably, as I claimed earlier, insulting my employer to get at my father is irrational: it may block the promotion I desire. But suppose I prefer insulting my father to getting the promotion; this preference will presumably be unconscious, if it is to lead me to insult my employer – but it is not clear how conscious and unconscious preferences are to be compared. Perhaps we should demand that to be rational the preference must be in equilibrium, in the sense that it "withstands knowledge of its own causes" (*PE*: 349), as Nozick (*NR*: 31–2) seems to suggest. At any rate the question arises of comparing symbolic and causal utility, which Nozick does not discuss until *The Nature of Rationality*.

Decision theory normally distinguishes three relevant situations, involving certainty, risk and uncertainty; as we saw earlier, the difference between the last two is that with risk we assume the alternatives facing us have definite probabilities, as with tossing dice, while with uncertainty we are in the dark, except for assuming we know what the alternatives are. Nozick points out that this classification is not watertight. Not only can certainty (so far indeed as this exists: *NTIC*: 11) be a special case of risk, where the probabilities are one and zero, but risk can be seen as certainty that the probabilities are what they are. But his main point here is different. In logic the propositional calculus treats propositions as either identical or distinct, without analyzing them further. But for the predicate calculus they can be distinct without being independent; they are treated at a deeper level. "Butter is yellow" and "Something is yellow" are distinct but the former entails the latter. Rather similarly Nozick wants to treat decision and choice as applying not to different situations, of certainty, risk or uncertainty, but to the same situations treated at different levels of structural description, namely of risk, certainty and uncertainty (*NTIC*: 20–21). A simple example of the levels (mine, not Nozick's) might be this: If I enter this lottery I shall certainly spend a pound on the ticket; I shall have a one per cent chance of winning the mystery prize; and there is some chance, but I am uncertain what, that I shall enjoy it if I do.

Before going on to the technical developments mentioned above Nozick adds a chapter, which is perfectly accessible, on preference and indifference. What we prefer, he thinks, is not objects (for our attitude to these will depend on circumstances and what we want them for), nor states of affairs (for we may view these differently according to how they are described), but that certain statements be true. He rejects behaviouristic accounts of preferring in terms of how we act, or the proportion of cases in which we would choose one way rather then another, and offers a tentative account in terms of what we would be willing or unwilling to do in certain circumstances. But interesting and subtly developed though the chapter is, it would take us too far afield to discuss it in detail.

Decision theory I: the first two discussions

Much of recent decision theory has been dominated by two special problems called Newcomb's Problem and the Prisoner's Dilemma. The Prisoner's Dilemma was introduced first, in or before 1957, but Nozick is particularly associated with Newcomb's Problem, which he introduced to the public in 1969, with the permission of its inventor, an American physicist called William Newcomb, so let us concentrate on that.

Imagine being presented by some being, perhaps "a graduate student from another planet, checking a theory of terrestrial psychology" (*SP*: 74), with two boxes, one transparent and containing £1,000 and the other opaque. You can take either the opaque box alone or both boxes, but you are told that the being is predicting your choice, and if he predicts you will take only the opaque box he puts £1,000,000 in it, but otherwise (including the case where you randomize your choice) nothing. You know from previous occasions that he is extremely reliable; all or virtually all one-boxers have ended up rich, and all or virtually all two-boxers have received a mere £1,000. The predictor knows that you know all this, and you know that he knows it, and so on. What should you do?

There have been two general approaches, corresponding to the two options. Perhaps the most obvious goes like this: The predictor has already put the money in, or not, so whichever he has done you will do better to take both boxes, getting either £1,001,000 or £1,000, while if you take only the one you will get £1,000,000 or nothing. Taking both boxes is therefore said to "dominate" taking only the one. This seems pretty compelling – until one realizes that it ignores the evidence of the predictor's previous successes. As one commentator puts it (Hurley 1994: 65) "Well, if you're so clever, why aren't you rich", like the one-boxers? (Hurley evidently assumes the chooser has chosen previously too.) The situation envisaged may seem spooky but it is not incoherent. Where incoherence *would* loom, at least, would be if it were claimed that the predictor *knew* how you would choose. That would raise the problem that troubled the followers of Milton's Satan about "fixed fate, free will, foreknowledge absolute" (*Paradise Lost* 2.560), for the predictor could never take into account *all* the estimates you might make about his own predictions, including this one itself. (This may be relevant to the discussion of certainty at *SP*: 71–2.)

Nozick has three discussions of Newcomb's Problem, in *The Normative Theory of Individual Choice*, *Socratic Puzzles* and *The Nature of Rationality*. His first discussion, in *The Normative Theory of Individual Choice*, comes towards the end of a complex and difficult discussion, in Chapter 5, of the work of Savage on decision theory in general. (At that time, 1963, Nozick had only just come across Newcomb's Problem.) The account is far too complex to expound in detail, but the general idea is this. He first develops the two approaches of the last paragraph. This involves the notion of probabilistic independence: does my choice affect the probabilities of the states between which I am choosing? Is the probability that the opaque box contains £1,000,000 affected by whether I choose it? He then suggests that if, but only if, the states in question are probabilistically independent of the choices made I should do the dominant action (if one is available). Otherwise I should go by the expected utility of the outcomes, where an outcome's expected utility is the product of its utility, should it occur, and the probability that it will occur if the agent so acts (*NTIC*: 230, 236, 262; cf. also *SP*: 55). (According to *SP*: 346 n.4 and 349 n.20, Jeffrey (1965), i.e. two years after Nozick's dissertation, also distinguished the two approaches, but recommended always following expected utility . Incidentally I am omitting a complication that occupies Nozick for several pages and which arises because he claims that, except when the states have the same probability as each other, the situation can always be described in two different ways, in one of which the states are probabilistically independent of the choices made while in the other they are not: see *NTIC*: 225–30 and *SP*: 50–52.)

In the case of Newcomb's Problem if we go by the evidence from previous trials we find that the states of the boxes are not probabilistically independent of the choices made, and so Nozick's principle tells us to adopt the expected utility argument rather than the dominance argument, and so to be one-boxers. Actually Nozick feels more confident about this in the case of two other examples he uses, one involving a horse race, which dispenses with the predictor's free will (*NTIC*: 227–8), and one involving a rigged roulette wheel, where there is a clear causal link between the choice made and the state of the wheel. With Newcomb's Problem he is impressed by the force of the dominance argument, but declares himself unconvinced by it, although he cannot yet answer it (*NTIC*: 233).

The 1969 article in which Nozick introduced Newcomb's Problem to the public was reprinted in *Socratic Puzzles*, along with his comments from 1974 on the 650 plus pages of letters written to *Scientific American* when it featured the problem in 1973, none of which satisfied him as a solution (a verdict *NR*: 43 extends to everything so far published). This was his second attempt on the problem (*The Normative Theory of Individual Choice* of course was not published until 1990).

The exposition of the problem here is the same as in *The Normative Theory of Individual Choice*, but Nozick now takes much more seriously the misgivings just referred to. He now thinks the dominance argument is indeed the right approach for Newcomb's Problem, but is left with the question why one is so tempted to apply the expected utility argument. The reason for his change of view is that he now realizes that probabilistic dependence or independence is not the central issue. What matters is rather causal influence, a notion he had already appealed to in *The Normative Theory of Individual Choice* (e.g. *NTIC*: 233), but without sufficiently distinguishing it from probabilistic dependence. That the notions are distinct can be seen from cases where two events are probabilistically linked because they have a common cause, without either of them causally influencing the other. Hurley (1994: 67) in her critical discussion gives an example (beloved of tobacco manufacturers) whereby a gene might cause both a desire to smoke and a predisposition to cancer. If such a gene exists it will plainly be irrational to try to avoid cancer by resisting one's desire to smoke; if one has the desire, and so the gene, one is in line for cancer anyway . Later Nozick points out (*NR*: 188 n.2), following Gibbard and Harper (in Campbell & Sowden 1985: 146) that there can also be causal influence without probabilistic dependence, which gives a fourth row to the matrix in *Socratic Puzzles* (*SP*: 63). This is because one feature, *A*, could causally affect another, *B*, while being associated with a third feature, *C*, whose *absence* also causally affects *B*.

Nozick himself gives similar examples to Hurley's, emphasizing that when considering probabilistic links we should take account of which way the explanation goes, if it does: low barometer readings are correlated with depressions (my example), but it is the depression that explains the reading, not vice versa. He adds that what matters is not so much whether the state (e.g. of the opaque box) is already fixed, but whether our choice can "*influence* or *affect*" it (*SP*: 63, with a rather coy footnote on these terms at *SP*: 350 n.20), because the predictor could start a process that only ended after our choosing, or could make his prediction after, although in ignorance of, our choosing. This however, is really only a point about the appositeness of "already" rather than of "fixed".

So why is one tempted to give the expected utility answer to Newcomb's Problem? Nozick warns us not to confuse two questions: What distinguishes Newcomb's Problem from cases where the expected utility answer is right? And what distinguishes it from cases where that answer is wrong but *clearly* wrong? Plainly these questions cannot have the same answer. Actually, Nozick (*NTIC*: 230) was in some danger of ignoring this advice by introducing the roulette example as a "clear" one, but later (*SP*: 54) it has become just "another" example. Newcomb's Problem, he suggests, involves an *illusion* of influence, because although the explanation of what is in the opaque box does not refer directly to our choice, it does in a way refer to it indirectly by referring to the predictor's beliefs about it. He compares explaining an action not by its result but by a pre-existing desire for that result – but then adds that cannot be the whole story, as we are not tempted to give the wrong answer in the desire case. The rest of the story, he thinks (*SP*: 68–9) may be that "by the conditions of the problem" the predictor will almost certainly be right, which leads us to gloss over the difference between the predictor's believing something and its being true. We will return to this point shortly.

If the predictor were only, say, 60% likely to be right, the expected utility of taking only the one box would be greater than that of taking both, Nozick argues (*SP*: 70–71), yet surely we would then all take both, so that expected utility cannot be what tempts us in the original case to take only the one. This may be right, but what it seems to show is that expected utility is not a kind of utility but a sort of amalgam of utility and expectation. Also on Nozick's own view we are influenced by an illusion, so why should we not be influenced too by failing to make the mathematical calculations he himself makes?

Decision theory II: the third discussion

The Nature of Rationality gives us Nozick's third and so far final attempt on Newcomb's Problem. *The Normative Theory of Individual Choice* had with reservations favoured expected utility, and *Socratic Puzzles* came out clearly for dominance, but now he wavers and proposes a new line: combining both approaches, each being given a certain weighting, in a new notion he calls decision-value – although Lowe (1995: 398) suspects this may be no more than a "temporary compromise".

Gibbard and Harper distinguish two kinds of expected utility, based roughly on what the action in question would be likely to cause and what its commission would be evidence of (in Campbell & Sowden 1985: 137, 143–4). They think the former kind is more properly called "utility" than the latter (145), and indeed the latter, which does often seem to underlie the position of one-boxers, may be helped by a certain confusion. Suppose I say, "*X* would be the courageous act, so let me do it": am I trying to *show* that I am *already* courageous (perhaps to bolster my self-esteem), or am I trying to *become* courageous? Perhaps both of these have some utility, but they are very different.

At any rate Gibbard and Harper go on to say: "Nozick treats [Newcomb's Problem in *Socratic Puzzles*] as a conflict between the principle of expected utility maximization and the principle of dominance. On the view we have propounded in this paper, the problem is rather a conflict between two kinds of expected utility maximization" (Campbell & Sowden 1985: 150; they also distinguish two corresponding versions of dominance (1985, 149), adding that Nozick endorses both but without distinguishing them (1985, 158 n.8)).

The Nature of Rationality accepts this, and Nozick now distinguishes causal and evidential expected utility, the combination of which (with another factor to be mentioned shortly) gives decision-value. The terms of Newcomb's Problem can of course be varied. Not only can the predictor's skill vary, as we have seen, but so can the contents of the boxes, and Nozick thinks that our intuitions may vary with the amount in the transparent box in particular. If it approaches the amount in (or not in) the opaque box one-boxers may think it worthwhile becoming two-boxers, while if it very small two-boxers may think it safer to become one-boxers. But here there is a certain ambivalence in Nozick's position. Does he think the two-boxers in this last case have an altered intuition? Or do they simply hesitate to rely too much on the intuitions they do have? It is one thing to confess modestly that one might be wrong, while continuing to hold one's view, and quite another to assign a positive value to an opposing view. Being modest *about* one's view is not the same as holding another view. If this is so, we may lack any reason yet to combine the approaches rather than choosing between them. Nozick insists that this is not so (*NR*: 45), but it is not clear why, nor how far he is concerned with people's actual intuitions or with what he thinks they should be. Different people may weight the two principles differently, yet these weights measure not their uncertainty but the "legitimate force" (*NR*: 45) of each principle. Who decides on this?

Christensen (1995), a two-boxer even if the transparent box were empty, praises Nozick in his review for raising the question, "what happens when we treat the choice of decision theory as a decision problem in itself?" (1995: 262), but rightly adds that "we must be careful to distinguish between the rationality of adopting a decision-policy . . . and the rationality of particular decisions made in accord with that policy" (1995: 262). It might be rational to become a one-boxer (because the predictor rewards one-boxers) without the one-boxer's choice being itself intrinsically rational. If threatened with execution unless one gave silly answers to questions it might be rational to give the silly answers – but they would still be silly. A rather similar point is made by Gibbard and Harper, who conclude that: "if someone is very good at predicting behaviour and rewards predicted irrationality richly, then irrationality will be richly rewarded" (Campbell & Sowden 1985: 151) (quoted by Nozick at *NR*: 57). Actually Nozick himself will later distinguish the rationality of what is believed from the rationality of believing it (see *NR*: 70), although this seems to go against a reliability analysis of rationality if that is "that rationality applies, in the first instance, to a process or procedure and, derivatively, to a particular inference, belief, or action as an instance of that procedure" (*NR* 66n.).

There is (*NR*: 47) some interesting discussion about the relations between the two principles (of causal and evidential utility) and whether they can recommend each other sometimes – a question reminiscent of Nozick's interest, seen especially in *Philosophical Explanations*, in "self-subsumption", or whether principles can apply

147

to or instantiate themselves. He treats the answer as empirical, depending on what the world is like. But there are limits to this appeal to what the world is like: can the question – is it rational to base one's actions on what the world is like? – itself depend on what the world is like?

The question why we have varying intuitions in different cases is discussed by Hurley (1994) who points out that the different answers Nozick gives in *Socratic Puzzles* (illusion of influence) and *The Nature of Rationality* (weighting of evidential principle) apply at best to different questions, whereas we need a unified account of both the variations discussed in *Socratic Puzzles* and those discussed in *The Nature of Rationality*. She suggests replacing evidentialist reasoning for this purpose by cooperative reasoning, where this involves the *collective* causal power of agents acting together to do what neither can do separately. The details are too complex to summarize, but the point is that we regard the predictor as like a parent who can benefit us if we cooperate.

An alternative explanation might be that we use induction, but instead of saying, "The predictor has previously been right about our actions, so he will continue to be so", which might make us realize we were treating our actions as events outside our control, we simply say, "One-boxers have been rich in the past, so they'll go on being so".

I promised above to return to Nozick's phrase "by the conditions of the problem" (at *SP*: 68). As philosophers we set the conditions of the problem by fiat, and give ourselves a God's-eye view. But if we were actually in a Newcomb situation, we would know that something odd was afoot – but what? Perhaps our choice does influence what is in the opaque box? (Have we not all been deceived sometimes by conjurors? Cf. Seabright 1993.) Perhaps backward causation does make sense (cf. *SP*: 80), or perhaps some hitherto unknown forward causal law is in play? As philosophers outside the situation we can exclude this by fiat, but not as agents inside it. I will make two comments on this suggestion. First, what if the far side of the opaque box is transparent and an observer or recording camera later confirms that nothing in it changed (cf. *SP*: 76–7)? This simply complicates the case: perhaps some strange law affects the observer's memory or the camera's working. Secondly, the present argument, however, would only apply to the full-blooded Newcomb's Problem or similar spooky cases and not to other versions, such as where the predictor is less successful, or related problems, like the Prisoner's Dilemma.

The Prisoner's Dilemma has many versions, but the general idea is this: Two prisoners, who cannot communicate but are, and assume each other to be, both rational and self-interested, are offered terms such that if both stay silent both will be better off than if both confess, but the best option for each is to confess while the other stays silent, and the worst option for each is to stay silent while the other confesses. What should such prisoners do?

Unlike Newcomb's Problem, the Prisoner's Dilemma is not at all spooky (except in idealized versions when total rationality and exact similarity of the participants is assumed) and has widespread applications, such as in superpower cold wars. It represents the general problem of securing cooperation when this is in the general interest but individuals can do better for themselves by defecting (cf. the "free-rider" problem). How it relates to Newcomb's Problem is disputed. Lewis (in Campbell & Sowden 1985: 251–5) thinks it is a form of Newcomb's Problem, although following articles criticize this, while Hurley (1994) claims that Newcomb's Problem is rather a form of the Prisoner's Dilemma. Nozick's main discussion of the Prisoner's Dilemma comes in *The Nature of Rationality*; however, *Socratic Puzzles* (especially 61–3) has a few remarks, and *The Normative Theory of Individual Choice* (272) has a passing reference, where he claims that, contrary to common belief, it does not belong to game theory (cf. *NTIC*: 269–73). He thinks the Prisoner's Dilemma at least "parallels" Newcomb's Problem (*NR*: 51), and treats them to a large extent in an analogous way, with confessing being analogous to being a two-boxer and staying silent analogous to being a one-boxer.

Decision theory III: symbolic utility again

I have discussed Newcomb's Problem at greater length than the Prisoner's Dilemma because despite the wider applicability of the latter, and its equal standing with the former in *The Nature of Rationality*, the former is particularly associated with Nozick and receives greater treatment from him overall. But one notion that appears in his treatment of both problems, as well as in that of principles, and perhaps has greater relevance for the Prisoner's Dilemma (because of its emphasis on cooperation) is symbolic utility, which of course we have already met in another context at the end of Chapter 4.

Nozick's most striking and controversial claim now is that we should add it as a separate item, with its own weighting, in the construction of decision-value, alongside causally and evidentially expected utility. Symbolic utility is not a different kind of utility, but a different kind of connection to ordinary utility (*NR*: 48).

In the case of acting on principle backsliding may be easier to avoid if one regards any breach as symbolizing a general rejection of the principle, and more generally regards any act of a certain kind as symbolizing a policy of that kind. In the Prisoner's Dilemma one may regard acting cooperatively as symbolizing the desirable characteristic of being a cooperative person, or doing the dominant action may symbolize "being rational, not being swayed by sentimentality" (*NR*: 57).

The reality of symbolic value is widely accepted, and Nozick has made a useful contribution by drawing attention to this, although Talbott (1995: 325–6) notes the heterogeneous nature of Nozick's examples of it and queries whether he has adequately distinguished rational from irrational cases of it. But the role Nozick gives it as a separate item in decision-value has been strongly criticized by Christensen (1995), who detects three reasons Nozick gives for his claim, all inadequate. One, that we give symbolic utility different weight in different choice situations, he thinks is not peculiar to symbolic utility. Another is that a partial chance (say a half) of realizing a goal need not have a symbolic utility with the same proportion (a half) of that of the goal itself; this he thinks is irrelevant and does not prove what Nozick wants. The third reason is that an act's symbolic utility may depend on its context and the alternative acts available; but this again is not peculiar to symbolic utility, and simply requires that acts be individuated sufficiently finely. Christensen also thinks that symbolic utility is not a *connection* to ordinary utility, since what is symbolized may not even exist; rather it is a *source* of value, which comes from the symbolizing rather than from what is symbolized. As for symbolizing what does not exist, Nozick talks of minimum wage legislation as symbolizing helping the poor (*NR*: 27), implying that it doesn't really help them, and of the desirability of harming one's enemy symbolically rather than actually (*NR*: 31); but one might wonder here whether the value of the symbolizing does not depend upon the belief, or at least half-belief, that what is symbolized does exist.

All in all one must distinguish the reality of symbolic utility itself from the role Nozick gives it in his decision theory. It is probably fair to say in general that the former has been much more sympathetically received than the latter.

Belief and acceptance

You can accept a statement without believing it, or even thinking it more likely to be true than false. Walking through the jungle you are stung by an insect which you judge, by the fleeting glance you have of it, is 30% likely to be a bee, 30% likely to be a wasp, and 40% likely to be a hornet. If you do nothing you will die. You have all three antidotes, but if you take the wrong one you will die painfully. What do you do? Presumably take the hornet antidote. You accept that the insect was a hornet, and act accordingly, but you do not believe it was, for it was only 40% likely to be so, and 60% likely to be either a bee or a wasp. But unfortunately the disjunctive statement that it was either-a-bee-or-a-wasp is not one you can act on as such – you could act on its being a bee, say, but that would be only 30% likely to be true. Scientists often accept a hypothesis they know faces cogent counterevidence because no alternative hypothesis is as yet available, and Nozick shows a certain tolerance towards inconsistency, in both *The Nature of Rationality* and *Philosophical Explanations* (see their indexes).

An important difference between belief and acceptance is that acceptance is plainly voluntary while belief is only indirectly so (one could engineer a belief in oneself by fabricating evidence and then taking a pill to make one forget the fabricating process). Nozick is presumably aware of all this, but he never explicitly distinguishes the terms (although *NR*: 97 lines 20–23 hovers over doing so), and uses them both often with a cheerful indifference. He talks of "rules of acceptance for what is to be believed" (*NR*: 94; cf. 85), and often talks of deciding what to believe – where this doesn't mean, as it often does, deciding what one does believe. ("I couldn't decide whether to believe him" may mean either: "whether to accept what he said" or: "whether I did believe him", but these are not the same.) The nearest he comes to our insect example is much earlier (at *NTIC*: 7), a passage already quoted above ("Practical rationality in the dissertation"): "Though [action] *A* is not believed likely to achieve what would be intended in doing it, it might be believed to be more likely to achieve it than any other action available, each of which yields bad consequences, and would be the rational thing to do".

We saw earlier that Nozick distinguishes the rationality of what is believed from that of believing it (*NR*: 70), but the following paragraph wavers and the situation is only saved (from subordinating the former to the latter when believing a falsehood would have good effects) by the symbolic utility of believing only truths (*NR*: 71). There does seem to be some confusion here though: why should the rationality of believing something false (that I am cancer-free when I am not, or in Nozick's example that my son is innocent) even tend to suggest (as the "wavering" paragraph seems to think) that *what is believed* is rational? Arrington (1994: 90) complains that the utility of averting my gaze from my son's obvious guilt may explain why I am irrational but does not make a case of irrationality one of rationality, and he doubts whether Nozick can successfully "combine epistemic credibility and utility into a unified theory of rationality. Most likely the concepts of rational belief and rational action are distinct and defy unification". Christensen (1995: 271) similarly asks "how plausible it is that the practical value of holding a belief helps determine its rationality" and Seabright (1993) doubts whether *both* credibility value and the usefulness of believing can play important roles. Arrington (1994: 90) also complains, as I have done, that for Nozick "believing something is a voluntary action". Perhaps Nozick is only thinking of believing as indirectly voluntary in the way I sketched above, but he certainly often writes as though he had something more direct in mind.

On the rationality question the trouble is that Nozick does seem to want to distinguish theoretical and practical rationality (as the remark at *NR*: 70 shows), but never seems to disentangle them unambiguously. Part of the reason may be that he is reluctant to limit cognitive goals to truth, or even to that plus "explanatory power, testability, and theoretical fruitfulness" (*NR*: 67), but is tempted to add in simplicity, ease in computation, and even mystical insight and oriental "enlightenment", which makes it easier to blur the line between cognitive and practical goals. This approach is well in line with the sort of inclusive and outgoing attitude to philosophy that he came to after *Anarchy, State, and Utopia*, as we saw at the outset. We must be responsive to reasons in a way that recalls the tracking of *Philosophical Explanations* (*NR*: 72, with *NR*: 193 n.15), and this leads him to develop a model of reasoning based on the notions of neural networks and parallel distributed processing currently popular in philosophy of mind. The general idea is that of a network of processes and goals interacting with each other, sometimes to reinforce and sometimes to inhibit, rather than of a single linear process of reasoning. This leads to the notion of a "credibility value" for a statement (*NR*: 84), which involves six or seven "rules of acceptance" that can be reduced to the two "rules to govern rational belief" of the initial summary (*NR*: xiv): "not believing any statement less credible than some incompatible alternative – the intellectual component – but then believing a statement only if the expected utility (or decision-value) of doing so is greater than that of not believing it – the practical component". The treatment of these as two "components" of a single notion illustrates the failure to disentangle that I mentioned above, but Nozick uses his rules to solve the "lottery paradox", that in a large lottery one will probably believe that some ticket will win, but also believe of each separate ticket that it will not win (see especially *NR*: 89–90).

Beliefs cannot be dispensed with in favour of the mere assignment of probabilities, as the "radical Bayesian" holds, for somewhere along the line, Nozick thinks, we must simply take something for granted, if only that probability- assignments are called for. Nozick (*NR*: 95–6) seems to think this objection could be answered, but he still rejects the position, and substitutes a "radical contextualism", where whether we accept (and for Nozick therefore believe) something may depend on the context; a scientist may demand more rigorous standards than a layman, for instance.

Before leaving this section let me mention that Christensen (1995: 269–70) also criticizes a technical notion of "measure" that Nozick introduces (*NR*: 83). The criticism (too complex to state in detail), as well as pointing out that the formulation of the notion is ambiguous, is to the effect that a certain incoherence is involved because terms of the formula that are supposed to have independent values in any given case cannot in fact be given their values independently, and also that (connectedly) putting the formula to its intended use (using some evidence to confirm a hypothesis) involves counting a certain quantity twice.

Evolution and its role

Where does our reason come from, and why should we rely on it? I mentioned at the start of this chapter a "transcendental" argument in favour of reason. Nozick claims that we have good inductive grounds for supposing that the injunction to believe or act on only what can be shown to be rational cannot itself be shown to be rational – "no one has done it yet, despite very serious efforts" (for which he gives no references: *NR*: 204 n.27, with text at *NR*: 122–3). Heil (1994: 558), commenting on this and on a certain paradox Nozick draws from it, warns against falling into a regress of arguments justifying rationality which involve steps which must themselves be justified by further steps, and so on, and suggests validating itself is "something it may make no sense to require of reason". The point may perhaps be expressed by saying that whether or not a transcendental justification (if one can be given) counts as rational, deductive reason cannot be deductively justified. Heil goes on to say, "This [his point just quoted] might be just what we ought to have expected given the biological basis of reason".

This biological basis, evolution by natural selection, forms a major tool for Nozick. But what is selected? Nozick, as we saw, distinguishes whether something believed is rational from whether it is rational to believe it (*NR*: 70). It is on the second that natural selection works (*NR*: 113). In *Philosophical Explanations* (261) Nozick insisted that the evidential relation is factual, not logical; it is for the world to tell us what is evidence for what. Now, however (*NR*: 108), he modifies this to take account of the plausibility of calling the relation a priori. (He adds that evidence might be purely factual even if being a reason was not, but in fact he seems to keep them on a level.) What evolution selects is creatures to whom certain factual relations *seem* self-evident, or more than factual; it is not "the capacity to recognise independently existing rational connections that is selected for" (*NR*: 108). This explains why, for Nozick, we think of things like induction as self-evident, and even why we think of Euclidian geometry as self-evidently applying to space, although strictly it is no more than an approximation. Evolution has made us like this because we are then fitter for survival than creatures otherwise constituted.

It is here that Nozick makes his striking claim to reverse what Kant called his "Copernican Revolution" to the effect that "objects must conform to our knowledge, to the constitution of the faculty of our intuition" (*NR*: 111, with *NR*: 202 n.11), i.e. we cannot know objects as they are in themselves, but only as they appear to us according to the constitution of our minds. Nozick's reversal of this says that "it is *reason* that is the dependent variable, shaped by the facts, and its dependence upon the facts explains the correlation and correspondence between them" (*NR*: 112; cf. 176).

This position is open to, and has received, criticism. Nozick is trying to explain our rational faculties causally, not to justify them, as Talbott (1995: 328 n.9) and Nagel (1997: 134) point out, although Nagel is puzzled in a footnote about how we can, as Nozick thinks we can, go beyond our evolutionary inheritance and pursue truth for its own sake, not just for its usefulness (see *NR*: 112–13, 124, 132, 176–8). One reviewer puts the problem like this: "Do we have any reason to suppose that human rationality, if it is indeed just a product of evolution by natural selection, is good enough for us to be justified in believing in the truth of its deliverances, including the theory of evolution itself?" (Lowe 1995: 399). Similarly Nagel (1997: 135) says that this natural theory would give us "no reason to trust [reasoning's] results in mathematics and science for example", adding that "the recognition of logical arguments as independently valid is a *precondition* of the acceptability of an evolutionary story about the source of that recognition", and "an evolutionary explanation of rationality is . . . necessarily incomplete" (Nagel (1997: 136–7).

At first this might seem rather unfair, since Nozick does not think that the explanation is complete, as we have just seen. But the trouble is, can he consistently deny this? Once we admit that some of our intuitions have been engineered by natural selection, and may not even be true (as in the geometry example), how can we know where to stop, and which intuitions we have independently of natural selection? He admits that something's seeming evident to us is no guarantee of its validity (*NR*: 109).

Well, is this any worse than acknowledging, as we must, that our intuitions are sometimes fallible? Yes, if mistaken intuitions are parasitic on genuine ones, and due to psychological etc. distorting factors. For Nozick the intuitions natural selection gives us must promote survival, and therefore *usually* be true – but this is contingent and they may not always be so; sometimes false beliefs may promote survival, as Nozick is well aware (cf., at any rate, his insistence on our adopting a belief only if it is useful to do so). He seems to think that evolution could make practically anything seem evident to us, if only it was useful. But could it? Is it simply lack of survival value that stops us solving problems about induction, other minds, or the external world as Nozick (*NR*: 121, 176) seems to suggest? Granted, we make mistakes, sometimes wild ones, but only in a context of correct views. Correct? But who says? Here we return to the question of justifying reason, and the transcendental argument I referred to earlier. Can we make sense of creatures whose intuitions (not just beliefs) are systematically and wildly at variance with our own, and cannot be brought into line with ours by reflection (on all our parts perhaps)? If not, then we must think of reason as that "capacity to recognise independently valid rational connections" which Nozick is "not suggesting" is selected for (*NR*: 108). We are back with Kant, or perhaps rather Aristotle. Of course whatever evolution selects *for*, it may be only because of evolution that rational creatures exist.

Other criticisms of Nozick here have been made. He claims an affinity with Wittgenstein (*NR*: 123), which leads Arrington (1994: 92) to comment that "Nozick's evolutionary hypothesis is nothing more than armchair speculation – the very kind of pseudo-scientific philosophizing that Wittgenstein condemned", and to contrast Wittgenstein's outlook with Nozick's "teleological interpretation of reason".

Nozick goes on to claim that phrases such as "the survival of the fittest" are not mere tautologies, and to offer a new definition of "function", and then to discuss some functions of reasons; but we must pass on.

Types and limits of rationality

At least one type of rationality is instrumental, concerning the means to achieve our goals, although Nozick includes ways of achieving them, and lets an action's goal include the value of doing it (*NR*: 133). But are there other kinds? Nozick thinks yes. We have seen that Newcomb's Problem led him to a notion of decision-value as an amalgam of causally and evidentially expected utility and symbolic utility (*NR*: 42–6). Instrumental rationality is wholly captured by the first of these (*NR*: 137), so that introducing the other two goes beyond it. The issue, however, is not all that clear. Obviously one form of rationality lies in drawing inferences (deductive, inductive, or whatever) about what something is evidence for as well as about what it will cause, and we may be motivated by simple intellectual curiosity. Of course such thinking would be a means to an end, satisfying our curiosity, but in that sense so would everything we deliberately do. But Nozick is evidently thinking here of the appeal to evidentially expected utility in cases like Newcomb's Problem, which we discussed earlier (cf. also *NR*: 137–8). The position is rather clearer when he insists that it is rational to pursue symbolic utility.

Is it simply the pursuit of evidential and symbolic utility that takes rationality beyond the instrumental? Nozick writes as though it is, but as we have just seen he takes a wide view of the instrumental. One might expect something on the rationality of ends, a discussion perhaps of Aristotle's claim that deliberation is of means, not of ends (although Nozick could argue that Aristotle was taking a similarly wide view of the instrumental), or of Nagel's (1970) attempt to show the rationality of altruism. Nozick doesn't ignore this issue altogether. He offers (without insisting on the details) 23 rules governing "rational preferences", which he describes as "contentful conditions" (*NR*: 163) that "go beyond the usual normative conditions" (*NR*: 162), i.e. those demanding consistency and coherence by satisfying the axioms of the probability calculus, but evidently feels he has made only limited progress in this area, and does indeed reject Kant's attempt to derive goals from mere rationality alone (*NR*: 163). He describes the 23 rules as "conditions on the rationality of goals", but adds that they don't fully specify the "substantive" rationality of them (*NR*: 176). They concern such things as not desiring what one knows is impossible, and preferring that, other things being equal, one satisfies the structural conditions for both rational desires and rational beliefs (e.g. not preferring X to Y and Y to Z but Z to X). If one prefers X to Y but prefers that one did not, one lacks "rational integration", but one can still be rational if one prefers not to be in that predicament (*NR*: 141–2). (Heil (1994: 559) thinks Nozick's insistence that rational preferences must be produced by processes that *reliably* produce ones satisfying the normative structural conditions he has sketched may serve to exclude extreme selfishness. This insistence, however, will only satisfy an externalist on rationality.)

A question arises here that Nozick touches on but does not really discuss. One can be burdened with unwelcome and conflicting desires, but how far can these (or even beliefs one cannot get rid of, although aware of the evidence against them) define one's rationality? Should not that be something which is "up to us", to use an Aristotelian phrase? But what does that involve? We cannot (directly) choose our beliefs, nor our desires, but whereas beliefs could not be simply at our choice without ceasing to be beliefs in any useful sense, it is not obvious, at any rate, that this is true of desires. The issue is pertinent to Nozick because of the parallelism that he wants to see in all this discussion between beliefs and desires or preferences. How far *can* rationality be regarded as parallel in these two spheres? Note incidentally that "preference" has an ambivalence in respect of being voluntary corresponding to what we saw in the case of acceptance and belief (see, e.g. principle VII at *NR*: 143; *NR*: 144 distinguishes preferences and desires, but without affecting this point).

Before leaving the search for rational goals Nozick rejects three further attempts to find them (*NR*: 151–63), the second of which leads him to a critical discussion of Davidson's claim that radically different conceptual schemes cannot be envisaged, and of what are now known as the interpretive principles of "charity" and "humanity".

Finally Nozick adds some interesting remarks on how to approach philosophical problems when no cut-and-dried method, or algorithm, is available (philosophical heuristics), and on the relations between rationality and imagination.

Summary

After introducing rationality as more "internalist" than knowledge, and objective, although able at the second level to prescribe its own suspension at the first level, *The Nature of Rationality* turns to principles. Having briefly compared ethical with legal and scientific principles, Nozick claims that ethical (and prudential) ones help us to avoid temptations, and deals at some length with our tendency to prefer earlier lesser goods to later greater ones (time preference). He also uses this idea to defend at least partially the honouring of "sunk costs", i.e. costs already incurred, although economists usually call this irrational, and Steele claims Nozick's example doesn't really involve them. Nozick ignores sunk costs incurred and to be honoured by others, and whether treatments of time preference can be extended to cover selfishness and altruism. The treatment here of principles as "teleological devices" with "functions" suggests a possible difference in attitude, at least, from *Anarchy, State, and Utopia*.

The Normative Theory of Individual Choice gives Nozick's first discussion of Newcomb's Problem, after some miscellaneous points on practical rationality (and some technical material we omitted). He sketches two solutions – the "dominance" one, of choosing both boxes because their contents are already fixed, and the "expected utility" one, of choosing only the opaque box because one-boxers have become rich – and prefers the latter because the contents of the boxes are not probabilistically independent of the choice. But in his second, and first published, discussion (reprinted in *Socratic Puzzles*) he prefers the dominance solution because he now distinguishes probabilistic dependence from causal influence, adding that the expected utility solution tempts us because of an *illusion* of causal influence. The third discussion, in *The Nature of Rationality*, accepts from Gibbard and Harper that the conflict has really been between causal and evidential expected utility, not between expected utility and dominance, which he now treats as two components of "decision-value". He also discusses the effects of varying the boxes' contents and the predictor's skill, albeit with some ambiguity in his position. Critics have distinguished the rationality of a policy from that of actions under it, suggested that the solutions of *Socratic Puzzles* and *The Nature of Rationality* are to different questions, and replaced evidentialist reasoning by cooperative reasoning. We also mentioned different inductive approaches, and the distinction between staged problems and real life ones, and briefly discussed the Prisoner's Dilemma and its relations to Newcomb's Problem. In a striking and original, although hotly disputed and generally rejected, move Nozick treats symbolic utility (in itself less controversial) as a third component of decision-value.

Apart from a near mention in *The Normative Theory of Individual Choice*, Nozick never explicitly distinguishes belief from acceptance, and although he does distinguish the rationality of believing from that of what is believed he does not always seem to keep either them or practical and theoretical rationality properly distinct, partly perhaps because following the outgoing approach of his later writings he adds things like simplicity and ease of computation to truth as *cognitive* goals.

Another striking claim by Nozick (his reversal of Kant's "Copernican Revolution") is that we owe our reason to evolution, which selects not creatures who recognize objective rational connections but creatures to whom certain factual relations *seem* self-evident, such as induction and Euclidian geometry. This separation of reason from the objectively valid has been hotly criticized. Granted, intuitions are fallible, but these are parasitic on genuine ones, it is said, and without presupposing these how could we believe anything our reason told us, including the theory of evolution itself?

Rationality for Nozick goes beyond the instrumental to include pursuing evidential and symbolic utility, but he claims only limited progress towards saying goals can be rational, and faces objections to his attempt to treat beliefs and desires or preferences in parallel. *The Nature of Rationality* ends with some interesting remarks on philosophical heuristics and rationality and imagination.

Chapter 7

Metaphysics I: personal identity

Introduction: identity in general

Personal identity is only one problem among many in the general area of identity, but it is a particularly important and sometimes psychologically pressing one, and Nozick devotes most, but not all, of the first chapter of *Philosophical Explanations* to it. But let us begin, as he himself in effect does, by looking at identity in general.

When is one thing identical with another? This question sounds absurd, for surely something can be identical only with itself – yet that sounds trivial, if not senseless. Perhaps we should ask instead when what looks like one thing is identical with what looks like another, as in the famous case of the evening star and the morning star. As this example suggests, many (but not all) problems about identity involve time: when is something at one time identical with something at another?

We might try saying: when they have all their properties in common. But how about identical twins? Leibniz thought that strictly speaking such cases were impossible, and had fun mocking a gentleman who searched frantically round the garden for two identical leaves. Nowadays the gentleman might be better advised to look for ball-bearings, or molecules, although even two molecules will be in different places. Perhaps then we should insist that "all their properties" should include spatial and temporal properties, for surely two things cannot occupy the same place at the same time. Actually this has been disputed. Can a statue and the lump of clay from which it is made be the same if the lump can outlast the statue (which is, say, knocked out of shape)? Here the lump and the statue do not share *all* their temporal properties, since the lump will exist at a time when the statue does not. But suppose they are both destroyed together (and created together): are they then identical? If not, then it seems that two things can share *all* their properties (and even in the former case it seems that two things can coincide for part of their history). But if they *are* identical, then it seems that whether (what seem to be) two things are identical at one time depends on what happens to them (it?) at another time. (Let us ignore the question of modal predicates such as "might have been squeezed into a ball and not destroyed", which seems to apply to the lump and not to the statue; for the example and discussion of it see Noonan 1985.)

This brings us within sight of a very plausible principle which might be called the principle that identity is intrinsic, i.e. that whether one thing is identical with (what looks like) another cannot depend on whether or not some third thing exists; if it can so depend, identity is extrinsic. An example where this issue becomes salient is the problem made famous by Hobbes of the "ship of Theseus". Suppose the ship that brought Theseus back to Athens after he destroyed the Cretan Minotaur was preserved as a sacred relic; as it gradually decayed its planks were replaced until eventually every plank had been replaced. But then the old planks (preserved in aspic) were reassembled into a ship. Which ship was now the ship of Theseus? Before the reassembling the gradually repaired ship was presumably the ship of Theseus – for at what stage did it cease to be so? Yet there is a strong intuition that if the old planks are reassembled then they form the real ship of Theseus, which the pilgrims should visit. (Suppose the repairing and the reassembling go on in parallel.) But then it seems that whether the repaired ship is the ship of Theseus depends on whether the reassembled ship exists, and so identity is extrinsic.

Nozick's theory

We can now return to Nozick. We saw in Chapter 5 that in constructing his view of knowledge Nozick appealed to a controversial principle, that knowledge is not closed under known entailment. Similarly when discussing personal identity he appeals to another controversial principle, that identity is extrinsic, which he applies to identity in general (this is why I said above that he in effect starts from identity in general). His own contribution here is the "closest continuer" theory of identity over time (although he acknowledges an anticipation of it in Shoemaker (*PE*: 655 n.5)). Which of two or more objects at one time is identical with a given object at another time depends on which of them most closely continues it (or, if the given object comes later, on which of them it most closely continues, but the discussion mainly concerns the former case). If y and z are equally close continuers of x and there is none closer then neither of them is identical with x and x no longer exists, but had only y (say) existed then x would have gone on existing as y, and had there been a yet closer w then x would have continued as w, whether or not y and z existed.

Although being the closest continuer is necessary if y is to be identical with x, more is needed. y must also be sufficiently close, an important qualification, one would think, which Nozick says less about, although he adds that the degree of closeness required depends on the kind of entity x is (*PE*: 34). We will see more of this later.

The other way the account needs filling out concerns what counts as being close. Similarity is one obvious candidate. But a mere replica will not count as identical, as we saw with the identical twins. The properties of a continuer of x must "grow out of x's properties, [be] causally produced by them, . . . be explained by x's having earlier had explained its properties, and so forth" (*PE*: 35). At this point Nozick refers to his notion of tracking, meaning presumably that the properties of x's continuer must track those of x rather as knowledge tracks the truth.

However, as at least two reviewers point out, even similarity and causation together will not do. Holland (1983: 118) claims that if Queen Elizabeth died suddenly Prince Charles might count as her closest continuer for Nozick, being relevantly similar and partly caused by her, and A. I. Goldman (1983: 82) makes a similar point about Athena springing full-grown from the head of Zeus (assuming Zeus had just died), attributing the core of the point to David Lloyd Thomas. Nozick must exclude *being born of* as a relevant causal relation – but on what grounds?

A problem that concerns Nozick, primarily about people but also other things, is that of overlap. It seems plausible that the gradually repaired ship of Theseus is the closest continuer of the original and so identical with it (*PE*: 33 rejects mereological essentialism – the view that it is essential to something which continues to exist that it retains all and only its original parts; cf. also *PE*: 100–104). But suppose the old planks are reassembled and the next day the repaired ship catches fire (*PE*: 45–6). Does the fire destroy the ship, or does it "jump" to what is now its closest continuer, the reassembled ship?

Nozick sees this puzzle as endemic to any view that allows identity to larger things than "atomic-point-instants". Any such view "trades off depth to gain breadth" by sacrificing some similarity. "The closest continuer theory is the best Parmenides can do in an almost Heraclitean world" (*PE*: 46). Nozick does not give a definitive solution, but sees the puzzle as representing a tension between local and global versions of his theory (*PE*: 47),where, roughly, the local opts for depth and lets the ship disappear, while the global opts for breadth by seeking a continuer that lasts longer, and so identifies the reassembled ship with the original. Of course other cases could be conceived, such as where the reassembled ship only lasts a very short time (cf. *PE*: 47), or there is a gap between the fire and the reassembling. Intermittency may not matter (a watch dismantled and reassembled is the same watch: *PE*: 45), but the tension will increase when the advantage of one solution over another is minute.

That identity is problematic once we get beyond what Nozick calls "atomic-point-instants" is true and important, and is probably the main motivation behind mereological essentialism, which can lead to the sort of dissolution of identity seen in at least some forms of Buddhism, especially when physics tells us (as *PE*: 61 notes), that to talk of reidentifying subatomic particles may make no sense. Elsewhere Nozick exhibits a certain fondness for various Eastern forms of thought, although apart from a casual reference right at the start he does not mention them in this first half of the chapter. In many contexts identity may seem to involve problems that may safely be left to philosophers. Does it really matter which ship is the ship of Theseus, except for sentimental reasons, and perhaps legal ones, although some other basis might be found for these? But apart from the fact that philosophy is what we are doing, there is one case where identity is certainly of interest to all of us, and that brings the main player of this chapter onto the scene.

Personal identity I: general considerations

The closest continuer theory is introduced as a general theory of identity, but embedded in a discussion of personal identity, which is clearly Nozick's main interest. As with most discussions of this topic the examples tend to be fictional and fantastic – which leads one reviewer (Fogelin 1983: 824) to ask whether one should expect any general theory to exist which covers exotic cases. As Fogelin admits, this is a Wittgensteinian approach, where terms like "person" derive their meaning from their use, which itself naturally derives from ordinary and not exotic cases, and may simply break down in these. This, however, is a controversial approach, associated with the now largely abandoned linguistic philosophy of the mid-twentieth century, and at least one of the "exotic" cases, namely brain bisection, is admittedly rare but actually does occur, and can hardly be swept under the carpet (see Nagel 1971b for its most famous discussion). As for the cases we will mention soon, who knows what the future holds? Admittedly the Wittgensteinian might claim that the concept of *person* might change to accommodate such cases, but there are objections to that, as we shall see.

A realistic example Nozick gives is that of the Vienna Circle, dispersed by Hitler and reconstituted (Nozick imagines) as two groups, one small, one large, but unaware of each other. The small group claims to be the Circle, and would be did the other not exist; but the other does exist and is the closer, because larger, continuer, and so is really the Circle. But as various reviewers have pointed out this makes an unjustified analogy between persons and groups. Groups, unlike persons, can survive in part (Williams in Paul 1981: 32), and can be dispersed and reassembled (Holland 1983: 119). Noonan (1985: 210–11) thinks that all the example shows is that the small group wrongly claims a *title*, not that an *entity* moves with the small group in one possible situation (where the large one does not exist) and with the large group in another (where it does). He presumably intends here a point he made earlier (1985: 206 with 227n. 15) about the ship of Theseus that identity will be in danger of becoming contingent in a sense he thinks absurd, namely that the reassembled ship will be identical with the original in one possible situation and distinct from it in another. It certainly seems strange that identity statements involving only rigid designators (i.e. ones that designate the same object in all possible situations where it exists) should be contingent. "Smith is the mayor" is contingent – he might not have been – but that is because "the mayor" is not a rigid designator; it is not contingent whether Smith is identical with that person who is *in fact* the mayor. Nozick, however, allows, albeit a little inconclusively, that his theory does require that identity can be contingent (see the long note at *PE*: 656–9).

This note also raises another point, relevant to both ships and persons, which is that Nozick often talks of objects as having temporal parts or stages, so that a ship-on-Monday and a ship-on-Tuesday may be parts of one ship; Noonan in fact (1985: 206–7) thinks he had better do this, and talk of ship-stages as being continuers of previous stages rather than of ships being identical, if he is to avoid calling identity contingent – although as we have just seen it is not clear that Nozick does claim, or perhaps even want, to avoid this. But Nozick sometimes talks loosely as though stages were identical with what they are stages of, as when he uses the example "Robert Nozick = RN", where RN is a temporal stage of Robert Nozick. He might have done better to talk in terms of *genidentity*, where a stage is genidentical to another if they are both stages of the same object.

The sort of exotic cases that crop up in discussions of personal identity involve such things as brain transplants and teleportation. The brain has two halves, with different but overlapping functions, either of which can approximately replace the other half if it is damaged, and philosophers usually assume for convenience that the two halves are exactly similar, since it seems that they could have been. Teleportation (short for "teletransportation") involves "reading" a complete molecule-by-molecule description of the brain onto computers and transmitting it by radio to some station where it is fed into a suitable brain-shaped piece of protoplasm in a body exactly like the original one, which then has all the physical and psychological characteristics, including (apparent) memories, of the original. Not only is this absurdly artificial in practice, it may even be impossible in principle, because of quantum indeterminism, but it *seems* coherent, and the questions it raises about personal identity cry out for an answer, so that Nozick like many other philosophers makes free use of it.

We have no space to discuss all the cases Nozick constructs to test our intuitions, which culminate in the overlap problem we have already discussed. The general idea, in Nozick as in other writers like Williams and Parfit, is to construct cases where things that usually go together, such as the body, the brain, its two halves, and psychological things like memory, skills, habits and character, are split apart, so that we can better see which of them, according to our intuitions, carries the identity of the person. Suppose for instance we thought that psychological characteristics and memory were what mattered: if a duplicate of ourselves were made which seemed to itself to have exactly our memories etc. (Nozick's Case 1), we might then think that spatiotemporal continuity of the embodiment of these was what mattered after all. Suppose though that you died as the duplicating was being done (Nozick's Case 3): the closest continuer theory would then allow that you had survived as the duplicate after all.

Holland (1983: 119–20) criticizes this whole notion of a duplicate, since unlike its original, or any other person, it would have no relevant history, and there would be no place for it in the world (Holland says that he is a university teacher so the duplicate must be one too, but that owing to the cuts this would be impossible!). This raises some big issues about such fantasy cases. What Nozick wants is someone indistinguishable from the inside, as it were, and it seems that a molecule-for-molecule duplicate must have the same inner life, however illusory it might be – its past would be a virtual reality. (To use a technical distinction, its thoughts would have the same narrow content as the original's but different wide content.) As for the cuts, the transmogrified Holland would simply find himself out of a job – a fate not unknown! Or Nozick might say that the duplicate's memories would be not virtual but real memories of the original Holland, although only if the original Holland died. Also the overlap problem might arise: if the original Holland died a few minutes, or seconds, after the duplicate came to life, would its memories suddenly change from being virtual to being real? (For some interesting discussion of further problems about transferring memories etc. see Schechtman 1990 and also for some related issues Noonan 1985: 217.)

Personal identity II: ties and caring

I said earlier ("Nozick's theory) that we might not care much about which ship was which but we certainly do care about which future (or indeed, as in cases of assigning responsibility, past) person, if any, is identical with ourselves. Nozick takes this up in his subsection on "Ties and Caring" (*PE*: 62–70). We may care for our children, but there is a quite different sense in which we care for ourselves, however altruistic we may be, as we can see in the case of fear. Fearing future pain to ourselves is a quite different experience from fearing future pain for our children, even if we may feel that latter more urgently and take more urgent steps to prevent it; Nozick's discussion seems to be directed to the sort of case we feel for ourselves, although not unambiguously so.

Basically we care for our closest continuer, but we also care for other continuers, provided they are close enough, in proportion to their closeness (*PE*: 64) . But the whole subsection is dominated, as its title suggests, by the possibility of a tie for closeness. This could most obviously happen if the two halves of our brain were transplanted separately into otherwise brainless bodies, or we were teleported onto two separate bodies, our original body being destroyed. The notion of a tie has its problems – would a single molecule be enough to break it? – but let us ignore these, as Nozick does for most of the time, although he does acknowledge that "[v]arying closeness slightly can produce a large change in care" (*PE*: 64), and makes a similar point en passant about overlap (*PE*: 47).

This possibility of a tie leads Nozick to a problem, since he considers, tentatively (*PE*: 64), that we care for our closest continuer, if there is one, but do not mind if there isn't one, provided the tied continuers are close enough. Why, he asks, is this? The puzzle arises because if *a* has two equally close continuers *b* and *c* and none closer, and if identity is closest continuity (given that it is close enough), then they cannot both be closest continuers of, and so identical with, *a* without being identical with each other, and it would be arbitrary to pick one of them, so *a* has no closest continuer but perishes. Yet *a* would care for *b* and *c* (Nozick thinks), as for all sufficiently close continuers, but more so than if there were a still closer *d* to carry the identity; *a* would be "no longer there" but it would not be "like death" (*PE*: 68). But why, since *b* and *c* do *not* carry the identity?

Nozick first compares the way we think it important that a baby continues to exist but not important that it should have been conceived in the first place. This, however, is different and is a moral matter, since the baby has its own interests and no predecessor is even in the offing. Incidentally Nozick does not distinguish the care we feel for our future projects, which we might partly forward through our children, and the care we feel to avoid pain etc., which is why I said above that his treatment is not unambiguous.

We saw concerning the overlap problem that Nozick distinguishes local and global versions of his theory, where the global takes, as it were, a wider perspective. He now takes a wider perspective still to solve the present puzzle by broadening the closest continuer view to ask instead for the best instantiated realization of *a*'s identity, since *a* has no closest continuer, so that *b* and *c* will do, and *a* will care for them as much as for a closest continuer, i.e. they get more care than they would if there *were* a closest continuer, *d*.

However, Noonan (1985: 217 ff., esp. 220–21) points out that one can hardly talk of a "best realisation" of identity in a case where identity does not exist, and then adds that far from solving his puzzles about why we care for our tied continuers Nozick simply postulates that we do. (Noonan claims that he himself can do better on this point, but fortunately discussion of his own rather difficult view is outside our scope.) Perhaps Nozick should talk of best "approximations to" rather than "continuers of". Presumably he is allowed to modify his view to cope with special cases. But the issue seems to be whether it is enough for him simply to describe his modified view, or whether he should justify it, or somehow derive it from his original view, on pain of its being merely ad hoc.

Holland (1983: 119) accuses the closest continuer theory of being "disguised nonsense", because on it "if you cease to exist you continue to exist", and you could be murdered with impunity. This, however, is rather unfair. Apart from the fact that there might be no sufficiently close continuer, Nozick could reply that for him (except in the ties case we have just considered) death is the end of the body, or of this phase of the person's existence, or even this phase of the body's existence if, like the ship, it too can be continued – in another lump of matter, but bodies change their matter anyway; the change would be discontinuous, but this could be seen as a form of intermittency, which Nozick allows (*PE*: 45).

Personal identity III: closeness

So far we have said little about closeness, except for mentioning similarity and causation and the Elizabeth/Charles objection. But Kolak and Martin (1987) think that causality is not necessary for identity, and is demanded only because once we have stopped treating the self as a Cartesian substance, as most philosophers now have, we seem to need some glue to hold together the stages that a relational view relates, and also to assuage our fear of death. For a more sympathetic view of the demand for glue see what Coburn (1985) calls the "natural" view. Kolak and Martin argue, against Nozick and others, that a spectrum of cases can be constructed where the causal link becomes weaker and weaker. Teleportation already involves a non-standard link, and we could imagine a computer which constructs random objects and compares them with a given person, and when it happens by chance to construct a replica it destroys the person and substitutes the replica, so that there is still a causal link, albeit very weak. Also Nozick allows some intermittency, and thinks we would not mind if a miracle destroyed us (perhaps during sleep) and another miracle reconstituted us a moment later. In fact science *might* show that our stages are only epiphenomenally linked, like shadows.

Kolak and Martin don't say what should replace causation, but there are at least two problems with their view, First, it is hard to test our intuitions against extreme cases, but with many concepts the existence, let alone possibility, of borderline areas where a definition only dubiously applies does not mean it does not definitely apply in central cases. Perhaps it is indeed indeterminate sometimes whether something counts as a person. (Are chimpanzees persons?) Secondly, perhaps causation itself is consistent with some (especially systematic) intermittency. Quantum physics with its particles popping out of and into the vacuum may indeed suggest that this is so, and "cause" may be no easier to define than "person".

A feature of Nozick's treatment of causation that has troubled several commentators is that he seems to allow the degree of closeness required for identity to depend not only on the kind of entity concerned, as we saw earlier, but also on individual choice, a feature much more prominent in the second half of the chapter (*PE*: 105–8). Kolak and Martin (1987: 347 n.12) contrast this en passant with his insistence on causation, and Coburn (1985: 382, point (A)) infers that an earlier and a later person might disagree on whether they were the same – as indeed Nozick is fully aware, but thinks it is balanced by the "dignity" the view gives us (*PE*: 107). (Coburn's article contains a number of criticisms along the general lines we have discussed, to the effect that for Nozick identity may depend on trivial considerations and have counterintuitive implications.) Goldman (1983: 83) makes a similar point to Coburn's, but in terms that will become relevant again a little later.

I said at the start of the last paragraph that Nozick "seems" to let identity depend on choice. Actually he vacillates on this. He allows it for ships but not for persons (*PE*: 34): "we are not willing to think that whether something is *us* can be a matter of (somewhat arbitrary) discussion or stipulation", and repeats the point (*PE*: 44), although more tentative in allowing it for ships etc. But he allows (*PE*: 69) that "what constitutes [people's] identity through time is partially determined by their own conception of themselves", which can, and "perhaps appropriately does", vary from person to person, and (in *PE*: 106–7) makes a similar point in different terms (cf. also *PE*: 108–10).

We shall meet this again shortly, but perhaps here we need again the distinction I made above between two kinds of care we feel for ourselves. Perhaps it *is* somewhat up to us what we should count as an adequate continuation of our own projects and ambitions. But suppose we are faced, in a typical fantasy case, with our mental life being teleported into Smith's body, and his into ours, are told that one body will be tortured tomorrow, and are asked which we prefer it to be: we may be deeply troubled about how to answer, but our trouble seems to concern which body *as a matter of fact* will be ours, not which body *to make or treat* as ours. (Cf. the view of Williams (1970: 174–5 (= Williams (1973: 58)) that we cannot regard our own future identity as an indeterminate matter.)

Interlude: the unity of Nozick's philosophy

The title of this section is perhaps optimistic. As I said right at the start, Nozick's foxlike nature prevents his philosophy from having all that much unity. Nevertheless there are certain unifying themes in it, although here we will treat them only very briefly.

In the course of distinguishing between local and global versions of his theory Nozick inserts a subsection on "Structuring Philosophical Concepts" (*PE*: 47–58). Here he elaborates five modes or stages of a progression for such structuring: I Intrinsic abstract structuring; II Relational; III Closest relative; IV Global; V Closest instantiated relation. We cannot exhibit these in detail, but the closest continuer theory belongs basically to III, broadened to IV for overlap cases, and to V for ties. Strictly, however IV is a form of III, not an alternative to it (*PE*: 51), and (as pointed out at *PE*: 55) V is really III repeated "one level up". We are then given a table (*PE*: 52–3) classifying under I to IV different views on ten philosophical topics covering metaphysics, epistemology, philosophy of science, semantics and ethics.

Although for Nozick this structuring presents "a progression of modes of increasing logical power and complexity", he adds that "the correct view on each topic need not be of the highest type" (*PE*: 51). We are mainly interested in how he views his own philosophy, and Nozick makes it clear that the entitlement theory of justice in *Anarchy, State, and Utopia* belongs to II (*PE*: 48), because on it a distribution is just if it relates in a certain way to an earlier just distribution; a closest relative version of the theory holds that it must not relate equally closely to an earlier unjust distribution (*PE*: 660 n.16 adds a further complication). Similarly his view in Chapter 5 of what makes an action right belongs to III because one condition is that there must be no even more suitable action available, although it will belong to IV if we allow that an action not qualifying under III may be made right by some larger context to which it belongs. An example he does not mention here is one we met earlier (Chapter 4, "Organic unity as value") where he associates his theory of value with the closest continuer theory by calling organic unity value provided it is close enough and no candidate is closer (*PE*: 441–4).

The most important topic in *Philosophical Explanations*, as we have seen, is knowledge. Nozick classifies his initial naive theory, that a belief is knowledge if it tracks the truth, under II. His more sophisticated theory, that the belief must use a method M and not also use another method M' which outweighs M but does not track the truth, falls under III. He adds implicitly that his theory falls under V (*PE*: 54–5), in so far as there might be beings who tracked the truth over a far wider range of possible worlds than those envisaged in the theory as he presents it; in that case what we now call knowledge would not be knowledge, for our beliefs would not then stand in the relationship to truth which best instantiated knowledge.

On the question of content there are a few recurrent themes in his philosophy. The one we have come across most often is the notion of value as organic unity, which we have seen underlying such things as our duty to feed the poor, and ethical responsiveness generally, as well as retribution, symbolic utility, and even the value of knowledge. A theme that Nozick himself emphasizes is that of self-subsumption and the related notions, some of which we are about to meet, of self-shaping, self-synthesis and self-choosing. It holds of responsiveness to reality, itself grounded in value as organic unity, plays a substantial role in the discussion of why there is something rather than nothing, where its relations to the organic unity principle are discussed (*PE*: 148–9), and pops up in many other places. Another unifying theme is that of tracking, originally developed in connection with free will to elaborate a notion of desirable action (*PE*: 169–71) and then applied to knowledge; he applies it briefly to the closest continuer theory of personal identity (*PE*: 66), itself akin to the fivefold scheme above.

Finally, if not quite relevantly, let me note the interesting discussion in Lucy (1990) of Nozick's earlier views on personal identity, which I have referred to in the "Guide to further reading" for Chapter 2.

Personal identity IV: the nature of the self

Although, like Nozick, we have been mainly concentrating on personal identity, the closest continuer theory is really a theory of identity as such and we have seen little on what persons or selves really are. Apart from a possible hint (at *PE*: 112) Nozick does not distinguish persons and selves, in this chapter entitled "The identity of the self" talking of persons in the first half (entitled "Personal identity through time") and selves in the second. "Person" is an everyday word and outside special contexts (e.g. the Trinity) suggests an embodied creature, while "self", outside pronouns like "myself" and compounds like "self-starter", "self-indulgent", is more a term of art used in focusing on certain philosophical problems. We call someone a "person of integrity" but not a "self of integrity".

Perhaps because of its narrower scope, and the obscurity and apparent implausibility of its central claim, which he himself calls "bizarre if not incoherent" (*PE*: 89), Nozick's treatment of the self has been less discussed than the closest continuer theory. He starts by asking a well-worn question: to what (if anything, some would add) does "I" refer? Roughly his answer is: to the self who is using it. But what does this user think of itself as referring to? I might wake up in hospital with amnesia after an accident, remembering neither my name nor anything else about myself, but still ask, "where am I"? What do I think I am asking the location of? Well, suppose I meant by "I" "the producer of this very token" (namely, "I". A token is, for our purposes, a word, phrase or sentence considered as uttered or written on a given occasion, and its utterer is said to be "tokening" it). By producing this token of "I" ("of", because here "I" is a general word, or "type", which can have many tokens) I confer on it the property of being produced by myself, and it is in virtue of having this property that it manages to refer in the way it does. Nozick sums up all this (and some further complications; see *PE*: 71–8) by saying: "so it seems we should understand 'I' as 'this very reflexive self-referrer', as 'the producer of this very token with this intention of involving a device of necessary self-reference in virtue of a property exhibited in the tokening'" (*PE*: 78).

But how do I know that it was I who produced the token? Not via a referring token, for I would have to know it referred to me. Nor by observing myself from the inside, which might tell me that it was I that was in pain, but would not show how I know, e.g., that I was born in Birmingham. "Reflexive access to ourselves, then, cannot be a special mode of relating to ourselves as objects" (*PE*: 81). So what is it?

It is here Nozick introduces his main original, and "bizarre", contribution, which he does "with great hesitation" (*PE*: 87). This is what he calls self-synthesis. Consider a set of ordinary acts *A1*, . . ., *An*, and then another act *A0* which is an act of "unification and synthesis which brings together" these acts and also itself, and so is "(partially) a reflexively self-referring act", which "unites these acts together as parts or components or things arising from the same entity *E*", which "thus synthesised is the doer of the acts, including *A0*". "[S]yntheses at different times can mesh into a larger continuing entity" without a "fresh creative act" each time (*PE*: 89). This synthesizing over time is done in accordance with the closest continuer theory (*PE*: 91) (not of course in conscious accordance with it, so it is no objection to say that not everyone holds that theory, which is simply a theory about how we do in fact synthesize ourselves).

Such in barest outline is Nozick's account, for which he sees a certain affinity with Fichte, as also with Zemach (1972). There is no pre-existing I, and this explains, he claims, why here we are "immune to error through misidentification", to borrow Shoemaker's phrase (*PE*: 90), and also why a self is essentially a self, i.e. something that can reflexively self-refer; a prince might turn into a frog, but not into a stone (despite Lot's wife?). A long and difficult footnote (*PE*: 664–6 n.51) claims that unity could emerge if a composite X + Y + Z uttered a token x + y + z which referred to X + Y + Z as a whole (i.e. it wasn't just that x referred X, y to Y, and z to Z, as with three people saying "I" in chorus). X + Y + Z could then apply the closest continuer theory to itself, i.e. consider itself as continuing as the closest continuer of X + Y + Z, not simply the closest continuer of X plus that of Y plus that of Z. (This incidentally comes in an interesting and useful discussion of unities and wholes (*PE*: 94–104) which would take us rather far afield.)

Is the theory circular? Nozick thinks not. He sees "no special problem about something *A* that refers to itself in virtue of a property it bestows on itself", since being its bestower it must be there to receive it; so reflexive self-referring is possible (*PE*: 93). But what is the property? Simply that of being referred to? But can something refer to itself, or anything else, *by* bestowing on it the property of being referred to? All Nozick says is "though the property was not previously enduring, it is bestowed by *A* as needed, and bestowed only on what is itself" (*PE*: 93). He does go on to ask whether any act at all doesn't presuppose an already existing agent. "I do not deny these difficulties", he replies cheerfully, adding that we ought not to mind, if we accept Lichtenberg's criticism of Descartes, that we can only say "Thinking is going on", not "I think" (*PE*: 93; cf. 87)! He adds further that the acts are done by a person existing before, but not necessarily "existing independently of the act of synthesis" (or as he puts it two paragraphs later, "of any act of synthesis") (*PE*: 93–4). He seems to offer the ensuing discussion, of unities and wholes etc., as answering all this, but interesting though it is, it is not clear that it does, although it does argue against the view that "unity can arise only out of unity" (*PE*: 100), as we saw in the last paragraph.

So far we have set no bounds what we can synthesize ourselves as (*PE*: 94), which leads Goldman (1983: 83) to ask whether he can synthesize himself so as to include a typewriter. This may be a bit unfair, as Nozick presumably intends us to synthesize only actions etc., or at least beings capable of acting (remember the prince who cannot become a stone), but he does say such selves "partially choose themselves" (*PE*: 106), which Goldman says would let a criminal escape by refusing to include the relevant act in his synthesizing. Nozick adds (*PE*: 107–8) that social constraints (presumably using some other criteria for identification) might limit deviant self-choosings. But it is not clear anyway that he needs to include choice in how individuals synthesize themselves differently, as he thinks they do. They could do so simply because they are the individuals they are, just as people differ in intelligence or even tastes without choosing to do so. But Goldman makes a more serious point when he says Nozick confuses a psychological notion of a "self-image" with a metaphysical notion of selfhood.

I might mention en passant that Nozick does not make very clear when he is asking an ontological question about what a self is and when an epistemological one about how a self knows itself. But this is not a very serious criticism, since obviously the questions are connected.

Finally, two critics who are basically sympathetic to Nozick suggest ways in which his account needs supplementing. First, Richards (1984) thinks Nozick blends intending with causal production, and risks circularity in his "X + Y + Z" example because he refers to an intention to bring about the productive activity, but seems to presuppose a subject to do the intending. The supplement he proposes, borrowing ideas from Castañeda, is to emphasize volitional thinking, or "[a]wareness of moving to act" (1984: 161); "*self-consciousness is consciousness of agency*" (1984: 149, his emphasis). The point seems to be to supplement the cognitive or theoretical notion of awareness, in the synthesizing process whereby the self becomes aware of itself, with a practical notion of what we might perhaps call "self-conscious intending" (my phrase, not his). One might, however, wonder whether his account (which of course is far more elaborate than this sketch) really succeeds, so far as the issue of circularity goes, in doing more than displacing it from the theoretical onto the practical.

Secondly, Mazoué (1990) (in a discussion that outdoes Nozick's own in obscurity) insists that Nozick needs to add an "Insulation Condition" to "preclude the possibility of an 'I' synthesising itself around episodes of sporadic interruption by another 'I'" (1990: 119), apparently by some sort of telepathic process. I will only comment that I am not sure why a thought transmitted to one telepathically (whatever that really means) should not count as one's own thought although *caused* by some outside agency, as one might be by a hypnotist, or even by a dominating friend one was over-impressed by. The thought might present itself as intrusive, but we often in reality are struck by unexpected or bizarre thoughts, which we may or may not then adopt. Perhaps the telepathic case lies at the strong end of a scale of degrees of mental influence, although it is true that one would not be aware of its source, as one could be of a hypnotist or friend.

Summary

Among the problems surrounding identity in general is whether it is intrinsic or extrinsic, a problem illustrated by the "ship of Theseus" example. For Nozick identity is extrinsic, and he introduces the "closest continuer" theory. Closeness raised problems, for neither similarity nor causation (two obvious candidates) seem adequate, even in combination, as reviewers point out; Nozick does say the continuer must be "sufficiently" close, but says little more than that this may depend on the kind of entity in question. Problems arise if two continuers are equally close, and also in cases of overlap, where continuer and continued exist together for a period. Identity is certainly problematic beyond "atomic-point-instants", and for modern physics even in those, which may support certain Buddhist views; but though it seldom matters with ships it does with persons.

As an example for his theory Nozick uses a group (the Vienna Circle), but groups behave differently from individuals. He also seems to allow that identity can be contingent, and accepts temporal parts or stages, although not entirely consistently. He follows the general tradition, which uses exotic examples like brain transplants and teleportation, the strategy being to take things which usually go together, like physical and psychological items, and imagine them coming apart, but the appeal to duplicates that this involves is criticized (inconclusively?) by Holland.

Problems arise if b and c tie for being closest continuers of a, for then (Nozick thinks) a faces extinction, but will still care about them as much as he would for a single closest continuer, in whom he would survive. Nozick (without properly distinguishing different kinds of care for ourselves) reacts by widening "closest continuer" to "best instantiated realisation", which allows this to count. But Noonan denies that a non-existent identity can have a "best realisation", and also thinks Nozick merely postulates his views about caring, while Holland accuses Nozick of contradiction, perhaps unfairly. Various critics have attacked Nozick's views on closeness, with varying effect, but perhaps his strangest, although tentative, view is that what continues us may partly depend on our choice.

Here we briefly discussed the unity of Nozick's philosophy, in view of the fivefold structuring of philosophical concepts under which he classifies many parts of his own philosophy, and thereby brings out a unity among them. Turning to content we mentioned especially organic unity, self-subsumption and tracking.

Nozick himself calls his account of the self "bizarre", and it has been much less influential than his closest continuer theory, but not without its friends. It is hard to summarize briefly, but roughly he thinks that "I" refers to what utters it, in virtue of the property of being referred to bestowed on it by that very act of referring, and that the self synthesizes itself partly in a way it itself chooses. He claims this is not circular, and that it explains why here we cannot err through misidentification. His appeal to choice seems unnecessary in fact, but Goldman accuses him of confusing a psychological notion of a self-image with a metaphysical notion of selfhood. Finally two friendly critics try to supplement his account.

Chapter 8

Metaphysics II: explaining existence

Introduction: "Why is there something rather than nothing?"

We have seen how Nozick emphasizes explanation as the proper aim of philosophy. This comes to the fore in the title of the second chapter of *Philosophical Explanations*, "Why Is There Something Rather Than Nothing?", especially if, as Camacho (1986: 415) comments, this "quickly becomes the somehow different question of the limits of our understanding", and whether it is possible to explain everything. The question "why is there something rather than nothing?" probably occurs to most people sometimes, but is only rather rarely discussed by philosophers, partly because it is often assumed to be either senseless, or dispensable, or insoluble. It might be thought senseless by someone who thought, as a logical positivist would, that we cannot understand a question unless we know what would *count* as an answer to it, although it would always be open to us, as a positivist like Schlick would admit, to investigate further this last question (about what would count). The question might be thought dispensable if it were shown that it is a necessary fact that there is something, although this would need to be shown, and even that might not settle the question. I might verify, by going through all 1,000 of them individually, that any six-figure number of the form ABCABC is divisible by 77, and realize that being a mathematical fact this must be necessary, but still ask why. If a problem is *known* to be insoluble, like that of squaring the circle, or trisecting an angle using only ruler and compasses, we would indeed waste our time trying to solve it, but might still be left philosophically puzzled and unwilling to dismiss it as senseless. We might convince ourselves that no explanation could ever be given for why a certain brainstate, or set of them, is correlated with the experience of seeing red (because the hue *red* seems opaque to analysis), but still ask about the status of such brute facts.

So we ought not to dismiss out of hand the question, "why is there something rather than nothing?" But what are we asking? What counts as "something"? It seems that any material object could simply vanish (although this has been disputed: see Winch 1982), so perhaps – although this would not follow logically, because of the fallacy of composition – they all could, and might never have existed in the first place. If there were no material objects would there still be space, whether or not filled by fields of force or energy? (Let us leave aside the question whether energy, which Einstein tells us is convertible with matter, could exist all on its own.) Or would space itself disappear, as perhaps time would if there were no events (but on this see Shoemaker 1969), and how about God? But He is far too controversial an entity to rely on. Some would say He exists necessarily, but others would say that the very fact that if He existed He would necessarily exist shows that He does not exist.

But what about things like universals, numbers, or facts? Even if there were no objects would there not still be the fact that there were no objects, or an absence of objects, and the number 17, and the property of squareness? Could these too be abolished? There are two replies we might make. We could say that the question "Why is there something rather than nothing?" only refers to particulars, like material objects, space and time, or God. Or we could say that universals etc. depend ultimately on the existence of particulars; even the property of being a purple cow may exist only because it is a consistent combination of the properties *purple* and *cow* which are instantiated. There are infinitely many numbers and perhaps only finitely many particulars, but numbers could be generated from the null set – assuming that can somehow be accounted for. (See Lowe 1996.) But let us return to Nozick.

Nozick's approach

In keeping with his later philosophical outlook as we sketched it at the outset Nozick adopts a tentative attitude, claiming simply to take the question seriously and examine possible answers to it, without coming down decisively for any of them. Given the nature of the question and the prevalent tendency to ignore or dismiss it this seems a reasonable and helpful procedure.

The question of the limits of our understanding, and whether we could explain everything, may be "somehow different", as Camacho (1986) puts it, from Nozick's title question, but their connection is clear. To explain why there is *anything* we cannot simply assume a starting point without having to explain that too, which threatens a regress. It is here that Nozick brings in his main idea, self-subsumption. But before considering that let us look briefly at the distinction he makes between inegalitarian and egalitarian theories.

To explain why some proposition p holds is not necessarily the same as explaining why p rather than q holds. ("Why do you eat fish?" "Because I like it." "Why do you eat fish rather than meat, which you also like?" "Because I have become a semi-veggie.") Inegalitarian theories hold that some states are more "normal" than others, and so less in need of explanation. The question "why is there something *rather than nothing*?" seems to be of this sort, presupposing that the existence of nothing is what is to be expected in the absence of some special explanation for an alternative. (But more on this below.) In the days before Galileo's introduction of inertia and its development by Newton this evidently seemed more plausible than it does at present. Nozick (*PE*: 122n.) refers to the sixteenth-century Kabbalist Meir ben Gabbai for the view that without God's constant sustaining of it the universe would simply vanish. He might have referred less abstrusely to Descartes' *Principles of Philosophy* 1.21 (despite Descartes' writing after Galileo). Nozick (ibid.) contrasts a principle he quotes from R. Harré: "Enduring is in no need of explanation", a reflection of Newton's inertia that still suggests a privileged state, although not nothingness now.

One might attribute Nozick's title question to a quest for simplicity. After all, if there is nothing, there is nothing there to explain while if there is something there *is* something there to explain. This perhaps provides a motivation, but not necessarily a justification. The fact that there was nothing might still need explaining, even without us there to explain it. Nozick toys with the idea that nothingness itself could be a natural state containing a force that produces things (*PE*: 122–3), an idea which one commentator (J. W. Smith 1988: 6) calls "quite absurd, containing little more than an imaginative play upon words". Perhaps Nozick was thinking of the way a spatial vacuum (not the same of course as pure nothingness, which would involve an absence of dimensions) is treated by modern physics as a sort of boiling cauldron from which particles pop into being, annihilate each other, and pop out again (rather like humans, one might think). As Smith also notes (1988: 18 n.12), the mid-twentieth century steady-state cosmology posited the creation of hydrogen atoms out of the void. Both Smith and Nozick assume that such creation would involve a force, but why shouldn't the atoms simply come into being spontaneously? Quantum theory anyway seems happy enough with spontaneous activity.

But be that as it may, Nozick prefers an egalitarian theory where nothingness is no more natural than any other state and all states are on a level. He could say that the spontaneous creation theory (which incidentally would answer his 12-year-old daughter: *PE*: 125) is unsatisfyingly puzzling and to be avoided where possible.

There are many ways of being something but only one way of being nothing. Nozick uses this to introduce his egalitarianism, which puts all possibilities on a level, none being the "natural" alternative. He first appeals to the principle of indifference (that any alternative has the same probability as any other) to argue that the existence of something must have a probability of at least a half, if treated as a single alternative in contrast to the existence of nothing, or of more than half, if treated as covering many alternatives while the existence of nothing covers only one. This indeterminacy of the probability according to how the alternatives are divided up is a well known feature of the principle of indifference, and Nozick does not pursue this line, although he does call the idea behind it "illuminating" (*PE*: 128). He dismisses it because he thinks (although it is not entirely clear why) that it still treats the realization of a possibility as what needs explaining, and its remaining unrealized as the "natural state", and so is still ultimately inegalitarian.

Pure egalitarianism, Nozick thinks, must "eliminate the 'rather than'" from our why-question (*PE*: 127). But this seems confused. We must distinguish "*p* rather than *q*", which may indeed suggest that *q* is the "natural" state as distinct not only from *p* but from *r* etc. and "*p* rather than not-*p*", which might suggest that not-*p* is the "natural" state, but if it does, this is something endemic to the asking of why-questions at all, not something that can be eliminated from them. (Nozick does at one point ask why egalitarianism holds, and distinguishes this from asking why it rather than inegalitarianism holds by adding that "[w]e still want to understand [its] ground or basis" (*PE*: 130). But this seems to amount to treating it as a how-question rather than a why-question.)

Fecundity

We now enter some murky waters. To draw out the implications of his egalitarianism Nozick introduces a "fecundity assumption" (F), that all possibilities are realized. This is reminiscent of what Lovejoy (1936) calls the principle of plenitude, an idea that goes back to Aristotle and Hobbes, and says, in one formulation, that all permanent possibilities are realized – nothing could remain merely possible throughout eternity (although a possibility could be foreclosed, as the possibility of my going to Australia will be if I die before doing so). Nozick, however, distinguishes his position from the principle of plenitude, because that "refers to the maximum realization of possibilities in one actual universe" (*PE*: 70 n.10), whereas he wants all possibilities to exist in "independent noninteracting realms, in 'parallel universes'" (*PE*: 129). This is because he adopts the "strong modal realism", as it is usually called, of Lewis, at least for purposes of discussion. We met this in Chapter 5 ("Counterfactuals") and noted there that Nozick refuses to commit himself to it. We shall see shortly ("Self-subsumption") that F will be modified, but as it stands it plainly implies Lewis's strong modal realism or something equivalent to it.

This lets us avoid the question "why X rather than Y?", Nozick thinks, because both X and Y will obtain. But how about not-X? Nozick goes on to say that if X is the situation that all possibilities obtain, and Z is the situation, on the face of it inconsistent with X, that all possibilities but two obtain and those two don't, X and Z can still both exist but in independent "realms" (*PE*: 129). He seems here to be using "situation" for possible worlds, and "realm" (which in the quotation in the last paragraph referred to possible worlds) for second-order possible worlds whose contents are ordinary possible worlds, which leads to complications: what does F say now? Is it simply the same as X, so that Z entails not-F? If so, shall we need a second-order F to say that F and not-F both exist? And a third-order F, and so on? And what about the possibility that there is nothing at all, not only no objects but no possibilities either, and no possible worlds of any order? Is there a possible world in which this possibility obtains? Our murky waters seem to have become a maelstrom. Nozick first dismisses the question (*PE*: 130) "Why isn't there *only* nothing?" as inegalitarianly presupposing that nothingness is a privileged state, but then says that egalitarian and inegalitarian theories can both hold in independent realms while all possibilities hold in the union of the realms (cf. *PE*: 131n.). But the union of two realms is itself one realm, and Nozick seems to confuse saying that inconsistent possibilities can exist but only in different realms, and saying they can exist in one realm after all, the union of the different realms; he seems to confuse the union of two realms with the second-order realm whose members they are. But anyway as we saw earlier we could only use all this to avoid the question "Why X rather than Y?" by avoiding all why-questions altogether. (Could it be that the fertility of Nozick's philosophical imagination has led him to extend fecundity to subsume both itself and its rivals, rather as he extended the libertarianism of *Anarchy, State, and Utopia* to subsume both itself and its rivals in the framework for utopia?)

Self-subsumption

But suppose we accept F. This will resolve our question why there is something rather than nothing (by saying that all possibilities obtain and that the existence of something is one of them), but only if F itself is grounded. It is here that Nozick brings in an idea that we have already seen him use in various of his works, that of self-subsumption. A principle subsumes itself if it is an instance of itself. A principle that all principles of a certain kind are true will subsume itself if it is itself a principle of that kind. If it subsumes itself it will potentially explain itself in the same way that it explains anything else that it does explain, by letting us derive it from itself.

It is essential to note, however, that explaining is not the same as proving (as of course Nozick is well aware). In each case the premises and the conclusion must all be true, but a proof establishes the truth of the conclusion, while an explanation presupposes it. That is why I added "potentially" just above. Nozick gives "Every sentence of exactly eight words is true" as an example of a sentence that subsumes itself (it has exactly eight words) but is not true and so does not explain itself (*PE*: 119).

There is, however, a further requirement on explanation which, as Smith (1988: 8–9) points out, Nozick seems to ignore or at least to underplay, when introducing self-subsumption (at *PE*: 119). As an example Nozick gives:

P: any lawlike statement having characteristic C is true.

P is a lawlike statement with characteristic C.

Therefore P is true.

He then says the question is whether having C explains the conclusion if it is true, and in effect focuses on the first premise. But we also need the second premise to be true. But suppose the first premise is indeed true but is only a true universal generalization and not a lawlike statement. Then the second premise will be false, and although the conclusion will be true the argument, although still valid, will no more be sound (valid with all its premises true) than if the first premise were false. We shall no longer have a case of self-subsumption (which requires the second premise to be true, even if the first is not), and so no explanation of the conclusion. I don't say Nozick seriously intends to, but he does tend to write as though true generalizations always explain their instances; compare the offhand introduction of the words "general lawlike" in brackets in *Philosophical Explanations* (*PE:* 132 line 4).

None of this of course affects the question whether when we do have self-subsumption we have explanation. Nozick allows that explanation is generally thought to be irreflexive: nothing explains itself. But this, he says, is because people have not considered self-subsumption, although this will only help towards avoiding "brute" facts if we mean facts that cannot be explained at all, not facts that cannot be explained by something *else* (*PE*: 120–21). When something does explain itself it is derived from itself, so why can't we simply use the logical law that p implies p to explain just any (true) proposition? Nozick sometimes refers to facts that explain as "deep" facts. "If it is a very deep fact that all possibilities obtain, then that fact, being a possibility, obtains in virtue of the deep fact that all possibilities do" (*PE*: 131). He does not explain depth, but evidently laws are "deeper" than their instances, but the point might be, returning to the previous example, that the first premise states a generalization, while the conclusion says *of* that generalization that it is true. This won't quite do, as it says nothing about explanation, and it is P, not "P is true", that is supposed to be explained. But perhaps we can appeal to a distinction from Wittgenstein's *Tractatus* and say that the example does not say that P is explained but shows it.

Limited fecundity

So far we have accepted F for the sake of argument, despite objections to it, and asked what it would amount to for it to be grounded by subsuming itself. But at this point (*PE*: 132–3) Nozick has cold feet about F, and also about the Lewisian strong modal realism it implies. Our world has a high degree of explanatory unity – more than the minimum our existence requires, and F, by allowing a plethora of chaotic worlds, makes it a matter of chance that we inhabit such an organized one, which he considers "highly unwelcome". So he hopes we can replace F by some LF (limited fecundity) whose analogue to the characteristic C of the previous example will turn out to ensure that it only applies to the actual world (it must not be framed to do so, or it will not be explanatory; see Wedin 1985: 346 n.6), and also that it itself has C and so subsumes and explains itself. However, he goes on, rival principles LF′ might also subsume themselves, and explain themselves if true, so why should we accept LF? In a difficult passage (*PE*: 136–7) he hopes to find an LF that not only subsumes and necessarily applies to itself, but is also reflexively self-referring (an idea we met previously in his discussion of the self). This means that it will hold simply in virtue of its holding. However, this would apply to rivals to LF, if they held, and so it seems insufficient. Here he simply comments: "Now we can see that this apparent insufficiency marks the fundamental principle as reflexive. A reflexive fundamental principle will hold merely in virtue of holding, it holds 'from the inside'" (*PE*: 137). To go on asking why one self-subsuming LF holds rather than another, he thinks, implies the ultimate one will not be reflexive, "[b]ut what else could it be?" (ibid.). I cannot regard this as anything but obscure.

Be that as it may, Nozick admits that replacing F by LF reintroduces inegalitarianism (by privileging explanatorily unifying possibilities) and so will be acceptable only if some deepest principle can render this unarbitrary (*PE*: 136). (It would anyway, as Wedin (1985: 346 n.6) points out, still be arbitrary that our world has the particular organization it has.) The structure of the remainder of Nozick's chapter is not all that clear, but the demand for ultimacy first leads him to toy with the principle of sufficient reason, which after an interesting brief discussion of a dilemma generated by the statement "This statement has no sufficient reason" he rejects because of quantum mechanics, which insists that microevents can only be treated statistically, not individually. He ends up by looking for an explanation of why there is something in terms of something which is presupposed by there being either something or nothing. Such a presupposition might be supported just *by* explaining a known fact (that there is something, using inference to the best explanation), but must be accessible to us, if it is to explain anything, and here he thinks, or hopes, that mystical experience might help – although later (*PE*: 609) he is less sanguine about what such experience might show.

Wedin's criticisms

The most important criticisms of this discussion are those of Wedin (1985) (which I have tacitly relied on earlier). Wedin accuses Nozick of not distinguishing properly between possibilities and possible worlds. He himself does not define them precisely (but see the diagram at 1985: 338). One difference is that not all possibilities are mutually inconsistent, but different possible worlds must be, since they are, or involve, *total* descriptions of the world. Nozick's egalitarianism forces him into Lewis's strong modal realism (for our world must not be privileged in being alone actual), and so all possible worlds are actual, but only for themselves, not together; "actual" becomes a relative term. Now consider F. (Wedin treats LF as something Nozick merely "considers" (n.6), although I have argued in the last two paragraphs that it does play a structural role in Nozick's arguments). Does F refer to possible worlds or to possibilities? If to possible worlds, it cannot subsume itself, for it is not itself a possible world. But if to possibilities, it "may well be" false (Wedin 1985: 341). I am wearing a green pullover. Surely I could be without it? But if so, I *am* without it in a different possible world. To avoid this apparent contradiction, Wedin thinks, Nozick must adopt Lewis's "counterpart theory", whereby I exist only in this world but have green pullover-less counterparts in other possible worlds. But in that case the possibility that *I* am not wearing a green pullover does not obtain in any possible world, and so not all possibilities obtain. Nozick, who does not mention counterpart theory, might reply that there is no such possibility, and that real possibilities exist only in the worlds in which they obtain. Perhaps this is why Wedin says of the view under discussion only that it "may well be" false; but it would hardly be a comfortable position for Nozick.

Wedin's other main criticism concerns Nozick's attempt to ground F (or LF), now assumed for argument's sake to be possible, for if it is to explain anything it must be not just possible but true, and known to be so. (As we saw earlier, explaining is not proving, but here grounding must cover both.) Nozick argues that just as being coloured or uncoloured presupposes being spatial, and some things are not spatial, so to exist or not to exist – or, as he sometimes says, to "nonexist" – may carry a presupposition not satisfied by everything. (He instances Santa Claus as not existing – leading Wedin to compare Meinong – and Plotinus's "One" as beyond existence and nonexistence.) Similarly, he says, possibilities may exist or nonexist but the structure of all possibilities does neither, although "there may be no room for the question" why it does whatever it does do (*PE*: 156–7). Nozick introduces this structure simply as an example, although Wedin treats it as the main topic here, which Nozick is seeking a ground for. (Actually Nozick (*PE*: 156) says only that this is what the Vedic Hymn of Creation sought, and promises more later.) Wedin's argument is complex, but his main point is that Nozick's term "nonexists" misleads him into positing an illusory contrary (as against contradictory) to "exists", and so to posit a third alternative, which indeed he needs for his grounding but cannot justify.

We lack space to discuss Nozick's interesting treatment of mysticism, or Wedin's criticisms of it and of Nozick's use of it. Wedin sees no reason why anything mysticism provides should play the role Nozick wants for it, although Nozick does gesture towards such a reason in what he says about the contents of the Vedic Hymn etc.

Summary

The question "Why is there something rather than nothing?" should not be simply dismissed as senseless, dispensable or insoluble, although there is a question about what it is whose existence we are trying to explain. Nozick's approach is tentative, as befits his later outlook. He starts by distinguishing inegalitarian theories (whereby some states are more "normal", and so less needing explanation, than others) and egalitarian ones (whereby all states are equal). The title question is inegalitarian, privileging nothingness, and he toys with saying nothingness might be itself a productive force (which has not made him popular with critics), but prefers an egalitarian approach – leading him to a rather spurious attempt to eliminate the "rather than" from the title question, and then to a "fecundity assumption", that all possibilities are realized, which he distinguishes from the plenitude principle by adopting, at least for discussion, Lewis's strong modal realism. But he then pushes fecundity to an extreme, leading us to a comparison with *Anarchy, State, and Utopia*'s treatment of libertarianism.

But fecundity needs grounding, and it is here that Nozick first introduces self-subsumption: fecundity can explain itself, provided it is true. J. W. Smith, however, points out that Nozick's illustrative example may be unsound, if one of its premises is false. Nozick can avoid trivially letting any true proposition explain itself by implying itself by saying, as he does, that what explains must be sufficiently "deep", but he does not clarify this notion, and in the present case may need to borrow something from Wittgenstein.

However, Nozick then has cold feet about fecundity (and strong modal realism), and hopes to limit fecundity in a way that will only apply to the actual world, relying on reflexive self-reference, whose application here is obscure. This reintroduces inegalitarianism but Nozick hopes to make this unarbitrary by finding some ultimate principle presupposed by both existence and non-existence, at which point Wedin accuses him of being misled by his invented verb "nonexist" into seeking an illusory contrary to "exist" rather than a contradictory. Wedin also accuses him of confusing possibilities (which can be mutually consistent) and possible worlds (which cannot), and sees objections to fecundity referring to either of these (he plays down Nozick's replacement of fecundity by limited fecundity).

Chapter 9

Metaphysics III: free will and retribution

Introduction

Traditionally free will has been associated with responsibility, for how can we be morally responsible for something if we are not free? Discussions of it therefore straddle the line between metaphysics (or perhaps philosophy of mind) and ethics. Chapter 4 of *Philosophical Explanations* duly includes both metaphysics and ethics, but with a difference. Nozick treats free will not so much as a prerequisite for responsibility but as an intrinsically valuable feature of our status as human beings. The ethical discussion of punishment that ends the chapter is strictly therefore a side issue, although an important one (*PE*: 291).

Critics have tended to play down this chapter, not so much because of this awkwardness of its structure as because its metaphysical part in particular is inconclusive and, as Nozick himself admits (*PE*: 293), contains more "thrashing about" than the other chapters. However, this in itself need not disqualify it from having philosophical interest. Good philosophy can be done by asking the right questions as well as by giving the right answers, and this would fit comfortably enough with Nozick's attitude to philosophy that we discussed in our first chapter, where we also saw that an interest in the free will problem antedated his first serious work in political philosophy. In fact (as *PE*: 293 tells us), he has spent more time "banging [his] head against" this problem than against any other except perhaps the foundations of ethics. It seems then that Nozick's treatment of free will deserves at least a short discussion, although it has admittedly been less influential than much of the rest of his philosophy. Because of its connection with ethics, especially in its closing pages, this chapter might have been expected to come together with those on politics and value, but it presupposes too much from later material, and so has had to be postponed.

The indeterministic approach

The basic dilemma is easy enough to state: If nothing happens without a cause, then all our actions must be caused, and so must their causes, in a chain leading back before our birth, indeed to the Big Bang; it does not matter whether the immediate causes of my action are internal (decisions of mine, say) or external. So if everything is determined before my birth, how can I be free? But if my actions have no cause they are surely mere random happenings, and that will hardly satisfy our desire for free will.

Although he is well aware of the problem, it is not clear, even to himself, that Nozick can answer it satisfactorily. He tries to distinguish between being caused and being causally determined. Our actions are caused by our reasons for them, but they are not causally determined because our reasons only cause them if those reasons have sufficient weight with us, and in a subsection entitled with deliberate ambiguity "Weigh(t)ing reasons" he says that it is we who bestow the relevant weights on our reasons.

The obvious objection to this is that it simply throws the problem one step back. What determines the weights we bestow on the reasons? Or is that itself a random matter? Presumably not, but intuitively it seems that reasons occur to us as already having a certain weight. True, the weight may vary as we reflect on them and concentrate on one rather than another, but what determines how much reflecting and concentrating we do and in what directions?

What bestows the relevant weight on the reason that causes our act, Nozick replies, is our very decision to act. He first compares the way that in quantum mechanics measuring something collapses a wave packet into a previously undetermined definite state. This is different from basing freedom, as has been done, on quantum mechanical indeterminacies in our brains, but the analogy is a poor one. The problem concerns how the deciding occurs, while in quantum mechanics what is problematic is not how the measuring occurs but how it has the effects it has. But Nozick's main answer is to appeal to reflexive self-subsumption, which we have already met, especially when discussing explaining existence (Chapter 8, "Self-subsumption"), and which is akin to the self-referring and self-synthesis Nozick uses in describing the self (Chapter 7, "Personal identity IV: the nature of the self"; cf. also *PE*: 306; in fact *PE*: 305 worries that he may be overusing the notion). "The bestowal of weights yields both the action and (as a subsumption, not a repetition) that very bestowal" (*PE*: 300); also it is "a doing, not a happening merely" (*PE*: 309). We could have decided otherwise, so that our action, although caused by our having the reason we had, is not causally determined. But neither is our decision random, because it is explicable in terms of the weight of the reason, which we bestowed on that reason in the deciding. Nozick (*PE*: 302) draws the moral that we can understand why something occurred without understanding why it rather than something else (another decision) occurred then. (In the terms of Nozick's earlier discussion then we are concerned with an "inegalitarian" theory (see Chapter 8, "Nozick's approach"), or rather there are inegalitarian theories lurking in the background in so far as the two kinds of "why" questions are distinguishable and both can be asked.)

A. I. Goldman (1983), one of the few commentators who discusses Nozick's views on this issue, asks what all this has to do with free will. Presumably Nozick is trying to give some positive account of spontaneity that avoids the dilemma of determinism versus randomness, and if such an account could be given it would indeed be useful. He claims to have "sketched a view of how free will is possible, of how . . . a person could have acted differently (in precisely that situation)" without determination or arbitrariness, but he concludes, rightly, that "I admit the picture is somewhat cloudy" (*PE*: 307). He distinguishes two kinds of value, among others, originative and contributory, and wants us to be free so that we can have originative value, which is compatible with our actions being caused provided they are not causally determined (*PE*: 315). Goldman thinks that indetermination may be necessary for origination, but that if it is sufficient it is hard to see why origination should be valuable, and he adds that a determinist could well allow for invention or creativeness. This raises some interesting questions which Nozick doesn't discuss. We want to be free (from inner or outer compulsions etc.) to follow and construct rational arguments, within the limits of our intelligence. But we cannot *choose* what conclusions to come to; we are constrained by logic. Similarly Einstein did not *choose* to invent relativity theory – it occurred to him, although he did of course like many lesser mortals, choose to think about the problem. But had either Einstein or the person constrained by logic any *more* free will than their less originative fellows?

Tracking again

However, his discussion so far does not satisfy even Nozick himself, who compares indeterminism to "intellectual quicksand" (*PE*: 316), so he tries another tack, one clearly compatible with determinism. He again appeals to a notion he has used before, this time that of tracking. What we want, he thinks, is that people end up doing the best available action, whether by "best" we mean morally best or best in some other way – a point to remember in what follows – and we could talk of rightness instead of bestness. We want people to do this reliably, in the sense that knowledge is more reliable than true belief, and so we want them to track bestness, in the sense that they intentionally do what is best, wouldn't do it were it not best, and would do it were it best – where these last two conditions correspond to Variation and Adherence respectively in the account of knowledge. There is a slight complication, however, to deal with the difference between the permissible and the mandatory, and with ties for bestness. One satisfies Variation therefore if one would not do the act were it not permissible, or were some other act better, while one satisfies Adherence if one would do the act were it mandatory, or were all other alternatives worse.

How far does this analogy between belief and action go? Nozick devotes several pages to elaborating and discussing this. Presumably if we are to do the right thing other than by accident or for the wrong reasons we must have the right beliefs about what is right and also the right motives. Having the right motive Nozick compares to using the right method in the epistemological case. The situation we want is that our beliefs track rightness and our actions track our beliefs. This leads to one or two complications about Variation and Adherence, and also about the role of desire, and about self-deception, which we can ignore.

But what has all this to do with free will? Not much, according to Nozick, or anyway not enough. "Only if the structural consequences of this notion of tracking illuminate the conflicting ways we are pulled on (what is unquestionably) the topic of free will – as happened previously with the topic of knowledge – will it be clear that tracking bestness is a theory of free will" (*PE*: 328). He considers various cases where, for example, we might track rightness in one action without tracking it in something entailed by that action. For instance, I might rightly go dancing tonight because were that wrong (and I ought to visit my sick aunt) I would not do it. But dancing tonight entails dancing at least once this year, which is right (permissible). But I might not track *that* rightness, because were it wrong (because my aunt needed constant attention) I would still do it (I am not *that* virtuous). So if tracking rightness amounted to freedom this would show that I could be free to do something but not free to do something it entailed. However, although such considerations do have some interest, Nozick thinks they do not "cut deeply enough" (*PE*: 328) to really give us a theory of free will. Borrowing a notion from this discussion of personal identity he adds that even if tracking bestness were the best instantiated realization of the concept of free will it still might not be good enough (*PE*: 327).

The attempt to tie free will to rightness or rationality goes back at least to Kant, as Nozick realizes. For Kant we are only free when we act in accordance with reason, which for him amounts to saying, when we act in accordance with, or anyway not against, the moral law. Kant's view is underpinned by a controversial metaphysics, and also by his own ethical theory, which we need not discuss. But the obvious objection to it is that we are surely equally free when we act wrongly; otherwise how could we ever be responsible for doing so? But the issue has wider implications. Nozick, as we have seen, talks indifferently of tracking rightness or bestness, terms which each go well beyond the moral sphere, even if that is the sphere that mainly interests us concerning free will. Leaving aside morality and altruism for the moment, i.e. taking cases where they do not arise, we might feel that someone who did not track their own best interests, or what they considered to be such, was under some limitation, either of folly or weakness of will, and to that extent not fully free. Now let us add in morality, altruism, and any other normal motives, and ask whether the person tracks what he considers is the best thing to do overall. If he doesn't we might again feel that he was not fully free.

After some interesting discussion, which we must leave aside, on whether tracking bestness is undercut by neurophysiology or sociobiology (he says it isn't) Nozick returns to free will itself and tries now, if not to refute determinism, at least to reduce its sting. He first suggests that a necessary, but not sufficient, condition for it is that our actions should be in equilibrium, in the sense that if we knew what caused us to do them we would still do them, or want to do them. So far we have specified freedom in terms of outcome rather than, as seems desirable, of a process leading to an outcome. What we really want, he thinks, is to be "self-choosers", in the sense of being able to "choose radically new goals, and not be tied to modifications of the goals built into us" (*PE*: 353). This would give us the fullest autonomy – but unfortunately, he concludes, the notion is doubtfully coherent, and anyway we are clearly not self-choosers; the most we could hope for is to be some sort of approximation of self-choosers. Here we can only agree. The notion of self-choosing might perhaps be thought of as an ideal, and unattainable, limit of the self-shaping which, as we saw in Chapter 2, Nozick appealed to in his discussion of the grounding of libertarian rights. That self-shaping, however, required simply the ability, in some sense, to formulate and be guided by an overall plan of life, without the metaphysical baggage, alien to an ethico-political work like *Anarchy, State, and Utopia*, of a regress of choices of the stances from which one chooses. One might, however, see a certain structural analogy, in respect of this regress, between self-choosing and the metaphysical notion of self-synthesis that we met in Chapter 8. All in all we must value Nozick's whole discussion of free will less for the conclusions he reaches than for the questions he raises and his treatment of them.

Retribution

Retributive punishment has had a bad press in recent decades, although now it is more in favour again. The first question to be asked is, what is it? Its opponents tend to see it as revenge wearing respectable clothes, and its defenders try to distance it from revenge, but Walker (1995) praises Nozick for both taking revenge seriously and drawing out its similarities to retribution. Revenge is personal, involves the revenger's emotions, need not commit him to similar action on other occasions, and is not by its nature limited unless for "external reasons" (*PE*: 367) – which may or may not include the social norms that Walker thinks may often govern it. Retribution differs on all these four points, but shares a common structure with revenge, in particular that a penalty is inflicted for a reason (a wrong or injury) on someone who knows that it is being inflicted intentionally, and that he is intended to know all this and know that he is intended to know it. This analysis stems from H. P. Grice's analysis

of meaning in terms of communicative intentions, as Nozick emphasizes. The amount of the penalty is determined by the degree of
responsibility of the offender (r) and the magnitude of the wrong done
(H), and is proportional to the product of these, r × H, and must be
inflicted *after* the offender's "ill-gotten gains (including psychic ones)
are removed or counterbalanced" (*PE*: 363). The "psychic" ones
presumably include things like the satisfaction of having murdered
someone, but how these are "removed or counterbalanced" is not
made clear. A slight complication is raised here by compensation.
The offender must compensate surviving victims where possible, but
the amount can be deducted from the penalty, as though the loss to
the offender were treated as part of the penalty, and so deserved, but
compensation must still be paid for accidental injury where no
penalty is deserved. There are some further complications, but we
can ignore them.

The symbol "H" suggests it is harm that calls for retribution, but
Nozick talks rather in terms of wrong, for one might guiltlessly harm
someone (rejecting an unwanted suitor is his example: *PE*: 388), or
deserve greater condemnation for taking advantage of ignorance or
helplessness, or violating special responsibilities (*PE*: 719–20 n.85).
This raises large issues, which Nozick does not discuss (is contracep-
tion wrong?), but he does insist that "usually" (as an exception he
mentions torturing animals) retribution may only be inflicted in
response to a violation of rights (*PE*: 719 n.84) – as we might expect
from the rights-based philosophy of *Anarchy, State, and Utopia*.

What merits retribution? For Nozick it is flouting correct values.
What he has to say about values and their correctness we have
discussed in Chapter 4, but what counts as flouting? An act is needed,
he thinks. Of course that is not all that is relevant. We must also take
account of intention and motive. To flout correct values is to be "anti-
linked" to them, as he puts it, but one can be anti-linked to them
without flouting them (or so *PE*: 384 tells us; but *PE*: 383 suggests
the opposite: ". . . a person who does the right thing but for the wrong
reasons, although unconnected to correct values, is not anti-
connected: he is not flouting" – not even if his reasons are positively
immoral?). Why then not punish people simply for being anti-linked,
for having a defective character, or a disposition to do evil which for
some reason, perhaps just *force majeure*, is left unactualized? Here
Nozick has to go beyond his official rationale for retribution, which
we shall discuss shortly, and relies again on his theory of rights, now
those of the agent. We have a right to privacy and non-interference,

even when anti-linked to correct values, unless we actually violate others' rights. However, we can violate these by imposing risk without actual harm. Nozick would not deny, I think, that if I drive down a busy shopping street at 70 mph but happen not to hit anyone, I merit punishment.

Here we reach the area known as "moral luck", which has puzzled many moralists. If I fire a bullet at you but an unpredictable gust of wind deflects it and saves you, most systems would punish me less than if I had killed you, but why? My guilt is clearly unaffected. It may be a merit of Nozick's insistence on the need for actual violation of rights that it can explain this, given that I have violated your rights less by putting you at risk, however grave, than by killing you. But whether this is consistent with his rationale for retribution, which we now come on to, is another question (as is whether it distinguishes gross negligence from failed attempts).

The retributive theory of punishment is often called nonteleological, in contrast to teleological theories such as those of deterrence and reform, which justify punishment in terms of the result it should produce. The retributive theory has the advantage of catering more easily for our intuitions of justice, which forbid punishing the innocent, even if their characters might be improved thereby. But this only caters for the negative side: not punishing more than a certain amount. But why punish at all?

For Nozick we punish to connect the offender to correct values. (Cf. the note on Plato's *Gorgias* in the "Guide to further reading" for Chapter 2.) But this raises various problems. A. I. Goldman (1983) calls this whole idea "elusive", as well he might. It involves communicating to the offender that his act was bad and how bad it was, with the offender realizing that this is being communicated to him deliberately. Goldman asks why we could not simply tell the offender how bad his act was, or even (following a suggestion by Holly Smith) rewarding him in proportion to its badness, and telling him we were doing so; why must he suffer? Goldman seems to ignore a remark (at *PE*: 384) that the role of suffering is "to negate or lessen flouting by making it impossible to remain as pleased with one's previous anti-linkage". But one might not be pleased at *this*, which one might not have thought of (unless Nozick means: pleased at what in fact constitutes the anti-linkage), and anyway why is this pleasure what is important? Is the aim that the offender should *accept* the values being thrust upon him? But this would return us to the reform theory, and although Nozick insists that the offender must understand the message, he treats the need to accept it as a feature of the rival teleological theory (*PE*: 380 – although *PE*: 379 admits that this and the teleological theory are "intertwined").

Walker (1999: 603–4) congratulates Nozick for alone among "expressivists" (those who say punishment expresses something, such as society's condemnation, etc.) avoiding consequentialism, "if only by the skin of his teeth", because a "twitch of consequentialism" makes him say we should not punish those who have since ceased to understand moral issues, or who genuinely repent. Jacobs (1999: 545 n.17), who supports retribution because it "directly enacts appropriate sentiments of resentful opposition" (1999: 552–3), agrees with punishing the repentant because "he did the thing". But is the now insane man still connectable to correct values, and is the repenter not already so connected? And in either case is the person sufficiently the same "he" to ground the resentment? But these are controversial issues.

It is hardly true, as Walker (1995) contends, that apart from capital punishment, where he hesitates, Nozick ignores the need, on his communicative theory, to use talionic penalties where possible (see *PE*: 364–5). (Capital punishment, Nozick thinks, flouts the offender's own value – unless, like Hitler, in Nozick's opinion, he has no value to flout. But what would it be to connect Hitler to correct values?) But more importantly Walker thinks Nozick "leaves the Kantian gap unbridged" by not explaining "in non-consequential terms why it should be obligatory – or even merely desirable – to 'connect' the wrongdoer to better values" (1999: 604–5). Nozick says simply that doing so is "of value" (*PE*: 379), although he refers to his chapter on value for more (*PE*: 397). But he notes (*PE*: 365) that the discussion so far erodes the distinction between explanation and justification (or proof), which he had insisted on when discussing the nature of philosophy in the Introduction, since there is no sharp distinction between explaining why a moral principle holds and justifying it. This seems correct. But Nozick then claims not to justify retributive punishment, although he accepts it, but to explain how it is possible for it to be appropriate or demanded. This then seems to be all he says on the "Kantian gap"; however, he may not be entirely consistent in claiming not to justify retributive punishment if he intends, as Hailwood plausibly suggests, that for the wrongdoer to be connected to better values would fall under the rubric of organic unity. But perhaps the Kantian gap, still unbridged, could now take the form of asking why it should be us that do the connecting.

Finally what of free will? Nozick concludes by saying that although originative value requires it, retribution, based on degree of flouting, not of responsibility, does not. But he strangely adds that determinism may reduce, but not eliminate, the degree of flouting, and that while manipulation by impersonal causes does not excuse us, manipulation by other agents does, because then their intentions are operating. (But why does this affect the involvement of the agent's own?) He ends by borrowing from his discussion of personal identity the notion of "best instantiated relation" (*PE*: 394) or "closest relation" (*PE*: 395). But our verdict must surely be that here at least he is "thrashing about".

Summary

Free will has occupied Nozick for much of his life, but with inconclusive results, as critics have complained. He values it for its own sake, rather than as a basis for responsibility, and approaches the basic dilemma between determinism and randomness by saying our reasons cause our actions but do not causally determine them, because it is we who give weight to the reasons, which we do by the very act of decision which they cause. To avoid the charge of simply postponing the issue he brings in self-subsumption again: weighting our reasons yields both the action and that very weighting, which is a doing, not a happening, and we could have decided otherwise, he thinks, claiming only to show how free will is possible, so that we can have "originative value".

But all this does not satisfy Nozick himself, let alone his critic A. I. Goldman, so he allows determinism in and appeals to tracking: what we want is that people's actions track bestness or rightness. This, which may be a best instantiation of free will without being good enough, he thinks, suggests Kant's view that only right actions, not wrong ones, are free, but Nozick might perhaps ask first whether an imprudent act is really free, and then whether an immoral one is if it goes against what we think best overall. Then he tries to say determinism doesn't matter if we still accept our actions when knowing their causes. But he yearns for an admittedly incoherent notion of "self-choosing", which we compared and contrasted with the self-shaping of *Anarchy, State, and Utopia* and the self-synthesis we discussed in Chapter 8 above.

In a section he admits is a side issue to what precedes, Nozick tries to rehabilitate retribution by first distinguishing it from revenge and then claiming that what merits it is "flouting correct values". But a mere disposition to do evil is not enough; normally one must violate someone's rights, for otherwise the retribution would violate one's own right to privacy – which incidentally *may* explain why unsuccessful crimes are less punishable than successful ones: putting someone at risk violates his rights less than actually harming him. Although Nozick claims only to show how it is possible for retribution to be appropriate or demanded, not to justify it, it is not entirely clear how far he can really avoid teleology concerning the question "why punish?".

We ended by noting two strange claims Nozick makes in his inconclusive discussion of free will.

Chapter 10

The meaning of life

Introduction: conditions for meaningfulness

The question why there is something rather than nothing is one of those grand metaphysical questions that often exercise the popular imagination. Another such question concerns the meaning of life, and Nozick devotes the last chapter of *Philosophical Explanations* largely to this topic.

What are those who search for the meaning of life really looking for? "Meaning" has many senses, and after a bit of fun with mystic gurus in the Himalayas Nozick lists eight of them, promising to use these distinctions in his discussion of our title question, a promise he starts out to fulfil, although it rather fades into the background as the discussion proceeds. Perhaps the main distinction we need is between meaning as something subjective, as when something means a lot to us, or we mean to do something or to make something of our lives, and meaning as objective meaningfulness or importance, a sense suggested by the phrase "*the* meaning of Life". (In *The Examined Life*, Chapters 16 and 17, Nozick distinguishes meaning from importance and various other notions, but most of those distinctions (60 of them altogether) we can ignore here.)

Objective meaningfulness, when not just causal significance ("Those clouds mean rain"), one of Nozick's eight senses, is a problematic notion. What would count as life's having such a meaning? Some look to God's purpose in creating us. But would we be satisfied, Nozick asks, by playing some quite trivial role in God's plan, equivalent to "fixing a mildly annoying leaky faucet" (*PE*: 586), or providing "needed food for passing intergalactic travellers who *were*

199

important"? (ibid.). One might also ask why we should bother about God's purposes unless we thought them good, in which case we ought to pursue them anyway. But perhaps this might be answered by saying that a purpose is only worth pursuing if it has a reasonable chance of success, and God is needed to provide this. (Nozick discusses the role of God in relation to value at *PE*: 552–5, cf. 745 n.10, and at a lighter level cf. also the final item in *Socratic Puzzles*.)

If something is a source of meaning for something else, must it itself have meaning? This question and its implications are what primarily occupy Nozick here. Some people feel that life is meaningless if death is the end. This leads Nozick to some interesting discussion of questions such as that of Lucretius: why are we worried about coming to an end but not about having had a beginning? Compare the question about time preference that we discussed in Chapter 6. He omits, however, the idea that the fear of death may be an instinct encouraged by evolution – a strange omission in view of his emphasis on evolution in the admittedly later *The Nature of Rationality*.

One facet of the desire for immortality, Nozick thinks, is the desire to leave traces, preferably permanent ones. "[I]t shouldn't *ever* be as if you had never existed at all . . .To be wiped out completely, traces and all, goes a long way toward destroying the meaning of one's life" (*PE*: 582). Perhaps this adds a peculiar horror to the mass obliterations of Hiroshima, Dresden, etc.; it may be true that all life will perish in the heat death of the universe (cf. *PE*: 585), but for most of us that may be too remote to affect our imaginings – what we want is that traces of us survive for as long as any life does that can appreciate them (cf. *PE*: 583–4).

This search for permanence and unlimitedness leads Nozick to a problem, as he well recognizes. Mere permanence by itself would hardly be enough to give one's life meaning, but what else is needed? Meaning for Nozick involves the transcending of limits. "The problem of meaning is created by limits, by being just this, by being merely this" (*PE*: 595), and "[t]o ask something's meaning is to ask how it is connected, perhaps in specified ways, to other things" (*PE*: 594). To extend to infinity the life one already has would transcend its original limits, but would not be to connect it to other things outside itself. Even if an original segment of one's life were given meaning in this way, the question would still arise about one's life as a whole (and even the initial segment would hardly gain meaning unless it was integrated into a larger and structured whole, and not simply repeated).

If something is to gain meaning by being part of or related to a structured whole extending beyond itself, that whole must itself have meaning; not just any old whole gives meaning to its parts or to things related to it. But then that whole must itself gain its meaning from something beyond itself, and so on to infinity. This is what suggests that only what is infinite and permanent can be an ultimate source of meaning.

Not everything infinite will do, though, and not everything unbounded is infinite. A Riemannian space (or in two dimensions the surface of the earth) is unbounded but not infinite. The set of odd numbers is infinite but does not include the evens, and even the indenumerably infinite set of real numbers does not include poems or people (as *PE*: 600 puts it). Nozick claims that neither "infinite", "unlimited", "unbounded", or "endless", nor any other word of English, gives what he wants, which is something all-inclusive. He doesn't say why "all-inclusive" will not do, but introduces instead a Hebrew phrase *Ein Sof*, meaning, he tells us, "without end or limit" (*PE*: 600).

Ein Sof and its problems

At this point we enter some rarefied territory. The problem I referred to three paragraphs ago arises because two of Nozick's requirements clash: a thing has meaning by being related to something beyond itself, but that something must itself have meaning. This threatens a regress, but the situation is even worse. The first requirement has led us to Ein Sof, but Ein Sof is defined in such a way that it cannot have anything beyond itself. Ein Sof, it seems, must be intrinsically meaningful; but can it?

A further objection Nozick raises (*PE*: 598) is that meaning might evaporate in a long hierarchy. If A is given meaning by B, and B by C, and so on to Z, might not Z be so remote from A that A becomes quite insignificant by comparison? Nozick never seems to answer this, but one might perhaps suggest that A need not be deprived of meaning merely because something else has much more meaning. Stubbing my toe does not cease to be painful because of what goes on in torture chambers. A's contribution to Z may be minuscule, but it is by contributing to B that it gets its meaning, on the theory Nozick is espousing. The nail contributed little to the battle but much to the horseshoe – or anyway that is true of most nails in such circumstances.

An escape Nozick does consider is that a thing's meaning is not something it is related to, which would need a meaning of its own, but its relation to that something, which would "loosen the grip" of the picture that leads to the problem (*PE*: 599). He rejects this, however, because although there may be such a sense he cannot show that there is not the other sense too, so that the problem remains.

But to return to Ein Sof: this includes everything, not just actualities but possibilities too. Does it include impossibilities, like round squares? If not, it is less inclusive than Meinong's jungle (we can ignore the controversial question what Meinong himself actually held). If the jungle is an incoherent notion, is Ein Sof limited by not including it? J. W. Smith (1988) offers three criticisms of Nozick, but before doing so defends him to the extent of saying that Ein Sof is not so trivial as to make us contradict ourselves by truly asserting and truly denying that it contains all possibilities; the denial would be false. That there are no limits to Ein Sof does not mean there are none to what we can say about it (Smith 1988: 80). But Nozick insists that "[t]o be one way and not another is to have limits" (*PE*: 608). This seems to mean that Ein Sof must have all possible properties, including the property of not containing all possibilities. Does Smith's point, which seems right in itself, mean then that we could truly assert that it has that property but not truly deny that it also has the property of containing all possibilities? Is Ein Sof then saved from inconsistency? Only by a dodge: we can say it has property F, and property not-F, but not that it is not F, or in other words we can say it is not-F but not that it is-not F. But this surely is absurd. (Smith (1988: 80) is happy enough to call Ein Sof "both consistent and inconsistent . . . unlimited and limited".)

One question is what is meant by saying Ein Sof "contains" either all possibilities or all possible worlds, which leads Nozick into difficulties, as we saw in Chapter 8 ("Fecundity"). His own treatment of the consistency of Ein Sof is mainly relegated to a footnote (*PE*: 747–8 n.17), where he asks whether Ein Sof could be called ineffable because no predicates apply to it (because a predicate would say it was so and not otherwise, and so would limit it), and toys with a Russell-like type theory where "ineffable" would become a higher-order predicate which *would* apply; as an alternative he seems willing, without too many qualms, simply to let Ein Sof be inconsistent, or at least risk being so (this latter possibility, of inconsistency, is the first of the three objections raised by Smith (1988: 115–16)). Nozick also raises, without pursuing, the question whether Ein Sof might "transcend the pair of terms existent-nonexistent, not satisfying its presupposition" (that what exists must be one thing rather than another, or than nothing, and so is limited) (*PE*: 601). We saw something of presuppositions, and the force of "rather than", in Chapter 8.

The reason for this apparent insouciance is that Nozick is more interested in the role of Ein Sof in grounding meaning. Can it be intrinsically meaningful? But perhaps it does not need to be? Appealing again to presuppositions he wonders whether Ein Sof might transcend the notions of meaningful and meaningless on the grounds that those terms only apply to what has something beyond itself. But the trouble with this way out is that it is not clear why such a thing should render what connects up with it meaningful rather than meaningless, since it transcends both these notions equally. This is Smith's second criticism, which Nozick makes himself (at *PE*: 602 – as of course Smith realizes).

Self-subsumption again

So we return to whether Ein Sof can be intrinsically meaningful. Nozick's favoured solution brings in self-subsumption again, a notion we met in Chapter 8. Ein Sof is its own meaning, in a way corresponding to that in which a self-subsuming principle explains itself (*PE*: 610). But how? He has two suggestions. First he appeals to mathematics, where an infinite set, unlike a finite set, can be mapped onto a proper part of itself. The integers can be mapped onto the even integers (by associating each integer with its double), so that there are as many even integers as integers, despite the odd integers. He then applies the analogy, implicitly turning the mapping around so that the evens are mapped onto the integers (which is fair enough) by saying that similarly "[o]nly an unlimited being can have its 'wider' context be itself, and so be its own meaning" (*PE*: 603). This lets Smith make his third criticism, in two parts: first it is between their elements that the correspondence between two sets holds – the sets are not identical; and secondly if Ein Sof is given meaning by a "subset" of itself, and itself gives meaning to that "subset", we simply have a vicious circle. It is as though the integers, as the wider set, gave meaning to the evens, which then, being the same set because also infinite, swapped roles and gave meaning to the integers. (In this last sentence I am going beyond Smith, hopefully without distorting his point.) Smith concludes that his criticisms refute the whole idea that it is limits that create the problem of the meaning of life, although he does not elaborate on this.

The second suggestion for how Ein Sof is its own meaning is that a finite being gets meaning by being connected to something external, but not just anything; it must transcend its limits. Nozick promises more later on why it must (*PE*: 603), but this promise is not obviously fulfilled. (The nearest passage, but not very near, is perhaps *PE*: 606–8, mentioned below. *The Examined Life*, Chapters 15 to 17 discuss meaning and related notions at length, but do not seem to help on this question.) What he does say is that an infinite being has no limits to transcend, no external context from which it would be insignificant, and therefore "it itself is its own importance and meaning" (*PE*: 605). But he does not explain why it should have any meaning at all, i.e. he does not *justify* abandoning the idea that being meaningful or meaningless involves a presupposition which an infinite being does not satisfy; he seems to abandon it simply because it would not serve his purpose, as we saw two paragraphs ago. He does, however, make a comparison, significant for the unity of his philosophy, with his "closest continuer" theory of identity. As something's identity may depend on whether something else exists, so here "the context to ground meaning must be such that ... nothing else includes or dwarfs or undermines or secretly gives rise to, or is deeper than it" (*PE*; 605). But unlike the identity case he is here inclined to require also that there *could* be no such underminer. This would suggest that only Ein Sof, which includes all possibilities as well as actualities, would fit the bill.

One might wonder how Ein Sof gives meaning to lesser things. Nozick's discussion of this is opaque (*PE*: 606–8), saying that either meaning just "flows to us" from it, or that we ourselves may be "in our fundamental natures, unlimited and all-inclusive", a position he derives from the Indian Vedanta school, which we must leave to specialists in that area to consider.

Even if we do not agree with Smith that the failure of Nozick's arguments refutes his premise that it is limits that create the problem of the meaning of life, should we accept it? Nozick is commendable for taking the problem seriously and pursuing its ramifications, but has not his pursuit led him into regions so rarefied as to be remote from anything ordinary people are looking for? Are we not content if our lives contribute to a valuable pattern, or simply themselves have a valuable pattern, without going beyond themselves – a view that should surely appeal to anyone favouring organic unity?

The dialectic of meaning and value

In his next subsection (*PE*: 610–19) Nozick comes down to earth, at least partly. He still insists that meaning involves connection to something external, but this something may be not intrinsically meaningful but valuable, and this could get its value without transcending its limits, so that the regress no longer threatens. He introduces worth as an underlying notion of which meaning and value are partial aspects or facets, and which is what we care about. (The development of these notions in *The Examined Life* Chapters 15–17, which I mentioned above, does not seem to me to get far beyond mere classification.) He then develops this dichotomy in a way both fanciful and suggestive, contrasting classicism with romanticism. Roughly, classicism pursues order and balance and organic unity, the kernel of value, as we saw earlier, while romanticism pursues "overcoming obstacles, breaking bonds, powerful irrational emotions, titanic struggle", etc. (*PE*: 613), all of which associates it with transcending limits, and so with meaning.

However, this contrast between meaning and value, although interesting, is not entirely convincing. We seem to have gone rather away from the meaning of life where the transcending of limits is surely of a rather different kind from the "titanic struggle" of the romantics. And how is worth, as what we care about, really related to value, which is also surely what we care about? Are we not really confronted here simply with different kinds of value? (Nozick adds a bracket at *PE*: 613 saying that "[t]he Romantics highly valued organic unity also".) If the problem of the regress of meanings really exists does this introduction of value really solve it as Nozick hopes? Is there really such a contrast between seeking the meaning of life and seeking value for one's life? (In fact Hailwood suggests, privately, that this question is an important one for Nozick, and destructive of his position at this point. I take his point to be that if meaning and value differ by transcending and not transcending limits, and we are content to seek value in our lives, as Nozick's fondness for organic unity would encourage us to do, then what remains of this whole discussion of transcendence and Ein Sof etc.?)

Robert Nozick

Conclusion: philosophy and the arts and sciences

In the last 28 pages of *Philosophical Explanations* Nozick finally comes right down to earth and returns to his opening theme of the nature of philosophy, although now with the emphasis on giving philosophy its place among the arts and sciences. What he says is interesting and straightforward, without the abstruseness of the discussion of Ein Sof.

Science aims at truth and explanation, but it is the message rather than the medium which is important (to use my terms, not Nozick's). We see no scientific, as against antiquarian, interest in reading the work of great scientists at first hand. But with art and literature, Nozick thinks, the reverse is true. They do not pursue truth in the ordinary sense, and they lose their point in summaries or paraphrases. (One might wonder about "arrangements" of music, e.g. for modern instruments, but that lies outside Nozick's topic.)

Philosophy for Nozick combines both these features. It pursues truth, but needs to be read at first hand and not paraphrased. This is because the philosopher, like the artist, is responding to meaning and value (from now on the previous distinctions between these are ignored). He does not study them merely from the outside, like the anthropologist, nor respond in the way the practical agent might, but one mark of his so responding is that he does not try to reduce them to less than what they are. Nozick thinks this approach fits best his own view of philosophy as pursuing explanation and understanding rather than proof and conviction, a view we have discussed in Chapter 1. He thinks there are other legitimate ways of doing philosophy than this responsive one, but without elaborating. It might indeed be thought that one reason for reading philosophers at first hand is that their arguments are often less tangible and definitively statable than those of scientists; nuances of expression can more easily affect the point being made.

One feature of science is that it tends to encourage reductionism, the claim that X is "nothing but" Y. This may not be bad; we can happily accept that light is nothing but electromagnetic vibrations. But Nozick attacks what he sees as a prevalent tendency to reduce phenomena in a debunking way: religion is nothing but a projection of infantile psychology, voluntary behaviour is nothing but the effect of childhood experiences, evolutionarily instilled innate desires, or electrical and hormonal brain activity, reasoning is rationalization, and so on. (He does not discuss the appeal he will later make to evolution in *The Nature of Rationality*, where, to speak roughly, he does not claim that rationality is *merely* what evolution has instilled – there are good reasons why it instilled it. See Chapter 6 above, "Evolution and its role".)

This raises large questions which we have no space to discuss fully. Nozick first points out, in favour of his "debunking" charge, that reductions normally go from the valuable to the less valuable. We might say "Love is nothing but glandular secretion", but never "Glandular secretion is nothing but love". No, indeed; but here the reason is obvious. Even if all love can be reduced to glandular secretion it is certainly not true that all glandular secretion amounts to love. Also he ignores that some actions are more basic than others. To take another of his examples, we play a violin sonata *by* scraping catgut with horsehair, but we do not scrape catgut with horsehair *by* playing a violin sonata, as against *in* playing one. (But for an interesting apparent counterexample, which has been used to support backward causation, see Von Wright (1971: Ch. 2: 74–82).) He considers the defence that a reduction may be offered simply because it is true, and replies that it would be hard to reduce the intellectual effort involved in constructing reductions, and that at most some of them could be true, since they are not all compatible. The first point seems weak: why should this intellectual effort be harder to reduce than others? And anyway the reductionist need not reduce everything, including rational thought. The second point is fair enough, although even theories that are not true may have some good reasons in their favour. In fact Nozick toys, but not very seriously, with reducing reductionism itself, perhaps to "the opiate of the ressentimental" (*PE*: 631). (He is rather fond of attributing disreputable motives to people he disagrees with. Cf. *PE*: 626n., and also his "Why Do Intellectuals Oppose Capitalism?" in *Socratic Puzzles*.)

However, I do not wish to defend reductionism. Nozick goes on to develop his own positive views, largely by appeal to the notion of Verstehen, which we met in Chapter 1 ("Explanation and understanding").

Finally Nozick ends *Philosophical Explanations* with a short discussion of how far philosophy can be regarded as an art form. Let us give him the last word

> We can envisage a humanistic philosophy, a self-consciously artistic one, sculpting ideas, value, and meaning into new constellations, reverberative with mythic power, lifting and ennobling us by its content and by its creation, leading us to understand and to respond to value and meaning – to experience them and attain them anew (*PE*: 647).

Robert Nozick

Summary

What is one who seeks the meaning of life really seeking? Dismissing appeal to God as inadequate, Nozick suggests permanence and unlimitedness, so that only the infinite and permanent could be an ultimate source of meaning, and the infinite in question must be all-inclusive, or Ein Sof, as he calls it.

But if what gives meaning must have meaning, gainable only from something beyond it, we shall have a regress, apart from the danger of meaning evaporating over a long chain. Also Ein Sof itself is hard to describe without inconsistency (although as J. W. Smith, one of the few commentators to take this chapter of *Philosophical Explanations* seriously, points out, that Ein Sof lacks all limits does not imply our descriptions of it must too). Nozick seems insouciant about whether Ein Sof is inconsistent, but toys with the idea that it might transcend both meaningful and meaningless – but both Smith and Nozick himself point out that it would then be unclear why it should make other things meaningful rather than meaningless, if it relates equally to both notions.

So can Ein Sof be its own meaning? Nozick again appeals to his favoured self-subsumption, suggesting an analogy with mathematics that Smith criticizes on two grounds, and that Ein Sof cannot transcend its limits because it has none, but without explaining why it has any meaning at all. He does suggest, by analogy with his closest continuer theory of identity, that what ultimately grounds meaning must have, necessarily, no rival, but he remains obscure on how it does its grounding.

But ordinary people are surely content to seek value for their lives, and Nozick now allows value to replace meaning (adding an interesting, if not entirely relevant, account of how value and meaning respectively relate to classicism and romanticism). In fact there seems little contrast between seeking meaning and seeking value – which Hailwood, privately, suggests may destroy Nozick's position here, presumably by making transcendence and Ein Sof superfluous.

Philosophical Explanations ends by showing how philosophy combines features of both arts and sciences, and fits his view of it as stressing explanation and understanding rather than proof and conviction, which leads Nozick to a final attack on over-indulgence in reductionism.

Guide to further reading

Chapter 1

Nozick's own reading on and around the subjects he considers is immense, and his footnotes often contain long bibliographies on particular points, which I have sometimes used or referred to in the reading lists that follow, and which the reader can use to supplement them.

The journal *Ratio* (Vol. 3, 1996) has a symposium on "The rise of analytical philosophy"; see especially D. Føllesdal, "Analytical philosophy: What is it and why should one engage in it?", who takes it in roughly what I have called the wider sense, criticizing various attempts to define it in narrower senses. Dummett (1993) defines it as an outlook that emphasizes language and treats it as prior to thought. He omits its main figures, such as Frege, Russell and Wittgenstein, concentrating instead on its historic roots in the phenomenological movement in Germany and Austria. The main English representative of logical positivism is Ayer (1936), the second edition of which in 1946 is unchanged but has an important new Introduction. For other versions see Ayer (1959) and Hanfling (1981a), which are anthologies; Hanfling (1981b) is his own book about logical positivism. Ayer et al. (1956) provides a short account of how philosophy saw itself at that time, while Rorty (1967) is a larger collection, with a long introduction, on the relations between logic and language around that time. The January 1992 issue of the *Philosophical Review* consists of four substantial surveys of trends in four branches of philosophy during the previous 40 years.

Nozick's views on explanation were heavily influenced by Hempel (1965); see especially Chapter 12 for the claim that explanation always involves inference from laws or statistical generalizations plus initial conditions, and Dray (1957) for criticism of this claim in the case of history. For an example of an avowed following of Nozick's advice that philosophy should explain how something is possible see Rodriguez-Pereyra (2000).

One of the pioneers of dialetheism is Graham Priest. See Priest (1985–6), and for some discussion see Chapter 6 of Sainsbury (1995).

Many discussions of Zeno's paradoxes are collected in Salmon (1970).

On Verstehen, a notion often associated with W. Dilthey (1833–1911), Nozick gives several references in *Philosophical Explanations* (750 n.39) and *Socratic Puzzles* (355 n.23 and 356 nn.24, 25, and cf. 351 n.2). M. Martin (2000) is a sympathetic, although critical, general survey relating it to various relevant philosophical outlooks. *Socratic Puzzles* (121–3) is the passage from "On Austrian Methodology" referred to in *Philosophical Explanations* (750 n.39).

For foxes and hedgehogs see Berlin (1953).

Chapter 2

There are many introductions to political philosophy generally. Two modern ones are J. Wolff (1996) and Kymlicka (1990). Two modern anthologies are those jointly edited by Goodin and Pettit (1993 and 1997). Two of the most influential political theorists of recent decades have been Nozick himself and Rawls. Apart from Rawls (1971), two anthologies dealing in whole or part with his work are Corlett (1991) and Daniels (1975); see also Barry (1973).

For Kant on "reverence" for the moral law (*Achtung*, also translated "respect") see Paton (1948), the standard translation of Kant's most famous work on ethics; see in particular the second footnote on page 69.

For Plato on the interest we have in being punished for our sins see his *Gorgias* (especially 472d–81b). We might perhaps see some affinity between this and what Nozick says about retributive punishment as connecting the offender to correct values; see Chapter 9 above.

The most prominent, but not the only, kind of teleological or consequentialist theory (these are roughly the same) is utilitarianism. (Other kinds would include egoism and altruism.) Two famous expositions of it are Mill (1863) and Sidgwick (1874, revised in later editions); Sidgwick is much fuller and more thorough. For discussions of it see Lyons (1965) and the debate in Smart and Williams (1973, with annotated bibliography), and for consequentialism generally see the two anthologies by Scheffler (1988) and (fuller and more advanced) Pettit (1993). Slote (1985) balances consequentialism against common sense morality rather as Sidgwick does. Notable deontologists, apart from Kant (see Paton 1948), include Prichard (1949) and Ross (1939), which is summarized in its very full table of contents. For an anthology on rights see Waldron (1984).

Nozick gives some references to Ayn Rand (in Paul 1981: 222 (= *SP*: 378)), and a long list of discussions of her work is given in Paul (1981: 266).

On justice in acquisition see Schmidtz (1994), who claims that appropriation is not just consistent with, but in practice necessary for, leaving ample resources for future generations, since open access in not the same as, and often may not lead to, maximum access.

Personal identity is a topic Nozick does not discuss for its own sake until his next book, and it will occupy us in Chapter 7, but Lucy (1990) examines the treatment of it that Nozick relies on in his discussion of Rawls, arguing that he accuses Rawls of using too "thin" a conception of the self in sketching his original choosers (see *ASU*: 213 ff.), but could not himself elaborate consistently a suitably "thick" conception (i.e. one involving natural endowments or a connection with the body) without making adjustments that would take him back towards Rawls's position and vitiate his criticism of Rawls.

Rawls, like Nozick, has spawned an enormous literature. Barry (1973) is in effect a critical review of Rawls (1971), and Daniels (1975) is a collection of essays on it (cf. also Rawls 1977). Corlett (1991) is devoted half to Nozick and half to Rawls.

Chapter 3

R. P. Wolff (1970) is a perhaps rather reluctant defence of anarchism (he cannot see any way of defending the state); its 1976 edition adds a reply to a critical discussion it had received. Relevant to Nozick's discussion of the development of a state is Axelrod (1984), which will also be relevant re the Prisoner's Dilemma in Chapter 6 above.

Books on utopia and utopianism include Kolnai (1995), written from a somewhat phenomenological point of view, distinguishing utopianism from other outlooks, notably perfectionism, and also including some interesting discussion of the concepts of Left and Right in politics. Manuel (1979) is a massive survey of the whole period, preceded by a 28-page Introduction.

Chapter 4

For a (fairly advanced) survey of developments in ethics over the second half of the twentieth century see Darwall et al. (1992).

Hailwood (1996) is a pioneering attempt at a full-scale treatment of Nozick's ethical and political philosophy as a whole, including developments later than *Anarchy, State, and Utopia*; it takes liberal neutralism as a unifying theme.

Aristotle's views on virtue and a valuable life are given in Book 2 of his *Nicomachean Ethics*; compare also his discussion of strength and weakness of will in Book 7, and writings on virtue ethics, e.g. Slote (1986).

The idea that the only really valuable thing is some state of the valuer is put forward by Sidgwick (1907: Bk 4, Ch. 14). It is criticized by Wiggins (1976 reprinted in Wiggins 1987; see esp. §§ 1–6, 10–15). An interesting question with some, even if not immediate, bearing on this is whether some motives can be not merely outweighed but silenced by others, whether moral or not. For this notion of silencing see McDowell (1978: 26), an idea taken up but used rather differently by Dancy (1993, esp. 47–55). For a social rather than individual issue to which this is relevant consider the way opponents of hunting stress the immorality of cruelty to animals, while its supporters stress (among other things) the aesthetics of preserving the rural environment. Does morality trump aesthetics, or not?

Popper's "third world" (or "world 3", as he later preferred to call it) is introduced in Popper (1972). It bears some relation to Frege's "third realm" (see Frege 1956); for corrections to the translation see *Mind* **80** (1971: 303) and *Mind* **91** (1982: 599)); but it differs from it because Frege's third realm is a platonic realm of eternal and changeless entities, while the items in Popper's third world are autonomous but nevertheless depend on human activity and would not exist unless humans did.

An excellent account of K. Gödel's most famous proof is given in Nagel and Newman (1959), which gives the complete beginner a lucid account of the essence of the proof in 100 short pages. Church's theorem, given in Church (1936), with further reference given there, is that there can be no decision procedure for the predicate calculus (beyond the monadic).

The naturalistic fallacy is discussed in several of the items in Foot (1967) and is the main topic of Hudson (1969). See also Beck (1967) and Newell (1968), both of which attack the fact/value distinction. For a history of the topic see Prior (1949), discussed along with Moore in Gauthier (1967). For an example of later sophistications on the theme see Blackburn (1984).

On the "double effect" doctrine see Mangan (1949).

There is an excellent discussion of communitarianism in Kymlicka (1990: Ch. 6).

Chapter 5

Dancy (1985) is an elementary introduction to epistemology, which also discusses Nozick's treatment of Closure (see its index, and also Dancy 1984). Two general anthologies are Pappas and Swain (1978) and Vol. 5 (1980) of *Midwest Studies in Philosophy*. Gettier's epoch-making attack on internalism is in Gettier (1963), reprinted in Griffiths (1967), where the bibliography lists some of the initial reactions and the arabesques that attempts to answer Gettier led to. For an early example of externalism, although not so called, see Watling (1954–5). Radford (1966), with a brief note answering criticism at Radford (1967), claims that belief is not always required for knowledge, while Sartwell (1991, 1992) claims that knowledge simply is true belief and needs no further conditions (a striking and unusual claim). That knowledge does entail belief is maintained by Lehrer (1968) and Armstrong (1969–70). Harrison (1963) agrees, in a subtle discussion of why anyone might think otherwise. Craig (1990) approaches the question what knowledge is in a pragmatic spirit, asking what use we have for it; compare also his attack on Nozick in Craig (1989), which is answered by Brueckner (1991), with continued discussion by Garrett (1992) and Brueckner (1992).

The notion of possible worlds was introduced by Leibniz; see Parkinson in Jolley (1995), Chapter 7 (esp. 212–16), and (more elaborate) Mates (1986), Chapter 4. Lewis's strong modal realism is developed in Lewis (1986), but he had already applied the notion to the analysis of counterfactuals in Lewis (1973a, esp. Chs 1, 3 and 4), and to causation in Lewis (1973b). Stalnaker develops his own moderate

modal realism in Stalnaker (1984, esp. Chs 3 and 8). For a discussion
of various views on possible worlds see McMichael (1983), and for an
anthology on the topic see Loux (1979). For the Oswald/Kennedy
example see Adams (1970), and for Nixon and the nuclear button see
Fine (1975); both examples have been used by other writers too. On
backtracking conditionals see also Downing (1958–9).

On scepticism Nozick himself gives a long list of references in
Philosophical Explanations (686 n.42). The power of Descartes'
demon is brought out by Watling (1964). An article which in a way
supports scepticism by emphasizing the force of the Gettier examples
but tries to sideline them for epistemological purposes, with some
discussion of Nozick, is Kirkham (1984).

Critics who have accused Nozick of vagueness about individuating
methods include BonJour (1987), Hetherington (1992), Lipson
(1987), Shatz (1987) and Shope (1984).

Fermat's last theorem has been presented, together with the solution that has now been found for it, by Aczel (1996).

The notion of a BIV was introduced by Putnam (1981: Ch. 1), which
also offers his own solution to the problem it appears to involve, while
Lipson (1987) insists that the BIV and dreaming examples are not on
a level in their sceptical implications. A. I. Goldman (1983) refers to
his own (1976) for an elaboration of his suggested alternative counterfactual analysis of knowledge. Reliabilism has been criticized by
Pappas (1987), who thinks it cannot account for such cases as where
we suddenly remember something, and in various ways by Foley
(1985).

An article relevant to the computer/aardvark example in "Some
criticisms of Nozick" (p. 120), is Buchdahl (1961), a dialogue which
discusses how we acquire certain types of negative knowledge, such
as that the wall in front of us is not blue.

An elementary introduction to intentionality and intentional
contexts is Crane (1995), while Searle (1983) gives a more extended
discussion. The *Proceedings of the Aristotelian Society*, supplementary volume 42 (1968), contains four relevant articles in the form of
two symposia which discuss various questions both philosophical and
historical.

Luper-Foy's appeal to "contratracking", and his charge that
Nozick gets the direction of tracking wrong (a charge similarly made
by Foley (1987) in connection with evidence, as we saw in Chapter 5,
"Evidence"), is criticized as an interpretation of Nozick by Mazoué
(1986) while Duran (1994) mentions this point about the direction of

tracking, and also the argument of Luper-Foy and Klein that Closure can be defended by claiming that the sceptic begs the question, and then goes on to argue that Nozick's position is unrealistic because he unduly neglects the program of "naturalising" epistemology, i.e., roughly, studying how people do in fact argue rather than how they should in accordance with some a priori scheme. A seminal work here is Quine's essay "Epistemology naturalised" in Quine (1969), while Kitcher (1992) gives an extended survey of the growth, or revival, of naturalism in metaphysics and epistemology; for an anthology on the topic see the journal *Midwest Studies in Philosophy* **19** (1995). An approach with some affinity to those mentioned above in this paragraph is that of Hetherington (1992), who insists on distinguishing sceptical and nonsceptical methods for gaining knowledge. Sosa (1988) attacks the coherence of Nozick's position when we bring in our justified beliefs as well as our knowledge.

The distinction in Aristotle (referred to in Chapter 5, "Evidence") is between what is "more knowable in itself" and what is "more knowable to us", and comes at *Posterior Analytics* (71 b 33-2a5).

Lewis Carroll's point about a deductive regress is made in Carroll (1895), a brief note on pages 278–80. Discussions of it include Rees (1951) and then Blackburn (1995), Schueler (1995) and Smiley (1995), all these three in *Mind* 1995, which also reprints Carroll's note. On the question of an inductive regress see Swinburne (1974), especially the items in it by Achinstein, Black and Braithwaite.

For the D. H. Lawrence story see Lawrence (1957).

On Nozick and tracking and scepticism, see also Williamson (2000: especially 147–56).

Chapter 6

Aristotle's anticipation of Kant's notion of a transcendental argument comes in his *Metaphysics*, Book 4, Chapter 4 (as we noted in Chapter 1), where, however, it is bound up with his doctrine of substance. In Kant himself the notion is deeply embedded in his whole philosophy.

For Kant's views on universalizability in ethics see Paton (1948). A modern development of them comes in Singer (1963). The article "The trivializability of universalizability" is by Locke (1968). The rationality of altruistic behaviour is defended by Nagel (1970), which is critically discussed by Sturgeon (1974). For some older discussions on the rationality and coherence of egoism see Ewing (1953: Ch. 2), Frankena (1963: 14, 16–21), Graham (1961: Chs 5 and 6, raising some questions about what egoism implies), and Kalin (1968, defending its rationality against various objections).

On the curve-fitting problem Nozick himself gives some references (at *NR*: 183–4 n.7).

Steele (1996) on sunk costs, referred to briefly in the text, is a thorough discussion of Nozick vis-à-vis the economists on the topic.

On preference as preference for the truth of certain statements see Scheffler (1959), which Nozick refers to (at *NTIC*: 34).

Newcomb's Problem and the Prisoner's Dilemma are the subject of a collection of articles, of varying degrees of difficulty, in Campbell and Sowden (1985). These discuss not only the problems themselves but also the relations between them, and include an article by R. Axelrod (see *SP*: 191 n.25, which also refers to Axelrod (1984), which we mentioned in the further reading to Chapter 3 above). In *Socratic Puzzles* (349 n.15) Nozick refers to Luce and Raiffa (1957: 94–102) for the Prisoner's Dilemma, which they in turn (at 94) attribute, without further reference, to A. W. Tucker. A pioneering discussion of some of the difficulties in self-prediction or mutual prediction is Popper (1950–1).

Parallel distributed processing is given a brief introduction in McClelland et al. (1992: 269–88). A longer account is given in Bechtel and Abrahamsen (1991).

We have already seen references to naturalized epistemology in the further reading for Chapter 5, which is relevant here in so far as Nozick is trying to explain rather than justify our rational faculties. Here let me mention a further item, Plantinga (1993: Ch. 12), which argues that what Plantinga calls naturalistic epistemology can only work in a supernatural (theistic) metaphysical framework. More directly relevant to Nozick (whom Plantinga does not discuss because they were writing simultaneously) is Robinson (1996), which argues that self-evident beliefs are not the *sort* of thing that evolution could select, for it works at a more primitive level, selecting features or processes directly relevant for survival. Seabright (1993), reviewing *The Nature of Rationality*, is more favourable about Nozick's appeal to evolution, although making various other criticisms, some of which we have seen.

Aristotle's claim that deliberation is of means, not of ends, comes in his *Nicomachean Ethics*, Book 3, Chapter 3. An opposite view is put forward by Kolnai (1961–2; revised in Kolnai 1997), while

Wiggins (1975–6) is a complex (and fairly difficult) exploration of the whole issue.

For Davidson on conceptual schemes see Davidson (1984, Essay 13), and for the principles of charity and humanity see Hacking (1975) and Evnine (1991).

Chapter 7

General anthologies on identity and personal identity include Noonan (1983a,b) and Rorty (1976). On the evening and morning stars see Frege (1952).

Leibniz mentions the gentleman in the garden in his 4th paper to S. Clarke, § 4; compare his 5th paper, §§ 25–6. His point is that for there to be two identical leaves etc. would not be logically impossible but would breach the principle of sufficient reason. See Alexander (1956: 36, 62–3).

Hobbes introduces the ship of Theseus example in his *Concerning Body* (*De Corpore*), which forms Part 2 of Volume 1 of Hobbes (1839); see Chapter 11, especially pages 136–7. For a discussion of it see Hughes (1997a), itself discussed by Simons (1997), with Hughes's reply in Hughes (1997b). Also relevant is Gibbard (1975), which defends the view that identity is sometimes contingent against Kripke's (1980) insistence that it is always necessary (Kripke also introduces "rigid designators" there).

Shoemaker's anticipation of the closest continuer theory comes in his review of Wiggins at Shoemaker (1970). For the views of Parmenides and Heraclitus that Nozick refers to see any standard history of early Greek philosophy. A partial defence of Nozick against Kripke is given by Chaudhury (1989). On genidentity see Chisholm (1976), especially Chapter 7 and Appendix A.

Problems concerning brain transplants etc. are discussed by Williams (1970), reprinted in Williams (1973), and Parfit (1984), among others.

The notions of wide and narrow content date effectively from Burge (1979); see also Burge (1986). Burge defends the claim that content as such is wide, but for an opposing view see Fodor (1987: Ch. 2).

On the reference of "I" Nozick (*PE*: 662 n.31) gives several references to H.-N. Castañeda, and also to Perry (1979), who argues that belief states must be distinguished from the objects of belief, and to Lewis (1979), who adds to the traditional de re/de dicto distinction (for one discussion of which see Plantinga 1969) the notion of de se ("about oneself"). For a more Wittgensteinian approach see Anscombe (1975).

For Lichtenberg's criticism of Descartes see Lichtenberg (1990: 168), which is aphorism 18 of Notebook K in the editor's numbering and was written between 1793 and 1796.

Chapter 8

The question why there is something rather than nothing would have been answered traditionally, had anyone asked it, by saying that the universe was created by God, Himself a necessary being. Leibniz in his essay "On the ultimate origination of things" (1697; see Leibniz 1973: 136–44) tried to do a bit better by asking why God created the universe and answering in effect in terms of the principle of plenitude. This goes back as far as Aristotle (*On the Heavens*, Book 1, Chapter 12) and Hobbes (1839, Vol. 1, Pt 2 (*Concerning Body*), Chapter 10, § 4), and has its standard treatment in Lovejoy (1936). The general idea is that it is metaphysically necessary that reality be as "full" as possible. For a general modern discussion of the question "Why is there anything at all?" see the symposium under that title between Van Inwagen and Lowe in the *Proceedings of the Aristotelian Society*, supplementary volume 70 (1996), together with the revised version of the chairman's comments in Baldwin (1996), and further discussion in Rodriguez-Pereyra (1997). The traditional argument that if God is even possible then He exists, and exists necessarily, is turned on its head by Findlay (1948), claiming that no being can exist necessarily, so that God does not exist, and therefore is not even possible. An attempt to show a priori that there must be something rather than nothing is Goldstick (1979–80), while Q. Smith (1999) argues along lines reminiscent of Nozick's appeal to self-subsumption that the universe exists because it caused itself to do so. Nozick's own use of self-subsumption is briefly criticized by Fogelin (1983: 820).

The principle of indifference is briefly but clearly criticized by Kneale (1949: 147–50). It is defended, and Kneale's own view at Kneale (1949: 172–3) is developed, by Blackburn (1973: Ch. 6).

For a further (and rather difficult) discussion of the distinction between possibilities and possible worlds see Lewis (1982: 24–32).

On presuppositions Nozick himself gives a useful list of references (at *PE*: 678 n.28), to which add Linsky (1967: Ch. 6), commenting on the debate between Russell and Strawson.

Chapter 9

Two excellent anthologies on free will and related issues are Berofsky (1966) and Watson (1982). Two opposing outlooks (incompatibilism and compatibilism) are presented by Van Inwagen (1983) and Dennett (1984a) respectively, and they join issue in shorter compass in Dennett (1984b) and Van Inwagen (1984). Hill (1988) discusses in detail under what conditions I am responsible for something I do freely except that had I tried to do the opposite I would have been prevented: I decide to stay at home by the fire rather than brave the snow to visit my dying aunt – but unknown to me the door of my room has been locked from the outside (my example).

Kant's views on freedom are developed in the third chapter of *The Groundwork of the Metaphysic of Morals*; see Paton (1948: Ch. 3).

An introduction to various views on punishment is Honderich (1969), while Acton (1969) is an anthology.

Questions about moral luck are discussed in a symposium between Nagel (1976) and Williams (1976), Nagel reprinted in Nagel (1979), and Williams in Williams (1981).

Ladenson (1976) discusses Nozick's earlier treatment of punishment in *Anarchy, State, and Utopia*.

Grice's views on meaning are collected together in Grice (1989).

Chapter 10

Recent philosophy has been reticent about such topics as the meaning of life, and Nozick's own discussion has not enthused reviewers, most of whom pass over it in silence, or worse. Nagel (1987) describes itself on its title-page as "a very short introduction to philosophy", and its final chapter is an even shorter introduction to the meaning of life (reprinted in Klemke 2000: 5–7), ending with a reference to the "absurd", which recalls a favourite theme of existentialism, and forms the subject of an article (Nagel 1971a, reprinted in Nagel 1979). On existentialism in general see Cooper (1990). Several of the chapters in *The Examined Life* develop Nozick's views on relevant topics. One book explicitly devoted to the meaning of life is Britton (1969), written from a Wittgensteinian point of view, while Klemke (2000) is an anthology.

Meinong's ontological views get their main development in Meinong (1983). See also his shorter work Meinong (1960).

The idea of doing one action *by* doing another has recently been discussed under the title of "basic actions"; see Candlish (1983–4), referring to other literature.

Bibliography

Works by Nozick

1962. (with R. Routley) Escaping the Good Samaritan Paradox. *Mind* **71**, 377–82.

1963. The Normative Theory of Individual Choice. Ph.D. thesis, Department of Philosophy, Princeton University.

1968a. Weighted Voting and 'One-Man, One Vote'. In *Representation: Nomos* **X**, J. R. Pennock and J. W. Chapman (eds), 217–25. Atherton Press. [In *Socratic Puzzles*.]

1968b. Moral Complications and Moral Structures. *Natural Law Forum* **13**, 1–50. [In *Socratic Puzzles*.]

1969a. Coercion. In *Philosophy, Science, and Method*, S. Morgenbesser *et al.* (eds), 440–72. St Martin's Press. [In *Socratic Puzzles*.]

1969b. Newcomb's Problem and Two Principles of Choice. In *Essays in Honor of C. G. Hempel*, N. Rescher *et al.* (eds), 114–46. Reidel.

1971a. On the Randian Argument. *The Personalist* **52**, 282–304. [In *Socratic Puzzles*, and also in Paul 1981: 206–31.]

1971b. Two Philosophical Fables (Testament, Teleology). *Mosaic* **12**, 24–8. [In *Socratic Puzzles*.]

1972a. Goodman, Nelson on Merit, Aesthetic. *Journal of Philosophy* **69**, 783–5. [In *Socratic Puzzles*.]

1972b. R.S.V.P. – A Story. *Commentary* **53**(3), 66–8. [In *Socratic Puzzles*, and also in Regis 1985.]

1973. Distributive Justice. *Philosophy and Public Affairs* **3**, 45–126. [A slightly different version of *Anarchy, State, and Utopia*, Chapter 7.]

1974a. *Anarchy, State, and Utopia*. Basic Books.

1974b. Reflections on Newcomb's Problem. *Scientific American* **230** (March), 102–4, 106, 108. [In *Socratic Puzzles*.]

1976a. Free Enterprise in America. *Encyclopedia Britannica Book of the Year* 1976, 14–6.

1976b. The Somebody Else Professor of Whatever It Is. *Harvard Magazine* (March).

1977a. On Austrian Methodology. *Synthèse* **36**, 353–92. [In *Socratic Puzzles*.]

1977b. Commentary on symposium: Equality and Efficiency: What Is the

Optimum Equality in Incomes? In *Income Redistribution*, Colin D. Campbell (ed.), 50– 55. American Enterprise Institute for Public Policy Research, Washington DC.

1977c. Religious Coercion in Israel. *Moment* (October).

1978a. Who Would Choose Socialism? *Reason* (May), 22–3. [In *Socratic Puzzles*.]

1978b. Total War, Nuclear Deterrence, Terrorism, Reprisals – Drawing Some Moral Lines. *Reason* (December), 19. [Review of Michael Walzer (1977), *Just and Unjust Wars: A Moral Argument with Historical Illustrations*. Basic Books; in *Socratic Puzzles* as War, Terrorism, Reprisals – Drawing Some Moral Lines.]

1978c. God – A Story. *Moment* (January–February).

1980. Fiction. *Ploughshares* **6**, 74–7. [In *Socratic Puzzles*, and also in Hofstadter & Dennett (1981), 461–4.]

1981a. *Philosophical Explanations*. Harvard University Press.

1981b. Excellence. In *Excellence*, T. Wolfe, R. Nozick *et al.* (eds). LTV Washington Seminar.

1983a. Simplicity as Fall-Out. In *How Many Questions?* L. Cauman, I. Levi, C. Parsons & R. Schwartz (eds), 105–19. Hackett.

1983b. Debate on the Rosenbergs. *The New Republic* **189**(3591), 42.

1983c. About Mammals and People. *New York Times Book Review* **88**(II), 11, 29–30. [In *Socratic Puzzles* as Do Animals Have Rights?, a review of T. Regan (1983), *The Case for Animal Rights*. University of California Press.]

1984. Man as an Ethical Being. In *Medicine, Science, and Society*, K. J. Isselbacher (ed.), 35–48. John Wiley.

1985a. Interpersonal Utility Theory. *Social Choice and Welfare* **2**, 161–79. [In *Socratic Puzzles*.]

1985b. Theological Explanations. *Ploughshares* **11**, 151–66. [Revised as Chapter 19 of *The Examined Life*.]

1985c. Symposium on the Public Benefits of the Arts and Humanities. *Art and the Law* **9**, 162–7, 173–5, 201–2, 207, 213.

1986a. Experience, Theory and Language. In *The Philosophy of W. V. Quine*, L. E. Hahn & P. A. Schilpp (eds), 339–63. Open Court. [In *Socratic Puzzles*.]

1986b. The Anti-Capitalism of the Intellectuals. In *The Future of Private Enterprise*, Vol. III, C. Aronoff, R. B. Goodwin & J. L. Ward (eds), 133–43. Georgia State University Business Press. [Revised in *Socratic Puzzles* as Why Do Intellectuals Oppose Capitalism?]

1989. *The Examined Life*. Simon and Schuster.

1990a. *The Normative Theory of Individual Choice*. Garland Press 1990. [Reprint of 1963 Ph.D. thesis.]

1990b. (ed.) *Harvard Dissertations in Philosophy*, 1930–1988. Garland Press.

1992. *Decisions of Principle, Principles of Decision*. Tanner Lectures on Human Value 14. University of Utah Press, 115–202. [Reprinted as Chapters 1 and 2 of *The Nature of Rationality*.]

1993. *The Nature of Rationality*. Princeton University Press.

1995a. Symbolic Utility. In *Essays in Honor of Amartya Sen*, P. K. Pattanaik (ed.), 110–40. Oxford University Press. [Extracted from the *Tanner Lectures on Human Value*.]

1995b. Socratic Puzzles. *Phronesis* **40**, 143–55.

1996. Moral Constraints and Justice in Deliberation (in Czech). *Filosof Cas* **44**, 969– 89.

1997. *Socratic Puzzles*. Harvard University Press.

References

Acton, H. B. (ed.) 1969. *The Philosophy of Punishment*. Macmillan.

Aczel, A. D. 1996. *Fermat's Last Theorem*. Four Walls Eight Windows.

Adams, E.W. 1970. Subjunctive and Indicative Conditionals. *Foundations of Language* **6**, 89–94.

Adler, M. J. 1970. *The Time of Our Lives: The Ethics of Common Sense*. Holt, Rinehart & Winston.

Alexander, H. G. (ed.) 1956. *The Leibniz-Clarke Correspondence*. Manchester University Press/Cambridge University Press.

Anscombe, G. E. M. 1975. The First Person. In *Mind and Language*, S. Guttenplan (ed.), 45–65. Clarendon Press.

Aristotle. *Metaphysics*.

Aristotle. *Nicomachean Ethics*.

Aristotle. *On the Heavens*.

Aristotle. *Posterior Analytics*.

Armstrong, D. M. 1969–70. Does Knowledge Entail Belief? *Proceedings of the Aristotelian Society* **70**, 21–36.

Arneson, R. J. 1982. The Principle of Fairness and Free-Rider Problems. *Ethics* **92**, 616–33.

Arrington, R. L. 1994. Review of Nozick, *The Nature of Rationality*. *Ratio* **7**, 88–93.

Axelrod, R. 1984. *The Evolution of Cooperation*. Basic Books.

Ayer, A. J. 1936. *Language, Truth and Logic*. Gollancz. [2nd edn (1946) has a new Introduction.]

Ayer, A. J. (ed.) 1959. *Logical Positivism*. Free Press.

Ayer, A. J., W. C. Kneale, G. A. Paul, D. F. Pears, P. F. Strawson, G. J. Warnock & R. A. Wollheim 1956. *The Revolution in Philosophy*. Macmillan.

Baldwin, T. 1996. There Might Be Nothing. *Analysis* **56**, 231–8.

Barker, S. F. 1987. Conditionals and Skepticism. See Luper-Foy (1987a), 282–96.

Barry, B. 1973. *The Liberal Theory of Justice*. Clarendon Press.

Barry, B. 1975. Review of Nozick, *Anarchy, State, and Utopia*. *Political Theory* **3**, 331–6.

Bechtel, W. & A. Abrahamsen 1991. *Connectionism and the Mind: An Introduction to Parallel Processing in Networks*. Blackwell.

Beck, C. 1967. Utterances Which Incorporate a Value Statement. *American Philosophical Quarterly* **4**, 291–9.

Bergson, H.-L. 1935. *Morality and Religion*. Macmillan. [French original 1932.]

Berlin, I. 1953. *The Hedgehog and the Fox*. Weidenfeld & Nicolson.

Berofsky, B. (ed.) 1966. *Free Will and Determinism*. Harper & Row.

Blackburn, S. 1973. *Reason and Prediction*. Cambridge University Press.

Blackburn, S. 1984. *Spreading the Word*. Clarendon Press.

Blackburn, S. 1995. Practical Tortoise Raising. *Mind* **104**, 695–711.

BonJour, L. 1987. Nozick, Externalism, and Skepticism. See Luper-Foy (1987a), 297–313.

Borradori, L. 1994. *The American Philosopher*. University of Chicago Press.

Brock, G. 1995. Is Redistribution to Help the Needy Unjust? *Analysis* **55**, 50–60.

Britton K. 1969. *Philosophy and the Meaning of Life*. Cambridge University Press.

Brueckner, A. L. 1985. Losing Track of the Sceptic. *Analysis* **45**, 103–4.

Brueckner, A. L. 1991. Unfair to Nozick. *Analysis* **51**, 61–4.

Brueckner, A. L. 1992. Losing Track of Nozick. *Ratio* **5**, 194–8.

Buchdahl, G. 1961. The Problem of Negation. *Philosophy & Phenomenological Research* **22**, 163–78.

Burge, T. 1979. Individualism and the Mental. *Midwest Studies in Philosophy* **4**, 73–121.

Burge, T. 1986. Individualism and Psychology. *Philosophical Review* **95**, 3–45.

Butler, J. 1914. Fifteen Sermons Preached at the Rolls Chapel. Bell. [Originally published 1726.]

Camacho, L. A. 1986. Review of Nozick, *Philosophical Explanations*. *Nous* **20**, 414–16.

Campbell, R. & L. Sowden (eds), 1985. *Paradoxes of Rationality and Cooperation*. University of British Columbia Press.

Candlish, S. 1983–4. Inner and Outer Basic Action. *Proceedings of the Aristotelian Society* **84**, 83–102.

Carroll, L. 1895. What the Tortoise Said to Achilles. *Mind* NS **4**, 278–80. [Reprinted in *Mind* **104** (1995), 691–3.]

Chaudhury, M. 1989. Identity as Necessity: Nozick's Objection – Kripke Replies. *Indian Philosophical Quarterly* **16**, 283–9.

Chisholm, R. M. 1976. *Person and Object*. Allen & Unwin.

Christensen, D. 1995. Review of Nozick, *The Nature of Rationality*. *Nous* **29**, 259–74.

Church, A. 1936. A Note on the Entscheidungsproblem. *Journal of Symbolic Logic* **1**, 40–41 (with correction at 101–2).

Clarke, S. 1978. A Discourse concerning the Unchangeable Obligations of Natural Religion (1705). In *The Works* (1738), Vol. II, 595–733. Garland Publishing.

Coburn, R. C. 1985. Personal Identity Revisited. *Canadian Journal of Philosophy* **15**, 379–403.

Cohen, G. A. 1977. Robert Nozick and Wilt Chamberlain: How Patterns Preserve Liberty. *Erkenntnis* **11**, 5–23.

Cooper, D. E. 1990. *The Existentialists: A Reconstruction*. Clarendon Press.

Corlett, J. A. (ed.) 1991. *Equality and Liberty: Analyzing Rawls and Nozick*. Macmillan.

Craig, E. 1989. Nozick and the Sceptic: The Thumbnail Version. *Analysis* **49**, 161–2.

Craig, E. 1990. *Knowledge and the State of Nature*. Clarendon Press.

Crane, T. 1995. *The Mechanical Mind: a Philosophical Introduction to Minds, Machines and Mental Representations*. Penguin.

Dancy, J. 1984. On the Tracks of the Sceptic. *Analysis* **44**, 121–6.

Dancy, J. 1985. *An Introduction to Contemporary Epistemology*. Oxford University Press.

Dancy, J. 1993. *Moral Reasons*. Blackwell.

Daniels, N. (ed.) 1975. *Reading Rawls*. Blackwell.

Danley, J. R. 1979. Robert Nozick and the Libertarian Paradox. *Mind* **88**, 419–23.

Darwall, S., A. Gibbard & P. Railton 1992. Towards *Fin de Siècle* Ethics: Some Trends. *Philosophical Review* **101**, 115–89.

Davidson, D. 1974. On the Very Idea of a Conceptual Scheme. *Proceedings and Addresses of the American Philosophical Association* **47**. [Reprinted in D. Davidson (1984), *Inquiries into Truth and Interpretation*, 183–98. Oxford University Press.]

Davis L. 1976. Comments on Nozick's Entitlement Theory. *Journal of Philosophy* **73**, 836–44. [In Paul (1981), 344–54.]

Bibliography

Dennett, D. C. 1984a. *Elbow Room*. Oxford University Press.
Dennett, D. C. 1984b. I Could Not Have Done Otherwise – So What? *Journal of Philosophy* **81**, 553–65.
Den Uyl, D. & D. Rasmussen 1978. Nozick on the Randian Argument. *The Personalist* **59**, 184–205. [In Paul (1981), 232–69.]
Downing, P. B. 1958–9. Subjunctive Conditionals, Time Order, and Causation. *Proceedings of the Aristotelian Society* **59**, 125–40.
Dray, W. H. 1957. *Laws and Explanation in History*. Clarendon Press.
Dretske, F. 1970. Epistemic Operators. *Journal of Philosophy* **67**, 1007–23.
Dummett, M. E. 1993. *Origins of Analytical Philosophy*. Duckworth.
Duran, J. 1994. Nozickian Tracking and Naturalization. *Metaphilosophy* **25**, 326–34.
Ehman, R. 1980. Rawls and Nozick: Justice as Well-Being. *Journal of Value Inquiry* **14**, 7–21. [In Corlett (1991), 313–29.]
Ellis, A. 1984. Review of Nozick, *Philosophical Explanations*. *Mind* **93**, 450–55.
Evnine, S. 1991. *Donald Davidson*. Polity/Blackwell.
Ewing, A. C. 1953. *Ethics*. English Universities Press.
Findlay, J. N. 1948. Can God's Existence be Disproved? *Mind* **57**, 176–83.
Fine, K. 1975. Review of D. Lewis, *Counterfactuals*. *Mind* **84**, 451–8.
Fodor, J. A. 1987. *Psychosemantics*. Massachusetts Institute of Technology Press.
Fogelin, R. J. 1983. Review of Nozick, *Philosophical Explanations*. *Journal of Philosophy* **80**, 819–25.
Foley, R. 1985. What's Wrong with Reliabilism? *Monist* **68**, 188–202.
Foley, R. 1987. Evidence as a Tracking Relation. See Luper-Foy (1987a), 119–36.
Föllesdal, D. 1996. Analytical Philosophy: What Is It and Why Should One Engage in It? *Ratio* **3**, 193–208.
Foot, P. 1958–9. Moral Beliefs. *Proceedings of the Aristotelian Society* **59**, 83–104. [Also in Foot 1967: 83–100.]
Foot, P. (ed.) 1967. *Theories of Ethics*. Oxford University Press.
Forbes, G. 1984. Nozick on Scepticism. *Philosophical Quarterly* **34**, 43–52.
Forbes, G. 1985. Response to Mazoué and Brueckner. *Philosophical Quarterly* **35**, 196–8.
Fowler, M. 1980. Stability and Utopia; A Critique of Nozick's Framework Argument. *Ethics* **90**, 550–63. [In Corlett (1991), 245–60.]
Frankena, W. 1963. *Ethics*. Prentice-Hall.
Frege, G. 1952. Sense and Reference. In *Translations from the Philosophical Writings of Gottlob Frege*, P. Geach & M. Black (eds), 56–78. Blackwell. [Originally published 1892 as Sinn und Bedeutung. Translations of these terms vary.]
Frege, G. 1956. The Thought: A Logical Inquiry. *Mind* **65**, 289–311. [German original 1918–19.]
Fumerton, R. A. 1987. Nozick's Epistemology. See Luper-Foy (1987a), 163–81.
Garrett, B. J. 1983. Nozick on Knowledge. *Analysis* **43**, 181–4.
Garrett, B. J. 1984. Nozick on Knowledge – A Rejoinder. *Analysis* **44**, 194–6.
Garrett, B. J. 1992. Keeping Track of Nozick's Trackers. *Ratio* **5**, 91–3.
Gauthier, D. P. 1967. Moore's Naturalistic Fallacy. *American Philosophical Quarterly* **4**, 315–20.
Gettier, E. L. 1963. Is Justified True Belief Knowledge? *Analysis* **23**, 121–3.
Gibbard, A. 1975. Contingent Identity. *Journal of Philosophical Logic* **4**, 187–221.
Gibbard, A. & W. Harper 1978. Counterfactuals and Two Kinds of Expected

Utility. In *Foundations and Applications of Decision Theory*, C. A. Hooker, J. J. Leach & E. F. McLennen (eds), **I** 125–62. Reidel. [Reprinted in Campbell & Sowden 1985: 133–58.]

Goldman, A. H. 1984. An Explanatory Analysis of Knowledge. *American Philosophical Quarterly* **21**, 101–8.

Goldman, A. H. 1987. Nozick on Knowledge: Finding the Right Connection. See Luper-Foy (1987a), 182–96.

Goldman, A. I. 1976. Discrimination and Perceptual Knowledge. *Journal of Philosophy* **73**, 771–91.

Goldman, A. I. 1983. Review of Nozick, *Philosophical Explanations*. *Philosophical Review* **92**, 81–8.

Goldstick, D. 1979–80. Why Is There Something Rather Than Nothing? *Philosophy and Phenomenological Research* **40**, 65–71.

Goodin, R. E. & P. Pettit 1993. *A Companion to Contemporary Political Philosophy*. Blackwell.

Goodin, R. E. & P. Pettit (eds), 1997. *Contemporary Political Philosophy: An Anthology*. Blackwell.

Goodman, N. 1954. *Fact, Fiction and Forecast*. Athlone Press.

Gordon, D. 1984. Knowledge, Reliable Methods, and Nozick. *Analysis* **44**, 30–33.

Graham, A. C. 1961. *The Problem of Value*. Hutchinson.

Greco, J. 1993. How to Beat the Sceptic Without Begging the Question. *Ratio* **6**, 1–15.

Grice, H. P. 1989. *Studies in the Way of Words*. Harvard University Press.

Grice, R. 1967. *The Grounds of Moral Judgement*. Cambridge University Press.

Griffin, J. 1986. *Well-Being*. Oxford University Press.

Griffiths, A. P. (ed.) 1967. *Knowledge and Belief*. Oxford University Press.

Hacking, I. 1975. *Why Does Language Matter to Philosophy?* Cambridge University Press.

Hailwood, S. A. 1996. *Exploring Nozick: Beyond Anarchy, State and Utopia*. Avebury.

Hanfling, O. (ed.) 1981a. *Essential Readings in Logical Positivism*. Blackwell.

Hanfling, O. 1981b. *Logical Positivism*. Blackwell.

Harrison, J. 1963. Does Knowing Imply Believing? *Philosophical Quarterly* **13**, 322–32.

Hart, H. L. A. 1955. Are There Any Natural Rights? *Philosophical Review* **64**, 175–191.

Heil, J. 1994. Review of Nozick, *The Nature of Rationality*. *Mind* **103**, 553–60.

Hempel, C. G. 1965. *Aspects of Scientific Explanation*. Free Press/Collier-Macmillan.

Hetherington, S. C. 1992. Nozick and Sceptical Realism. *Philosophical Papers* **21**, 33–44.

Hill, C. S. 1988. Causal Necessitation, Moral Responsibility, and Frankfurt-Nozick Counterexamples. *Behaviorism* **16**, 129–35.

Hobbes, T. 1651. *Leviathan*.

Hobbes, T. 1839. *English Works* (ed. J. Molesworth). John Bohn.

Hofstadter, D. & D. Dennett (eds) 1981. *The Mind's I*. Harvester Press.

Holland, R. F. 1983. Review of Nozick, *Philosophical Explanations*. *Philosophy* **58**, 118–21.

Holmes, R. L. 1977. Nozick on Anarchism. *Political Theory* **5**, 247–56. [In Paul (1981), 57–67.]

Honderich, T. 1969. *Punishment: The Supposed Justifications*. Hutchinson. [Rev. edn, 1976, Peregrine.]

Hudson, W. D. (ed.) 1969. *The Is / Ought Question*. MacMillan.

Hughes, C. 1996. Giving the Skeptic Her Due? *Epistemologia* **19**, 309–26.

Hughes, C. 1997a. Same-Kind Coincidence and the Ship of Theseus. *Mind* **106**, 53–67.

Hughes, C. 1997b. An Incredible Coincidence? *Mind* **106**, 769–72.

Hume, D. 1739–40. *A Treatise of Human Nature*.

Hurley, S. 1994. A New Take from Nozick on Newcomb's Problem and Prisoners' Dilemma. *Analysis* **54**, 65–72.

Jacobs, J. 1999. Luck and Retribution. *Philosophy* **74**, 535–55.

Jeffrey, H. 1965. *The Logic of Decision*. McGraw-Hill.

Jolley, K. (ed.) 1995. *The Cambridge Companion to Leibniz*. Cambridge University Press.

Kalin, J. 1968. On Ethical Egoism. *American Philosophical Quarterly Monograph* **I**, 26–41.

Kavka, G. S. 1982. An Internal Critique of Nozick's Entitlement Theory. *Pacific Philosophical Quarterly* **63**, 371–80. [In Corlett (1991), 298–310.]

Kirkham, R. L. 1984. Does the Gettier Problem Rest on a Mistake? *Mind* **93**, 501–13.

Kirzner, I. M. 1978. Entrepreneurship, Entitlement, and Economic Justice. *Eastern Economic Journal* **4**. [In Paul (1981), 383–411.]

Kitcher, P. 1992. The Naturalists Return. *Philosophical Review* **101**, 53–113.

Klein, P. 1987. On Behalf of the Skeptic. See Luper-Foy (1987a), 267–81.

Klemke, E. D. (ed.) 2000. *The Meaning of Life*, 2nd edn. Oxford University Press.

Kneale, W. 1949. *Probability and Induction*. Clarendon Press.

Kolak, D. & R. Martin 1987. Personal Identity and Causality: Becoming Unglued. *American Philosophical Quarterly* **24**, 339–47.

Kolnai, A. T. 1961–2. Deliberation Is of Ends. *Proceedings of the Aristotelian Society* **62**, 195–218.

Kolnai. A. T. 1977. *Ethics, Value and Reality*. Athlone Press.

Kolnai, A. T. 1995. *Utopian Mind and Other Papers* (ed. F. Dunlop). Athlone Press.

Korsgaard, C. M. 1983. Two Distinctions in Goodness. *Philosophical Review* **92**, 169–95.

Kripke, S. 1980. *Naming and Necessity*. Blackwell.

Kymlicka, W. 1990. *Contemporary Political Philosophy: An Introduction*. Clarendon Press.

Ladenson, R. F. 1976. Does the Deterrence Theory of Punishment Exist? A Response to Nozick. *Philosophy Research Archives* **2**, 392–405.

Lawrence, D. H. 1957. *The Rocking-Horse Winner*. The Complete Short Stories of D. H. Lawrence 3, 790–804. Heinemann.

Lederkramer, D. M. 1979. Quest on the Entitlement Theory. *Analysis* **34**, 219–22.

Lehrer, K. 1968. Belief and Knowledge. *Philosophical Review* **77**, 491–9.

Leibniz, G.W . 1973. *Leibniz: Philosophical Writings* (ed. G. H. R. Parkinson). Dent.

Lewis, D. K. 1973a. *Counterfactuals*. Blackwell.

Lewis, D. K. 1973b. Causation. *Journal of Philosophy* **70**, 556–67. [Reprinted in E. Sosa & M. Tooley (eds) 1993. *Causation*, 193–204. Oxford University Press.]

Lewis, D. K. 1979. Attitudes De Dicto and De Se. *Philosophical Review* **88**, 513–43.

Lewis, D. K. 1982. Individuation by Acquaintance and by Stipulation. *Philosophical Review* **92**, 3–32.

Lewis, D. K. 1986. *On the Plurality of Worlds*. Blackwell.

Lichtenberg, G. C. 1990. *Aphorisms*. Penguin.

Linsky, L. (ed.) 1967. *Referring*. Routledge & Kegan Paul.

Lipson, M. 1987. Nozick and the Sceptic. *Australasian Journal of Philosophy* **65**, 327–34.

Locke, D. 1968. The Trivializability of Universalizability. *Philosophical Review* **77**, 25–44.

Locke, J. 1690. *Two Treatises of Government*.

Loux, M. J. (ed.) 1979. *The Possible and the Actual*. Oxford University Press.

Lovejoy, A. O. 1936. *The Great Chain of Being*. Harvard University Press.

Lowe, E. J. 1995. Review of Nozick, *The Nature of Rationality*. *Philosophical Quarterly* **45**, 397–9.

Lowe, E. J. 1996. Why Is There Anything at All? *Proceedings of the Aristotelian Society*, supplementary volume **70**, 111–20.

Luce, R. D. & H. Raiffa 1957. *Games and Decisions*. Wiley.

Lucy, W. N. R. 1990. Nozick's Identity Crisis, *Journal of Applied Philosophy* **7**, 203–12.

Luper-Foy, S. 1984a. What Sceptics Don't Know Refutes Them. *Pacific Philosophical Quarterly* **65**, 86–96.

Luper-Foy, S. 1984b. The Epistemic Predicament: Knowledge, Nozickian Tracking, and Scepticism. *Australasian Journal of Philosophy* **62**, 26–49.

Luper-Foy, S. (ed.) 1987a. *The Possibility of Knowledge: Nozick and His Critics*. Rowman & Littlefield.

Luper-Foy, S. 1987b. The Possibility of Skepticism. See Luper-Foy (1987a), 219–41.

Lyons, D. 1965. *Forms and Limits of Utilitarianism*. Oxford University Press.

Lyons, D. 1977. The New Indian Claims and Original Rights to Land. *Social Theory and Practice* **4**, 249–72. [In Paul (1981), 355–79.]

Mack, E. 1981a. How to Derive Libertarian Rights. See Paul (1981), 286–302.

Mack, E. 1981b. Nozick on Unproductivity: The Unintended Consequences. See Paul (1981), 169–90.

Mangan, J. T. 1949. An Historical Analysis of the Principle of Double Effect. *Theological Studies* **10**, 41–61.

Manuel, F. E. & F. P. 1979. *Utopian Thought in the Western World*. Blackwell.

Martin, M. 2000. *Verstehen: The Uses of Understanding in Social Science*. Transaction Publishers.

Martin, R. 1983. Tracking Nozick's Sceptic: A Better Method. *Analysis* **43**, 28–33.

Mates, B. 1986. *Philosophy of Leibniz*. Oxford University Press.

Mazoué, J. G. 1986. Some Remarks on Luper-Foy's Criticism of Nozick on Tracking. *Australasian Journal of Philosophy* **64**, 206–12.

Mazoué, J. G. 1990. Self-Synthesis, Self-Knowledge, and Skepticism. *Logos: Philosophic Issues in Christian Perspective* **11**, 111–25.

McClelland, J. L., D. E. Rumelhart & G. E. Hinton 1992. The Appeal of Parallel Distributed Processing. In *The Philosophy of Mind: Classical Problems / Contemporary Issues*, P. Beakley & P. Ludlow (eds), 269–88. Massachusetts Institute of Technology Press.

McDowell, J. 1978. Are Moral Requirements Hypothetical Imperatives? *Proceedings of the Aristotelian Society*, supplementary volume **52**, 13–29.

McGinn, C. 1984. The Concept of Knowledge. *Midwest Studies in Philosophy* **9**, 529–54.

McMichael, A. 1983. A Problem for Actualism about Possible Worlds. *Philosophical Review* **92**, 49–66.

Meinong, A. 1960. The Theory of Objects. In *Realism and the Background of Phenomenology*, R. M. Chisholm (ed.), 76–117. Free Press. [German original 1904.]

Meinong, A. 1983. *On Assumptions*. University of California Press. [German original 1910, revised from 1902.]

Mill, J. S. 1863. *Utilitarianism*. Longman, Green, Longman, Roberts & Green. [Originally in *Fraser's Magazine* (1861)]

Miller, D. 1981. Steiner on Rights and Powers. *Analysis* **41**, 222–3.

Miller, D. 1984. *Anarchism*. Dent & Sons.

Milton, J. 1677. *Paradise Lost*.

Moore, G. E. 1903. *Principia Ethica*. Cambridge University Press.

Nagel, E. & J. R. Newman 1959. *Gödel's Proof*. Routledge & Kegan Paul.

Nagel, T. 1970. *The Possibility of Altruism*. Clarendon Press.

Nagel, T. 1971a. The Absurd. *Journal of Philosophy* **68**, 716–27. [Reprinted in Nagel (1979), 11–23, and also in Klemke (2000), 176–85.]

Nagel, T. 1971b. Brain Bisection and the Unity of Consciousness. *Synthèse* **22**, 396–413. [Reprinted in Nagel (1979), 147–64.]

Nagel, T. 1975–6. Libertarianism without Foundations. *Yale Law Journal* **85**, 136–49. [Reprinted in Paul (1981), 191–205; a review of Nozick, *Anarchy, State, and Utopia*.]

Nagel, T. 1976. Moral Luck, *Proceedings of the Aristotelian Society, supplementary volume* **50**, 137–51. [Revised in Nagel (1979), 24–38.]

Nagel, T. 1979. *Mortal Questions*. Cambridge University Press.

Nagel, T. 1987. *What Does It All Mean? A Very Short Introduction to Philosophy*. Oxford University Press.

Nagel, T. 1997. *The Last Word*. Oxford University Press.

Newell, R.W. 1968. Ethics and Description. *Philosophy* **43**, 360–70.

Noonan, H. W. 1985. The Closest Continuer Theory of Identity. *Inquiry* **28**, 195–229.

Noonan, H. W. (ed.) 1993a. *Identity*. Dartmouth Publishing Company.

Noonan, H. W. (ed.) 1993b. *Personal Identity*. Dartmouth Publishing Company.

Pappas, G. S. 1987. Suddenly He Knows. See Luper-Foy (1987a), 152–62.

Pappas, G. S. & M. Swain (eds) 1978. *Essays on Knowledge and Justification*. Cornell University Press.

Parfit, D. 1984. *Reasons and Persons*. Clarendon Press.

Parkinson, G. H. R. 1995. Philosophy and Logic. See Jolley (1995), 199–223.

Paton, H. J. 1948. *The Moral Law: Kant's Groundwork of the Metaphisic of Morals*. Hutchinson.

Paul, E. F. 1979. The Time Frame Theory of Governmental Legitimacy. *The Personalist* **60**, 151–61. [Reprinted in Paul (1981), 270–85.]

Paul, J. 1979. The Withering of Nozick's Minimal State. *Philosophy Research Archives* **5** (1347). [Reprinted in Paul (1981), 68–76.]

Paul, J. (ed.) 1981. *Reading Nozick: Essays on Anarchy, State, and Utopia*. Blackwell.

Paxson, T. D. 1987. Evidence and the Case of Professor Nozick. See Luper-Foy (1987a), 137–51.

Perry, J. 1979. The Problem of the Essential Indexical. *Nous* **13**, 3–21.

Pettit, P. 1988. The Consequentialist Can Recognise Rights. *Philosophical Quarterly* **38**, 42–55.

Pettit, P. (ed.) 1993. *Consequentialism*. Dartmouth Publishing Company.

Plantinga, A. 1969. De Re et De Dicto. *Nous* **3**, 235–58.

Plantinga, A. 1993. *Warrant and Proper Function*. Oxford University Press.

Plato. *Gorgias*.

Plato. *Republic*.

Popper, K. R. 1950–1. Indeterminism in Quantum Physics and in Classical Physics. *British Journal for the Philosophy of Science* **1**, 117–33, 173–95. [Revised in K. R. Popper (1972), Ch. 6, and also in K. R. Popper, 1982. *The Open Universe: An Argument for Indeterminism*. Hutchinson; Rowman and Littlefield.]

Popper, K. R. 1972. *Objective Knowledge: An Evolutionary Approach*. Clarendon Press.

Prichard, H. A. 1949. *Moral Obligation*. Clarendon Press.

Priest, G. 1985–6. Contradiction, Belief and Rationality. *Proceedings of the Aristotelian Society* **86**, 99–116.

Prior, A. N. 1949. *Logic and the Basis of Ethics*. Oxford University Press.

Putnam, H. 1981. *Reason, Truth and History*. Cambridge University Press.

Quest, E. 1977. Whatever Arises from a Just Distribution by Just Steps Is Itself Just. *Analysis* **37**, 204–8.

Quine, W.V.O. 1969. *Ontological Relativity and Other Essays*. Columbia University Press.

Radford, C. 1966. Knowing but Not Believing. *Analysis* **27**, 1–11.

Radford, C. 1967. More about Knowing and Feeling Sure. *Analysis* **27**, 139–40.

Rawls, J. 1971. *A Theory of Justice*. Oxford University Press.

Rawls, J. 1977. The Basic Structure as Subject. *American Philosophical Quarterly* **14**, 159–65.

Rees, W. J. 1951. What Achilles Said to the Tortoise. *Mind* **60**, 241–6.

Regis, E. (ed.) 1985. *Extraterrestrials*. Cambridge University Press.

Richards, W. M. 1984. Self-Consciousness and Agency. *Synthèse* **61**, 149–71.

Robinson, W. S. 1996. Evolution and Self-Evidence. *Philosophica* (Gent) **57**, 33–51.

Rodriguez-Pereyra, G. 1997. There Might Be Nothing: The Subtraction Argument Improved. *Analysis* **59**, 159–66.

Rodrigues-Pereyra, G. 2000. What Is the Problem of Universals? *Mind* **109**, 255–73.

Rorty, A. O. (ed.) 1976. *The Identities of Persons*. University of California Press.

Rorty, R. (ed.) 1967. *The Linguistic Turn*. Chicago University Press.

Ross, W. D. 1939. *The Foundations of Ethics*. Clarendon Press.

Russell, P. 1987. Nozick, Need and Charity. *Journal of Applied Philosophy* **4**, 205–16.

Ryan, C.C. 1977. Yours, Mine, and Ours: Property Rights and Individual Liberty. *Ethics* **87**, 126–41. [Reprinted in Paul (1981), 323–43.]

Sainsbury, R. M. 1995. *Paradoxes*, 2nd edn. Cambridge University Press.

Salmon, W. C. (ed.) 1970. *Zeno's Paradoxes*. Bobbs-Merrill.

Sampson, G. 1978. Liberalism and Nozick's 'Minimal State'. *Mind* **87**, 93–7.

Sartwell, C. 1991. Knowledge Is Merely True Belief. *American Philosophical Quarterly* **28**, 157–63.

Sartwell, C. 1992. Why Knowledge Is Merely True Belief. *Journal of Philosophy* **89**, 167–80.

Sayward, C. & W. Wasserman 1981. Has Nozick Justified the State? *Pacific Philosophical Quarterly* **62**, 411–15. [Reprinted in Corlett (1991), 261–7.]

Schechtman, M. 1990. Personhood and Personal Identity. *Journal of Philosophy* **87**, 71–92.

Scheffler, I. 1959. Thoughts on Teleology. *British Journal for the Philosophy of Science* **9**, 265–84.

Scheffler, S. 1976. Natural Rights, Equality and the Minimal State. *Canadian Journal of Philosophy* **6**, 54–76. [Reprinted in Paul (1981), 148–68.]

Scheffler, S. (ed.) 1988. *Consequentialism and Its Critics*. Oxford University Press.

Schmidtz, D. 1994. The Institution of Property. *Social Philosophy & Policy* **11**, 42–62.

Schueler, G.F. 1995. Why 'Oughts' Are Not Facts (or What the Tortoise and Achilles Taught Mrs Ganderhoot and Me about Practical Reason). *Mind* **104**, 713–23.

Seabright, P. 1993. The Reasons for Our Reasons. *Times Literary Supplement* (18 June), 7–8.

Searle, J. 1983. *Intentionality: An Essay in the Philosophy of Mind*. Cambridge University Press.

Shatz, D. 1987. Nozick's Conception of Skepticism. See Luper-Foy (1987a), 219–41.

Shoemaker, S. 1969. Time without Change. *Journal of Philosophy* **66**, 363–91.

Shoemaker, S. 1970. Wiggins on Identity. *Philosophical Review* **79**, 529–44.

Shope, R. K. 1984. Cognitive Abilities, Conditionals, and Knowledge: A Response to Nozick. *Journal of Philosophy* **81**, 29–48.

Sidgwick, H. 1907 [orig. publ. 1874]. *The Methods of Ethics*. Macmillan.

Simons, P. 1997. On Being the Same Ship(s) – or Electron(s): Reply to Hughes. *Mind* **106**, 761–7.

Singer, M. G. 1963. *Generalization in Ethics*. Eyre and Spottiswoode.

Singer, P. 1975. The Right to be Rich or Poor. *The New York Review of Books* **22**(3), 19–24. [Reprinted in Paul (1981), 37–53.]

Slote, M. 1985. *Common Sense Morality and Consequentialism*. Routledge & Kegan Paul.

Slote, M. 1986. *From Morality to Virtue*. Oxford University Press.

Smart, J. J. C. & B. A. O. Williams 1973. *Utilitarianism: For and Against*. Cambridge University Press.

Smiley, T. 1995. A Tale of Two Tortoises. *Mind* **106**, 725–36.

Smith, J. W. 1988. *Essays on Ultimate Questions*. Avebury.

Smith, Q. 1999. The Reason the Universe Exists Is that It Caused Itself to Exist. *Philosophy* **74**, 579–86.

Sorensen, R. 1986. Nozick, Justice, and the Sorites. *Analysis* **46**, 102–6.

Sosa, E. 1988. Beyond Scepticism, to the Best of Our Knowledge. *Mind* **97**, 153–88.

Stalnaker, R. 1984. *Inquiry*. Massachusetts Institute of Technology Press.

Steele, D. R. 1996. Nozick on Sunk Costs. *Ethics* **106**, 605–20.

Steiner, H. 1977a. Justice and Entitlement. *Ethics* **87**, 150–52. [Reprinted in Paul (1981), 380–82.]

Steiner, H. 1977b. Review of Nozick, *Anarchy, State, and Utopia*. *Mind* **86**, 120–29.

Steiner, H. 1978. Nozick on Appropriation. *Mind* **87**, 109–10.

Steiner, H. 1981a. Liberty and Equality. *Political Studies* **29**, 555–69.

Steiner, H. 1981b. Nozick on Hart on the Right to Enforce. *Analysis* **41**, 50.

Steiner, H. 1982. Vanishing Powers: A Reply to Miller and Wilson. *Analysis* **42**, 97–8.

Sturgeon, N. 1974. Altruism, Solipsism, and the Objectivity of Reasons. *Philosophical Review* **83**, 374–402.

Swinburne, R. (ed.) 1974. *The Justification of Induction*. Oxford University Press.

Robert Nozick

Swinburne, R. 1983. Review of Nozick, *Philosophical Explanations*. *Australasian Journal of Philosophy* **61**, 303–7.
Talbott, W. J. 1995. Review of Nozick, *The Nature of Rationality*. *Philosophical Review* **104**, 324–9.
Thomson, J. J. 1977. Some Ruminations on Rights. **19** *Arizona Law Review* **45**. [Reprinted in Paul (1981), 130–47.]
Van Inwagen, P. 1983. *An Essay on Free Will*. Oxford University Press.
Van Inwagen, P. 1984. Dennett on 'Could Have Done Otherwise.' (Abstract.) *Journal of Philosophy* **81**, 565–7.
Van Inwagen, P. 1996. Why is There Anything at All? *Proceedings of the Aristotelian* Society, supplementary volume **70**, 95–111.
Vogel, J. 1987. Tracking, Closure, and Inductive Knowledge. See Luper-Foy (1987a), 197–215.
Von Wright, G. H. 1971. *Explanation and Understanding*. Routledge & Kegan Paul.
Waldron, J. (ed.) 1984. *Theories of Rights*. Oxford University Press.
Walker, N. 1995. Nozick's Revenge. *Philosophy* **70**, 581–6.
Walker, N. 1999. Even More Varieties of Retribution. *Philosophy* **74**, 595–605.
Watling, J. L. 1954–5. Inference from the Known to the Unknown. *Proceedings of the Aristotelian Society* **55**, 87–108.
Watling, J. L. 1964. Descartes. In *A Critical History of Western Philosophy*, J. O'Connor (ed.), 70–86. Free Press.
Watson, G. (ed.) 1982. *Freewill*. Oxford University Press.
Wedin, M. V. 1985. Nozick on Explaining Nothing. *Philosophy Research Archive* **10**, 337–46.
Wertheimer, A. 1987. *Coercion*. Princeton University Press.
Wiggins, D. 1975–6. Deliberation and Practical Reason. *Proceedings of the Aristotelian Society* **76**, 29–51.
Wiggins, D. 1976. Truth, Invention and the Meaning of Life. (Pamphlet.) *Proceedings of the British Academy*.
Wiggins, D. 1987. *Needs, Values, Truth*. Blackwell.
Williams, B. 1970. The Self and the Future. *Philosophical Review* **79**, 161–80. [Reprinted in Williams (1973), 46–63.]
Williams, B. 1973. *Problems of the Self*. Cambridge University Press.
Williams, B. 1975. The Minimal State. *Times Literary Supplement*, 17 January. [Reprinted in Paul (1981), 27–36.]
Williams, B. 1976. Moral Luck. *Proceedings of the Aristotelian Society*. supplementary volume **50**, 115–35. [Reprinted in Williams (1981), 20–39.]
Williams, B. 1981. *Moral Luck*. Cambridge University Press.
Williamson, T. 2000. *Knowledge and its Limits*. Oxford Univeristy Press.
Wilson, P. 1981. Steiner on Nozick on the Right to Enforce. *Analysis* **41**, 219–21.
Winch, P. 1982. Ceasing to Exist. *Proceedings of the British Academy* **68**, 329–53.
Wittgenstein, L. 1922. *Tractatus Logico-Philosophicus* (transl. C. K. Ogden). Routledge & Kegan Paul. [Rev. transl. D.F. Pears & B. F. McGuinness (1961), Routledge & Kegan Paul; German original 1921 in *Annalen der Naturphilosophie*.]
Wolff, J. 1991. *Robert Nozick: Property, Justice and the Minimal State*. Polity Press.
Wolff, J. 1996. *An Introduction to Political Philosophy*. Oxford University Press.
Wolff, R. P. 1970 [expanded edn 1976]. *In Defense of Anarchism*. Harper & Row.
Wolff, R. P. 1977. Robert Nozick's Derivation of the Minimal State. **19** *Arizona Law Review* **7**. [Reprinted in Paul (1981), 77–104.]

Wright, C. 1983. Keeping Track of Nozick. *Analysis* **43**, 139–40.

Young, F. C. 1986. Nozick and the Individualist Anarchist. *Journal of Libertarian Studies* **8**, 43–9. [Reprinted in Corlett (1991), 268–75.]

Zemach., E. M. 1972. The Reference of 'I'. *Philosophical Studies* **23**, 68–75.

Ziff, P. 1984. *Epistemic Analysis*. Reidel.

Index

This index does not cover the guide to further reading or bibliography

Eastern forms of thought 163, 186,
   204
egalitarianism 37, 38
   in metaphysics 179–80, 181, 184,
      185, 186, 187, 190
egoism 27, 33
   eudaemonistic 33, 34
   and libertarianism 33
   as possibly self-subsuming 94
Ehman, R. 43, 47
Ein Sof 201–4, 205, 206, 208
   consistency of 202, 208
   as giving meaning to other things
      204, 208
   and meaningfulness 203
   nature of 202
   as self-subsuming 203–4, 208
   as transcending existent/
      nonexistent pair 203, 208
Einstein, A. 121, 178, 190–1
Ellis, A. 84, 98
Empedocles 4
end-state 37
energy 178
entailment
   and known entailment (Closure
      under) 110
   principle 110, 122 *see also* Closure
entitlement theories 37, 38, 50, 51,
   54, 56, 71, 170–1
envy 49, 81, 82, 89, 207
equilibrium 192–3, 197
essentialism, mereological 162, 163
ethics
   and free will 188–9
   lexical priority of 77–8
   and motivation 74–8, 79, 81–2, 98
   Nozick's attitude to 188
   as objective 73
   and truth 87
   see also moral, morality
Euclidean geometry 154, 155, 159
evidence 18, 113, 125–30, 132, 133
   compared to problems re deduction
      and induction 130
   for conjunction without being so for
      each conjunct 126
   as contingent and empirical 129
   for evidence 129, 132
   factual, not logical 154
   involves tracking 125
   as nonobjective 128, 132

not closed under implication 126
Nozick's account as both too strong
   and too weak 129
Nozick's approach as back-to-front
   126–8, 132
Nozick as externalist 130
as objective but contingent 128
and possible regress 129–30
and probability 129
and rationality 128–9
as "real objective relation between
   belief and fact" 125, 128
and self-subsumption 130
strong and weak 125–6, 128, 132
and support 127–8, 132
for us (subjective) 127, 129, 132
evil, paradox of pursuing 81–2
evolution 200
   and knowledge 130
   limitations of 155
   and rationality 18, 135, 153–6,
      159, 206–7
   role of, for Nozick 154
exchanges
   productive and unproductive 45
   unproductive and Nozick's shift to
      teleology 45–6
existence and presuppositions 185–
   6, 187
existentialism 135
experience machine 26–8, 50, 78, 97
explanation 6, 13, 184, 185, 187, 206
   as aim of philosophy 6, 12–13, 14,
      16, 73–4, 177
   direction of, and Newcomb's
      problem 145
   evolutionary 154–5
   fundamental 55, 62
   invisible hand 62
   as irreflexive? 183
   and justification, of state 55
   and moral principles 94, 99
   and ought-statements 93
   potential 55, 182
   regress of 179
   and self-subsumption 94
   and understanding 13, 14, 19
   why there is something 177–80,
      186
   see also proof, self-subsumption
expressivism 84, 196
externalism 17, 122–5, 129, 130, 132

unity of his philosophy   17, 19, 28,
74, 97–8, 170–1, 176
use of other philosophers   5–6
numbers   178

objectively best community   70, 72
objectivism
in epistemology   124, 125
in ethics   87, 90, 99
offers and threats   10
open question argument   88
organic unity   28, 91, 98, 99, 101,
136, 205
in aesthetics   78, 85
and closest continuer view   171
definition of   80
and individual uniqueness   84
and retributive punishment   196
as supporting imperialism in
utopias   84–5
and symbolic utility   97–8, 171
unity and diversity in, as not
properly related   83
as unity in diversity, 78, 98
and unity of Nozick's philosophy
97–8
and value   78–80, 82–3, 171
value as, as recurrent theme in
Nozick   171, 176
Oswald/Kennedy example   102
other minds, problem of   155
ownership
and ability to use   47
rights   34

paraconsistency   8
paradigm case argument   122
parallel distributed processing   152
Parfit, D.   165
Parmenides   163
particulars   178
paternalism   26, 50, 69, 85, 92
patterned theories   37, 48–9, 84
Paul, E. F.   57
Paul, J.   20, 22, 44, 64, 65
Paxson, T. D.   129
Peano axioms   110
"Pedro" example   10
penalties, not always felt   76
person   164
and group   164
as indeterminate?   169

and self   172
Pettit, P.   41, 51
philosophy   196
aesthetic view of, decried   16
algorithms and heuristics in   158,
159
its alleged coercive nature   6, 8–9
anglophone, "Continental" and
Oriental   4, 5
and arts and sciences   206–7, 208
and explanation and justification
(or proof)   196, 206, 208
and its history   3–4, 5
and its history in Soviet universities   4
linguistic   164
as persuasive   16–16
post-analytic   4
and science   2–3
of science   5
and truth   14–16, 206
see also   analytical philosophy
placebos   86
Plato   25, 53, 75, 76, 77, 87, 109, 195
Platonism   87, 99
plenitude, principle of   181, 186
Plotinus   185
pluralism
and framework for utopia   17
in philosophy   15
political implications of Nozick's
change of view   95–8, 99
Popper, K. R.   68, 86
positivism, logical   2, 4, 6, 85, 177
possible worlds
and counterfactuals   104, 105–7,
131
degrees of closeness of, and
philosophical problems   111
and Ein Sof   202
and possibilities   181–2, 185, 187
preference
ambiguity of   157
equilibrium of   141
objects of   142
and reliability   157
rules for rational   157
principle of sufficient reason   184
principles   135–40, 158
adopting   138
avoidance of?   136
kinds of   135, 139, 158